# on excellence in teaching

Solution Tree | Press

a division of

Solution Tree

555 North Morton Street
Bloomington, IN 47404
800.733.6786 (toll free) / 812.336.7700
FAX: 812.336.7790

email: info@solution-tree.com

Printed in the United States of America

18   17   16   15   14                3   4   5

Library of Congress Cataloging-in-Publication Data
On excellence in teaching / edited by Robert J. Marzano.
    p. cm.
Includes bibliographical references and index.
ISBN 978-1-934009-58-1
1. Teaching.  I. Marzano, Robert J.
LB1025.3.O5 2009
371.102--dc22

                                                2009025676

*President:* Douglas Rife
*Publisher:* Robert D. Clouse
*Director of Production:* Gretchen Knapp
*Managing Editor of Production:* Caroline Wise
*Senior Production Editor:* Suzanne Kraszewski
*Proofreaders:* Elisabeth Abrams, Rachel Rosolina
*Text Designer:* Orlando Angel
*Cover Designer:* Grannan Design, Ltd.

# Acknowledgments

There are many individuals who deserve my thanks relative to this volume. Quite obviously the chapter authors are first on the list. When I put together my "dream team" of contributors to this anthology, I had no idea that they would all say yes. A simple thank you does not suffice to convey my gratitude to them.

From a production perspective, a "tip of the hat" is in order to Gretchen Knapp and Suzanne Kraszewski who performed flawlessly in their editorial and publishing roles. The quality of this book is a direct result of their effort, skill, and professionalism.

At a more general level, I owe a debt of gratitude to those individuals who provided me with opportunities to examine the research and theory early in my academic career. Larry Hutchins and Ron Brandt are two key individuals in my life, and I will never forget their contribution. From an institutional perspective, I will always be indebted to McREL (Mid-continent Research for Education and Learning) and ASCD (Association for Supervision and Curriculum Development), without whom I would never have had the opportunities to engage in a wide variety of exciting research and development projects that have shaped my perspective on education. I hope our relationships will continue far into the future and serve as positive forces in educational reform.

Finally, I must acknowledge Jeff Jones, president of Solution Tree, and cofounder of Marzano Research Laboratory. His partnership has brought new possibilities to my life. I am completely committed to translating those possibilities into practical and useful tools for K–12 educators.

# Table of Contents

# About the Editor

## Robert J. Marzano

Robert J. Marzano, Ph.D., is CEO of Marzano Research Laboratory. Robert Marzano focuses on translating research and theory into practical programs and tools K–12 teachers and administrators can put to use in their classrooms for immediate gains. During his forty years in education, Dr. Marzano has worked with educators in every U.S. state and a host of countries in Europe and Asia. He has authored more than 30 books, 150 articles and chapters, and 100 sets of curriculum materials. His work focuses on reading and writing, instruction, thinking skills, school effectiveness, restructuring, assessment, cognition, and standards implementation.

# Introduction

# A Focus on Teaching

Robert J. Marzano

From its conception, the purpose of *On Excellence in Teaching* was to gather the opinions and recommendations of the world's best educational researchers, theorists, and professional developers regarding the topic of effective instruction. That purpose has been realized. To my knowledge, no other anthology on teaching has ever assembled a list of authors quite like those in this volume. Even a casual perusal of the contributors to *On Excellence in Teaching* validates this assertion.

One cannot examine the research on educational policy and practice over the last four decades without becoming familiar with the names David Berliner, Jere Brophy, Thomas Good, and Richard Mayer. Their past and current research has been the bedrock on which the work of people like me is based. One cannot examine curricular and instructional reforms in K–12 schools without becoming familiar with the names Lynn Erickson, Heidi Hayes Jacobs, Jay McTighe, Carol Ann Tomlinson, and Grant Wiggins. Their work is shaping the basic structure of curriculum, instruction, and assessment in our schools. Finally, one cannot examine cutting-edge practices in professional development without becoming familiar with the names Barrie Bennett, Matthew Perini, Debra Pickering, and Harvey Silver.

Their work in schools and districts is changing the daily practice of teachers and students across North America and around the world. I am quite honored to have the name Marzano listed among this prestigious assemblage.

*On Excellence in Teaching* addresses what might arguably be considered the keystone of school effectiveness: the instructional skills of teachers. One can make a case that student achievement in schools would increase dramatically if improving the pedagogical skills of teachers was a reform priority. Indeed, as a result of their review of research on district leadership, Marzano and Waters (2009) have concluded that one of the "non-negotiable" goals in every district should be that every teacher improves every year. Additionally, districts should be organizations that explicitly and systematically help develop pedagogical competence in their teachers.

This book can be used as a guide to that end. It updates the knowledge base regarding effective teaching. It examines the process of teaching from a variety of perspectives. It provides clear suggestions about how instruction can improve, and it points out characteristics of the current system that are impediments to enhancing teacher effectiveness.

*On Excellence in Teaching* cuts a wide swath across the domain of instruction. Its chapters are organized into three major sections. The first section, Theories of Excellence, focuses on conceptual and theoretical issues that must be considered for effective reform in teaching. Grant Wiggins' chapter introduces this section. Wiggins poses and discusses the most basic or essential of questions professional educators should ask and answer: what is the job of the classroom teacher? An assumption underlying the chapter is that lack of clarity regarding this issue is at the root of many problems currently facing K–12 educators. Thomas Good's chapter follows with a panoramic view of the research on effective teaching since 1968. A basic message in the chapter is that we now know for sure that effective teachers make a difference in student learning, but there is still much to be learned about exactly how they make this difference. Additionally, what we do know about the specifics of effective teaching has not been applied well in schools. Barrie Bennett's chapter reminds us that effective teaching is as much art as it is science, and that what is learned from the research must be adapted by teachers over time to produce the best results for their particular environment. This section ends with Richard Mayer's chapter on the relationship between the science of learning and the science of instruction. In the chapter, he lays out a model of how these two domains, when considered in relation to one another, can greatly inform practice and policy regarding teaching.

The second section of the book, Systemic Excellence, deals with issues and innovations at the district and school levels. The section begins with the chapter by David Berliner. Here he describes how high-stakes testing, particularly as articulated in No Child Left Behind, works against the development of critical-thinking skills, social skills, skills related to work ethic, and other related sets of skills that should be the very focus of twenty-first century education. Debra Pickering's chapter complements Berliner's nicely as she describes the specifics of a curriculum that focuses on higher-order thinking. Lynn Erickson's chapter expands the discussion of higher-order thinking by articulating the conceptual underpinnings of a curriculum that enhances this type of thinking. Heidi Hayes Jacobs' chapter describes how curriculum mapping can be used as the foundation for comprehensive reform in curriculum, instruction, and assessment at the systems level. The section ends with Robert Marzano's chapter on developing expert teachers, which maintains that school systems can develop expert teachers if they are willing to devise comprehensive models of effective teaching and provide time for teachers to engage in deliberate practice relative to the skills articulated in the comprehensive model.

The third section, Classroom Excellence, addresses specific practices that teachers can employ to enhance their pedagogical expertise. This section begins with a chapter by Carol Ann Tomlinson in which she lays out the specifics of how teachers might effectively differentiate instruction in their classrooms. The next chapter by Jay McTighe describes the Understanding by Design (UbD) framework and shows how teaching to transferable concepts and processes can have long-term benefits for students. The chapter by Jere Brophy tackles the complex issue of student engagement and motivation. In this chapter, he presents a model for motivating and engaging instruction along with necessary curricular changes to support the model. The chapter by Harvey Silver and Matthew Perini also addresses the issue of engagement but from the perspective of learning styles. They describe how different strategies can be used for different learning styles to motivate and engage students. The final chapter in this section and the book is by Robert Marzano and Jana Marzano. This chapter focuses on teacher thoughts and perceptions and how they might hinder or help effective instruction. It presents strategies that teachers can use to metacognitively control their thoughts and perceptions with the intent of enhancing their teaching effectiveness.

As this brief review of the chapters indicates, *On Excellence in Teaching* provides multiple perspectives on the teaching/learning process. A careful reading of the chapters should provide a rich source of ideas and strategies with which K–12 practitioners can examine and enhance their practice.

### Reference

Marzano, R. J., & Waters, T. (2009). *District leadership that works: Striking the right balance.* Bloomington, IN: Solution Tree Press.

# Grant Wiggins

Grant Wiggins, Ed.D., is the president of Authentic Education in Hopewell, New Jersey, a consulting, research, and publishing organization. He consults with schools, districts, state education departments, and national education agencies on a variety of reform matters. He is the coauthor, with Jay McTighe, of *Understanding by Design* and *Schooling by Design*, the award-winning and highly successful materials on curriculum design. Dr. Wiggins is the author of *Educative Assessment* and *Assessing Student Performance*. His many articles have appeared in such journals as *Educational Leadership* and *Phi Delta Kappan*.

Over the past twenty years, Dr. Wiggins has worked on some of the most influential reform initiatives in the country, including Vermont's portfolio system and Ted Sizer's Coalition of Essential Schools. His work is grounded in fourteen years of secondary school teaching and coaching.

In this chapter, the author addresses the fact that fundamental school reform begins with a serious ongoing and in-depth dialogue about the essential question of teaching: what's the real job of a teacher? Once educators are clearer about their mission, the priority learning goals, and what the job logically demands from them, he argues, they will be more focused on outcomes instead of just inputs and good intentions. Thus, teachers will be more effective, and so will students.

# Chapter 1

## What's My Job? Defining the Role of the Classroom Teacher

### Grant Wiggins

During my nineteen-year career in the classroom, I taught for sixteen years in grades 9 through 12 in three good schools and for several years at the college level at an Ivy League institution. In all those years, I was never hired on the basis of a real job description or a performance-based test of my abilities. Rather, as in almost all teacher hiring, I responded to a notice about a content-area slot that needed to be filled. I was never required to directly show that I could teach. More importantly, perhaps, I was never given a real job description framed in terms of performance standards and learning goals. I merely had to provide references in which I was praised and that verified my paperwork was accurate concerning my readiness to handle the job to be filled. In my sixteen years as a secondary teacher, I was evaluated only twice, and those evaluations were based on a total of two class visits, with no review of any of my curriculum designs, lesson plans, or feedback to students.

This scenario is so common that we do not realize how odd and unfortunate it is. The glaring absence of true accountability in education can be traced right back to the moment of our hiring.

We almost never have to sign a contract committing ourselves to achieving results or standards of excellence. We usually are not required to meet any specific goals or results. Educators rarely have real job descriptions; rather, we need only fill a slot, keep our noses clean, and maintain order.

What do I mean by a "real job description"? I mean a description written around key learning goals and related responsibilities, not merely a description of the subjects I would be expected to teach and the roles I would take on, such as "You will teach U.S. history, participate in department and staff meetings, and coach the volleyball team." This is not a real job description. It does not demand that I do the job well, only that I will fulfill certain roles and cover certain content. It does not detail what I am responsible for causing: What are my priority goals? What growth am I expected to cause in students? In short, what am I supposed to *accomplish*? The answer to these questions forms the complete, real job description. It answers the question of what it means to be a teacher—what's my job?

Charlotte Danielson (2007) developed the widely known and used framework for teaching that answers some of the questions about what it is to be a good teacher. The framework identifies twenty-two components of being a teacher that fit into four domains:

1. Planning and Preparation
    + Demonstrating knowledge of content and pedagogy
    + Demonstrating knowledge of students
    + Setting instructional outcomes
    + Demonstrating knowledge of resources
    + Designing coherent instruction
    + Designing student assessments
2. The Classroom Environment
    + Creating an environment of respect and rapport

+ Establishing a culture for learning
+ Managing classroom procedures
+ Managing student behavior
+ Organizing physical space

3. Instruction

+ Communicating with students
+ Using questioning and discussion techniques
+ Engaging students in learning
+ Using assessment in instruction
+ Demonstrating flexibility and responsiveness

4. Professional Responsibilities

+ Reflecting on teaching
+ Maintaining accurate records
+ Communicating with families
+ Participating in a professional community
+ Growing and developing professionally
+ Showing professionalism

This is a thorough and extremely helpful list of roles. As Danielson argues, the framework defines good teaching: "Although they are not the only possible description of practice, these responsibilities seek to define what teachers should know and be able to do in the exercise of their profession" (p. 1); however, few of the domain components stress a teacher's need to *commit to* and *cause* results. Rather, the focus in the framework is on all the tasks that a teacher should do.

I believe this is part of the problem. We tend to define *teaching* by measuring all the things a teacher is supposed to *do* rather than what the teacher is supposed to *accomplish*. Could you not do three quarters of the components on the list well but not be an achiever of outstanding results? Or vice versa? I have known many teachers who do nothing but cause learning and would be found lacking many of the components in Danielson's list (for example, Jaime Escalante, who was awarded the Presidential Medal for Excellence in Education by former president Ronald Reagan, among other distinguished accomplishments).

Interestingly, job descriptions in other fields are often far more clear about linking roles to results. The following is a sample from a job description for a manager of marketing from the Indiana Department of Workforce Development (2009, italics added):

- Plan and prepare advertising and promotional material *to increase sales of products or services*, working with customers, company officials, sales departments, and advertising agencies.

- Inspect layouts and advertising copy and edit scripts, audio and video tapes, and other promotional material *for adherence to specifications*.

- Identify and develop contacts for promotional campaigns and industry programs *that meet identified buyer targets* such as dealers, distributors, or consumers.

- Monitor and analyze sales promotion results *to determine cost effectiveness* of promotion campaigns.

- Read trade journals and professional literature *to stay informed on trends, innovations, and changes* that affect media planning.

- Track program budgets and expenses and campaign response rates *to evaluate each campaign* based on program objectives and industry norms.

Notice how the italicized phrase in each bulleted item—to increase sales, for adherence to specifications, that meet identified buyer targets, to determine cost effectiveness, to stay informed, and to evaluate each campaign—establishes a performance goal for the role stated in the first phrase. Teachers are rarely hired based on the terms of contracts that specify desired outcomes like this.

What got me thinking hard about the issue of real job descriptions some years back was a conversation I once had with a high school principal. We were arguing about what to do about the problem of so many teachers merely marching through textbooks. I said to him, "Well, you're the principal—you can change this." "Whoa!" he retorted. "I don't have control over what they do. I just rent space to them in the mall." A tad sarcastic and overstated, perhaps, but nonetheless a sobering view of an all-too-common reality.

I think we can focus on three core obligations when defining the job of a teacher. A teacher in a school arguably has these three results-focused responsibilities:

1. Cause successful learning related to school, program, and course goals, as determined by appropriate local, state, and national assessments.

2. Cause greater interest in the subject and in learning than was there before, as determined by observations, surveys, and client (student, parent, teacher, and so on) feedback.

3. Cause greater confidence, feelings of efficacy, and intellectual direction in learners.

This seems straightforward enough, but many teachers do not think of themselves as beholden to bottom-line goals like this. Or, if they agree to such goals in the abstract, they quickly claim that such outcomes cannot be assessed and/or that a teacher should not be held accountable for them.

## Causing Successful Learning

The first core obligation—cause successful learning—is basic. *Successful* learning is the goal, not just learning, and to determine whether learning was successful, we have to have appropriate measures of and standards for it. Success is not defined by teachers on their own. Success depends upon institutional mission and mandate. Yet few teachers deliberately plan courses, units, and lessons to honor mission and program goal statements. Nor do they routinely set or discuss with supervisors measurable goals for themselves against these outcomes. During planning, far too many teachers think only about how to teach, not how to cause results. They rely on a list of grade-level topics to determine their teaching, rather than deriving lessons and assessments from program and course goals. Some high school teachers in our workshops admit readily that they do not refer to state standards when framing courses, though they are formally obligated to them. Rather, they teach (and are allowed to teach) the same old courses they always have, without looking to see what the state law, higher grade levels, colleges, or the real world demand.

The advent of detailed standards and explicit mission statements was of course meant to address this. Clarity about standards and mission means that teachers are reminded that a primary job responsibility is to serve the institution and its goals, not merely themselves and their comfort zone. Why has this point not yet been widely discussed and acted on at the school level? Why are school report cards and course syllabi not standards based, for example? I am not sure why school leaders have not seen this as fundamental to their jobs, but it underscores a point I make throughout this chapter: far too often in schools, faculty members are left on their own to do in good faith what they think the job requires.

## Causing Greater Interest

The second core obligation—cause greater interest—is a point on which educators often bristle, get defensive, or protest. This is one of what Collins (2001) calls the "brutal facts of reality" that all "good to great" institutions must address. Students find far too many classes to be boring—a word too many students use to define life in school. One veteran teacher I know shadowed a student for a day and was shocked at the level of boredom he witnessed in students and felt himself as he sat through one lifeless class after another—in fact, he went home and cried. This was part of groundwork research for the Coalition of Essential Schools, and the school in question was not only his place of employment but also his own alma mater! Research from the High School Survey of Student Engagement (Yazzie-Mintz, 2007) supports this common sense hunch. More than 81,000 students responded to the annual survey, which was administered in 110 high schools, ranging in size from thirty-seven students to nearly 4,000, across twenty-six states. The researchers found that "today's high school students say they are bored in class because they dislike the material and experience inadequate teacher interaction" ("Students Are Bored," 2007, para. 1). The findings show that two out of three students are bored in class every day, while 17 percent say they are bored in every class. And these data reflect only the self-selecting school sample that willingly joined the study.

Great Britain's Chief Inspector of Schools, Christine Gilbert, recently announced that this issue of boredom would be a focus of the British national education department (OFSTED):

> [The OFSTED] is to launch a crackdown on "boring" teaching in response to concerns that children's behaviour is deteriorating because they are not being stimulated enough in class.
>
> Inspectors will be told to give more finely tuned advice to struggling schools on what is going wrong in their lessons and why pupils are not paying attention. (Curtis, 2009, para. 1, 2)

John Goodlad's *A Place Called School* (1984), based on some of the most extensive research ever done, found more than twenty-five years ago that:

> The only [teachers] getting ratings of "very interesting" from more than a third of junior and senior high school students taking them were the arts, vocational education, physical education and foreign languages. . . .

It was especially distressing to see that the kinds of classroom practices found most often in school were liked by small percentages of students. (pp. 233, 236)

*Plus ça change.* For some reason, the issue of boredom is never directly addressed by teachers and administrators, even though it is arguably one of the greatest impediments to high levels of student achievement. Why would we not make the issue of student engagement a key factor in judging whether or not a teacher should be hired, retained, or promoted? Why does such conversation quickly lead to cynical student-bashing or tough teacher talk about learners needing to persevere, school cannot always be fun, and so on? This is an unfortunate and unprofessional response given the goals of teaching, and it is disingenuous: teachers would not sit still for a year of boring professional development. Indeed, Norton (2009) found that some teachers often make very clear from moment to moment in workshops when *they* are bored, with behavior that they would not tolerate in their own classrooms, such as reading the newspaper, having loud side conversations, and checking cell phone messages.

If the goal is for students to learn successfully, and yet a majority of students are bored, it creates a serious problem, same as if a doctor failed to help a majority of her patients or a comedian rarely made his audience laugh. The statement, "I'm a pretty good teacher, even though a good number of my students just tune out" is a contradiction in terms under any meaningful job description of teaching linked to learning goals.

## Making Students Feel More Competent and Confident

The third core obligation—make students feel more competent and confident—is critical to successful learning. We all know that students are not likely to learn in an environment that is impersonal or where they are not valued or expected to achieve. How many teachers spend the first week of school really getting to know the strengths, weaknesses, talents, interests, and styles of all their learners, and then take a few days to plan accordingly? Interestingly, almost all coaches do this—they hold early practices primarily to see who has what talent, how to make the most of that talent, and what goals to set. How many teachers help their students recognize their strengths as learners and use this information as a central part of planning, teaching, assessing, and reporting? This idea is summed up nicely by the Secretary's Commission on Achieving Necessary Skills (SCANS) report (2000): "students should leave school with a résumé, not a transcript" (p. 62). Goodlad (1984) also notes this problem:

> What do students perceive themselves to be learning? We asked [them] to write down the most important thing learned in school subjects. . . . Most commonly students listed a fact or topic. . . . Noticeably absent were responses implying the realization of having acquired some intellectual power. (p. 234)

School will never be successful at its core mission if students continue to feel that school assessment is a "gotcha!" exercise rather than a method for improvement and mastery, and if schoolwork leaves them feeling less rather than more competent and self-directed.

This all seems like common knowledge. Readers of this chapter will naturally be thinking, "Well, of course! We realize this already." But then why do we as professionals not honor this knowledge more often? Why, for example, do we lack personalized approaches to meeting state standards regarding how courses are built and conducted? Why are we arguably closer than ever to a false and undemocratic one-size-fits-all view of teaching and learning if we understand this? Stephen Covey astutely states in *The Seven Habits of Highly Effective People* (1989) that too often people cite external causes or a lack of self-discipline for a failure to act on beliefs when the real issue, he claims, is a lack of vision and habits to support it. I agree. Our lack of clear vision reveals itself the moment we hire, supervise, or evaluate staff members with the goal of mere slot filling, and as we continue to standardize the curriculum rather than the outcomes. In short, it is the job of the person hiring and supervising to make crystal clear what is expected, and the job of teachers to demand clarification of bottom-line outcomes. This is rarely done. Why? Because few of us—teachers or supervisors—have ever sat down and asked, What's the *point* of my teaching? What am I obligated to *cause*? For what results should I *willingly* hold myself responsible and be held accountable? The answers to these questions should constitute real learning goals.

## Real Versus Apparent Learning Goals

Can it be true that at a deep level, few of us really understand our job as teachers? Consider the following exercise: what would you say if I asked you to state your goals for a unit of study—an upcoming unit you will teach or a unit you once taught? You might answer as follows:

- My goal is to teach the Constitution and the three branches of government.

- My goal is to teach students to decode letters and words.

- My goal is for students to graph linear relationships.

These statements describe content and skills to be covered— *they are not real goals.* There is no commitment to any larger purpose or long-term goal related to the point of school. Compare these typical answers to the following three:

- My goal is to teach you about the three branches of government so that you will end up an informed and committed citizen, aware that our government was built to counter human flaws and fallibility, and be responsive to citizen feedback.

- My goal is to teach you decoding so that you are able to comprehend, eager to read, and can find value in any new text.

- My aim is to teach you to make sense of linear relationships so that in the end you will be able to solve any problem with either linear or nonlinear relationships and be able to recognize on your own which kind of relationship it is.

Do you see the difference? In all three later examples, a purpose justifies the teaching. The teacher has committed him- or herself to causing long-term accomplishments in students. Recall the earlier job description in the marketing example: the second half of each job responsibility identified the goals and related results of the position. With these goal statements, the teacher moves beyond just saying, "I am hired to teach stuff, test and grade it, and move on." The intention is quite different. Instead, the teacher is saying, "I am committed to causing my learners to realize important accomplishment by using the content."

More importantly, *how* we teach and assess (concerning the three branches, decoding, and graphing, for example) is now affected by our goals. I now have to teach the content and assess for achievement in a way that directly reflects the goals, what Jay McTighe and I call "backward design" from the desired results (Wiggins & McTighe, 2005). Just teaching the content will not cause the goals to be met. The teachers cited in the previous examples from history, reading, and math will need to do such things as the following:

- Help students see the dangers of too much power by any one branch of government or the government as a whole.

- Provide students with opportunities to influence government.

- Ask students to imagine an ideal government for school or an emerging democracy.

- Make clear that decoding is one way to make meaning of text.

- Teach other ways of comprehending, such as looking at clues from pictures and headings.

- Keep reinforcing the idea that the reader has to be proactive, like a detective, to figure out what a text means.

- Help students realize repeatedly that just knowing what the words are does not mean they understand the text.

- Give students linear and nonlinear data, without hints as to which is which, to see how they handle the ambiguity.

- Help students find, not just solve, linear relationships.

- Give them data with outliers to see how well they understand real-world analysis of data.

- Instruct them to do a research project on an area of interest in which they must find meaningful linear and nonlinear relationships.

We can generalize from these examples that the job of teaching is meant to cause understanding through meaning and transfer. Knowledge and skill are not, in fact, the long-term, bottom-line goals of teaching; they are the means to those goals, though few teachers grasp this point, and few supervisors and those responsible for hiring reinforce it. In other words, the point of school is not to learn stuff and get good at school. The point of school, as the core responsibilities suggest, is to be able to make helpful and interesting connections about what is learned, and to be able to effectively transfer what is learned in school to one's current and later life (see Wiggins & McTighe, 2005, 2007).

This analysis of job description makes us begin to see how many common school structures and policies end up undercutting job clarity. When we clarify our purpose as educators in this way, and thus clarify the purpose of the content we teach, we are forced to rethink processes such as student assessment, for example. The typical quizzes used in school will properly be seen as invalid measures of achievement. We will also see that typical grading habits and formulae make no sense and go against our long-term goals. Why calculate the mean of all tests if the goal is reaching a standard? Why grade only what is easy to grade instead of what matters most? The implications for other aspects of schooling are significant once we stay focused on results.

The earlier history, reading, and math examples indicate clearly what we call "curriculum writing," which is fundamentally flawed. There is a pressing need in schools today to write curriculum backward from performance goals, not based on content topics—a point Tyler (1948) made over sixty years ago when he talked about the error of defining curriculum categories by topics instead of "desirable changes in the learner." We have laid out a complete conception of just such an accomplishment-focused approach to curriculum design in *Schooling by Design* (Wiggins & McTighe, 2007).

There are many key questions to consider in revising our approach: What do we mean by "appropriate" measures and results? What are the most credible and useful measures of accomplishment? These questions are serious and are worthy of long and intense faculty conversation—and another publication (Wiggins, 1998). For now, I will simply say what follows from the discussion so far: the most appropriate results involve evidence that supervisors and teachers agree reflect the goals of the school, the program, and the course. The initial hiring would establish a mutual agreement about how success will be measured.

### "But I Have to Cover the Content!"

My conception of teaching clearly calls into question the good-faith but inappropriate view of the job that far too many educators have (or at least often express): my job is to cover content by touring the textbook. Marching page by page through a textbook should never be the job of a teacher—ever. The textbook is written completely independently of teachers' goals and students; it merely pulls together a comprehensive body of information in a logical package for use by hundreds of thousands of people with varying needs. Textbooks in the United States typically contain all the necessary information for adoption in all fifty states. They are not built around any specific learning goals or priorities. Indeed, how could they serve us all if they did? Textbooks are just designed to hold everything that any interest group with influence thinks they should, and to pass reviews by numerous textbook adoption committees. The form and function of most textbooks resemble a dictionary, encyclopedia, or software manual. While comprehensive and logically organized, no one feels compelled to read them from front to back. On the contrary, you would consult them *as needed* in light of a particular goal or need. That this rarely happens may be the biggest indicator of the pressing need to clarify the job of teacher.

So how should textbooks fit in with the real job description of teachers? Once the desired results for learners are clarified (as in our history, reading, and math examples), a teacher or group of teachers should consider the following questions (preferably before the school year begins):

- Which chapters in the textbook are central to my goals, the school's mission, and our standards?

- Which chapters are not vital, relating only somewhat to my goals, the school's mission, and our standards?

- Which chapters can be skipped since they are irrelevant to my goals, the school's mission, and our standards?

- What must I do to supplement the text in order to achieve my goals, the school's mission, and our standards?

The topics of coverage and teaching to the test inevitably initiate comments such as this in schools and staff development sessions: "No, you don't understand. My job is to cover the content, though I would do otherwise if I could. That's not my wish, but that's what I must do." I respectfully disagree. We must think about what these words really mean. They say that teaching equals casual mentioning. They imply that teachers have no responsibility for any learning being caused, only an obligation to ensure that certain things are covered. The words are thus egocentric. They say nothing about what you should be causing; they are merely describing what you will do, as if that were all that mattered in the job of a teacher. It seems a stretch to imply that a supervisor wants his or her teachers to "cover things" irrespective of resultant learning.

But what about standardized tests, which are really at the heart of the coverage issue and form the basis for "teaching to the test." It is perhaps more common to hear the statement: "No, you still don't get it! I have to cover all this content to prepare my students for the tests! That's the bottom line, not my goal, and I am hassled about it regularly. We have to prepare them for the test, so we have to cover everything."

This statement brings up an interesting point: no research that I know of says that mediocre and superficial coverage optimizes test performance. In fact, recent large-scale research on learning in higher education and in the sciences at the high school level suggests just the opposite (see Bain, 2004; and Schwartz, Sadler, Sonnert, & Tai, 2008). It defies common sense as well: the best teachers make their subject interesting and cohesive with big ideas and clear performance goals. Endless content coverage is actually the approach of someone who has no explicit course goals or strategy for staying focused on them. Turning pages in a textbook and doing whatever the textbook offers up is not a *plan* (see McTighe, Seif, & Wiggins, 2004; and Wiggins & McTighe, 2005). More than a half dozen states and countries (including Massachusetts, Florida, and New York at the high school level, and National Assessment of Educational Progress [NAEP] and Trends in International Mathematics and Science Study [TIMSS] at the national and international levels) release their tests *and* the results, so we have a trove of interesting data on what is tested and which questions are most likely to get answered incorrectly or scored the lowest. The questions that students get wrong most often have nothing to do with factoids and everything to do with transfer of learning, careful reading, nonroutine problem solving, and critical thinking.

Consider the released test results from Florida (Florida Department of Education, 2007) in figure 1. This question is ranked as "moderate" in difficulty. In the question in figure 1, 32 percent of students scored 0 points, 49 percent scored 1 point, and 20 percent scored 2 points on a 4-point scale.

Hipparchus, an astronomer in ancient Greece, proposed an Earth-centered model of the solar system. In this model, the Sun, Earth's moon, Mercury, Venus, Mars, Jupiter, and Saturn not only traveled around Earth, but also traveled in small circles called "epicycles." A simplified illustration of Hipparchus's solar system is shown below.

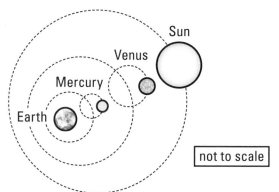

Explain how our current understanding of the solar system differs from Hipparchus's Earth-centered solar system.

AN EXPLANATION SIMILAR TO THE FOLLOWING:

We now know that the Sun is at the center of the solar system instead of Earth. We also know that the planets do not travel in epicycles; instead, they rotate on their axes as they revolve around the Sun.

**Figure 1: Test question and results released by the Florida Department of Education for Benchmark SC.E.1.3.1.**

Figure 2 shows a sample question from an elementary grade (Florida Department of Education, 2006).

The question tests students' skill at determining main idea/essential message from a text passage. The percentage of students who chose each answer appears to the left of each answer.

**Figure 2: Test question and results released by the Florida Department of Education for Benchmark LA.A.2.2.1.**

As these sample questions show, the tests do not *demand* superficial coverage; they demand whatever instruction will enable a student to handle a fairly small number of familiar or unfamiliar looking items, problems, prompts, and text samples related to the standards. The tests test for transfer, in other words. The hardest test questions require students to summarize or comment on author purpose in a *new* text, or take core information they learned and apply it to a novel situation, drawing, data, or problem. The easiest questions involve recall of simple facts and skills, and there are not that many of them.

If more teachers taught for understanding, student scores would rise. That is what test validity demands and common sense suggests. Only a lack of clarity about performance goals and our fear about tests and how to prepare for them hold us back.

## The Job of Being a Teacher Outside of the Classroom

Up until now, we have been considering the questions, What's my job when I am with students? What was I hired to accomplish with students? But now we begin to see that learning-goal clarity and careful analysis of state standards and assessments lead to these related vital questions:

- What is my job when I am *not* with students? What was I hired to accomplish before and after class to better achieve my goals with students?

- What is my job when I am with colleagues? What must we accomplish together in order to best serve students and our learning goals?

As McTighe and I argue in *Schooling by Design* (2007), there are numerous roles for teachers outside of class that should be made mandatory, not optional. We suggest that teachers must be contributors to the curriculum, analyzers of results, and continuous learners in their areas. Danielson's framework (2007) calls for optional participation in these roles for good teaching. We believe they should be mandatory because of how we defined the job earlier: given what all teachers are hired to accomplish, excellent learning can only occur if we work together as a team to ensure that the institution's efforts are coherent over time and devoted to continuous progress at our few bottom-line cross-classroom goals.

The great scandal in K–12 education is that almost every K–12 system is actually not a system at all. High school teachers in history rarely score papers or discuss writing with teachers of English, even though nonfiction writing is a state standard. Or, when elementary grade-level teams meet, they do not typically use the time to share and improve student performance deficits but instead put out the perpetual fires of daily schoolkeeping. As Covey put it (1989), many educators confuse the urgent with the important. This is inevitable when the job description is not clear. Middle school teachers rarely interact with high school teachers, resulting in great damage to many students' education. How can an eighth-grade student get a B+ in math only to get a D+ in algebra 1 in the very next semester in the same district? This would not and should not ever happen in a true *system*.

The K–12 system will only be truly systematic if the following happens:

- Teachers of all grades write curriculum together.

- Teachers of all grades score student work together.

- Teachers are required, as team members, to issue team reports each semester to the rest of the K–12 faculty on what worked, what did not, and what will be done to improve learning against goals and standards, mindful of best practice in the building as well as in the education world more generally.

The Greece, New York, school system's language arts program is an example of a system that truly works together as a system to address cohesion across grade levels and subjects. They have worked together to create common rubrics, themes, essential questions, and anchor papers. See their website (http://web001. greece.k12.ny.us/academics.cfm?subpage=311) for samples of the work they have done together.

Collaboration must be a requirement of the job, not an option. Our obligations clearly demand that we not merely teach in our "slot" (our individual content), but that we achieve cross-course and cross-grade goals related to standards and school mission. But few schools have structures and policies in place to ensure that the coherence of students' education makes it impossible for them to fall through the cracks between the slots. Our goals can only be met if we get out of our isolated classrooms and continually work on the key outcomes that cross room, subject-area, and school boundaries (McTighe, 2008).

## Agreeing to Agree and Agreeing to Disagree: Freedom and Obligation

Teachers might ask, "But what about our academic freedom? What about our professional prerogative as individual teachers?" These are important questions, of course—arguably two of the most important questions *never* adequately discussed in staff meetings in schools and universities. However, notice that the first question has little relationship to the second question. Academic freedom applies to original research and the rights of free speech; teaching obligations reflect the right of an institution to ensure that your individual teaching serves the needs and goals of the organization, that it honors what we know about how people learn, and that it reflects professional standards of conduct. In short, that you do your job.

For example, no teacher is free to construct, give, and grade an invalid test. No teacher is free to wander away from the established curriculum. No teacher is free to treat some students differently in terms of grading, learning opportunities, and other issues of fairness.

What teachers are free to do—quite properly—is develop methods of teaching and assessment that make it more likely that students will succeed at school mission and course-specific goals.

But this freedom is not without a significant caveat. As Jay McTighe and I have made clear (Wiggins & McTighe, 2008), once teachers realize that our goals require a focus on transfer and meaning making, not mere acquisition of content, then many habit-bound teaching practices would have to change based on a backward design analysis of what these two goals require of instruction. If transfer is the goal, then spending the most time in class lecturing is inappropriate; if meaning making is the goal, then instructional strategies have to involve students doing such things as research, Socratic seminar, and analysis of problems and cases (see McTighe's chapter in this volume on page 271 for more information).

Where it gets even stickier is when institutional demands require teachers—even good ones—to change time-honored approaches borne of work in isolation. Thus, though it makes impeccable sense for there to be common rubrics and grading standards across the organization so that we are all on the same page about what quality work looks like for key performances, few school systems have tackled this problem. Most teachers still weigh criteria, score, and grade independently of one another.

This demand for consistency of goals and means is not unattainable. The New England Association of Schools and Colleges (NEASC), the accrediting agency for the Northeast, now requires all high schools to develop and use rubrics for its key mission-related goals, and track performance over time as part of its self-study. Great Britain, as part of its national curriculum, has created longitudinal (developmental) rubrics for use across grade levels. And the American Council on the Teaching of Foreign Languages (ACTFL) proficiency guidelines anchor New Jersey's world language curriculum standards and local assessment. In short, any hope of achieving the goals of the job depends upon clarity and agreement about what that goal looks like, and having it be transparent to all parties.

## Gaining Focus

The job of being a teacher has arguably never been more challenging. But let us not conflate *challenging* with *stressful*. So much of the current real stress of teaching comes, like all stress, from a lack of conscious awareness about the point of it all, the absence of clarity about priorities, and the resultant feeling that little is in our control. But once we are clearer about what our mission is, what the priority learning goals are, and what the job logically demands from us, we will be less crazed and more focused—like the soccer coach or band director. And once we focus on outcomes instead of just inputs and good intentions, we will be more effective, and so will students. That will, ironically, make us feel far less stressed, but also more challenged with important goals that we must stretch to reach so there is always more to be done. Fundamental school reform thus arguably begins with a serious ongoing and in-depth dialogue about the essential question of teaching: what's my job as teacher *really*?

## References

Bain, K. (2004). *What the best college teachers do.* Cambridge, MA: Harvard University Press.

Collins, J. (2001). *Good to great: Why some companies make the leap . . . and others don't.* New York: HarperCollins.

Covey, S. (1989). *The seven habits of highly effective people.* New York: Simon & Schuster.

Curtis, P. (2009, January 5). Ofsted's new mission—to get rid of boring teachers. *The Guardian.* Accessed at www.guardian.co.uk/education/2009/jan/05/ofsted-boring-teachers on May 20, 2009.

Danielson, C. (2007). *Enhancing professional practice: A framework for teaching* (2nd ed.). Alexandria, VA: Association for Supervision and Curriculum Development.

Indiana Department of Workforce Development. (2009). *Advertising and promotions managers job description.* Indianapolis, IN: Author. Accessed at http://dwdonenet.in.gov/occupation.htm?onetCode=11-2011.00&familyId= on March 30, 2009.

Florida Department of Education. (2006). *Florida Comprehensive Assessment Test 2006: Released grade 3 reading sunshine state standards test book.* Accessed at http://fcat.fldoe.org/pdf/releasepdf/06/FL06_Rel_G3R_AK_Cwf001.pdf on March 1, 2009.

Florida Department of Education. (2007). *Florida Comprehensive Assessment Test 2007: Released grade 8 science sunshine state standards test book.* Accessed at http://fcat.fldoe.org/pdf/releasepdf/07/FL07_G8S_AK_Rel_WT_C001.pdf on March 1, 2009.

Goodlad, J. (1984). *A place called school.* New York: McGraw-Hill.

McTighe, J. (2008, May). Making the most of professional learning communities. *The Learning Principal, 3*(8), 1–7.

McTighe, J., Seif, E., & Wiggins, G. (2004, September). You *can* teach for meaning. *Educational Leadership, 62*(1), 26–31.

Norton, J. (2009, March 4). PD pet peeves: Teachers misbehaving. *Teacher Magazine.* Accessed at www.teachermagazine.org on March 4, 2009.

Schwartz, M., Sadler, P., Sonnert, G., & Tai, R. (2008, December). Depth versus breadth: How content coverage in high school science courses relates to later success in college science coursework. *Science Education,* 1–29.

Secretary of Labor Commission on Achieving Necessary Skills. (2000). *Learning a living: A blueprint for high performance: A scans report for America.* Washington, DC: Author.

Students are bored, many skip school, lack adult support. (2007, February 28). *IU News Room.* Accessed at http://newsinfo.iu.edu/news/page/normal/4948 .html on March 1, 2009.

Tyler, R. (1948). *Basic principles of curriculum and instruction.* Chicago: University of Chicago Press.

Wiggins, G. (1998). *Educative assessment.* San Francisco: Jossey-Bass.

Wiggins, G., & McTighe, J. (2005). *Understanding by design* (2nd ed.). Alexandria, VA: Association for Supervision and Curriculum Development.

Wiggins, G., & McTighe, J. (2007). *Schooling by design: Mission, action & achievement.* Alexandria, VA: Association for Supervision and Curriculum Development.

Wiggins, G., & McTighe, J. (2008, May). Put understanding first. *Educational Leadership, 65*(8), 36–41.

Yazzie-Mintz, E. (2007). *Voices of students on engagement: A report on the 2006 High School Study of Student Engagement.* Bloomington: Indiana University School of Education, Center for Evaluation and Education Policy.

# Thomas L. Good

Thomas L. Good, Ph.D., is a professor and head in the Department of Educational Psychology at the University of Arizona. His previous appointments were at the University of Texas at Austin and the University of Missouri-Columbia. His policy interests include school choice and youth. His research interests include the communication of performance expectations in classroom settings and the analysis of effective instruction, especially in schools that serve children who reside in poverty. His work has been supported by numerous agencies, including the National Science Foundation and the National Institute of Mental Health. Dr. Good has been a Fulbright Fellow (Australia) and was the editor of the *Elementary School Journal*. He has published numerous books in various languages, including Chinese, German, Japanese, and Spanish.

In this chapter, Dr. Good addresses the question, What do we know about research on teaching that we did not know in 1968? He examines the progress of research on teacher effectiveness, concluding that progress has been useful, but less than expected. He argues that research on teaching has not improved its capacity for theoretically (and empirically) explaining how teachers impact students' subject-matter learning. Dr. Good challenges the reader to think about what constitutes progress and the role of research in improving practice.

## Chapter 2

# Forty Years of Research on Teaching 1968–2008: What Do We Know Now That We Didn't Know Then?[1]

Thomas L. Good

### Forty Years Later: An Introduction

In this chapter, I examine the progress research on teacher effectiveness has made in the forty-year period 1968–2008. I conclude that the field's progress has been modest and useful, but less than expected. Before viewing this progress, I consider gains in society and in the social sciences. Progress in these fields has also been limited; for example, economists do not predict gross national product any better today than they did in 1968. So, in comparison to other social sciences, our limited progress in education may perhaps be typical. Despite the field's modest gains, there is some progress in research knowledge that merits celebration. Teachers do impact student achievement, and I

---

[1] A version of this paper was initially presented as an invited address at the University of Geneva, Geneva, Switzerland, on April 25, 2008.

describe some of the ways they do so. Then I suggest why the field has not accomplished more.

### Early Personal Memories

In 1968 I was a graduate student at Indiana University searching for a good dissertation topic. Lightning struck, so to speak, when I read three publications: Benjamin Bloom's "Learning for Mastery" (1968), Robert Rosenthal and Lenore Jacobson's *Pygmalion in the Classroom: Teacher Expectation and Pupils' Intellectual Development* (1968), and Philip Jackson's *Life in Classrooms* (1968). Bloom, Rosenthal, and Jacobson noted the malleability of student potential and the importance of teaching. Jackson provided a way to think about classrooms as social systems. While writing my dissertation, I found Nate Gage's (1968) work that provided a broader intellectual grounding in the field of research on teaching.

Subsequently, I conducted a study describing how teachers interacted differently with students they believed to be high or low achievers. This dissertation (Good, 1968) was subsequently published in 1970 in the *Elementary School Journal*—a journal that I was to subsequently edit from 1980–2008[2] and was once edited by Phil Jackson, who had influenced my early research interests. In 1971, I joined the Department of Educational Psychology (EDP) at the University of Texas. That same year, Jere Brophy also joined EDP. Jere arrived from the University of Chicago where he had studied dyadic interaction between mothers and children. Our mutual research interests in dyadic interactions led to a collaboration (Brophy & Good, 1970) that continues today (Good & Brophy, 2008).

---

[2]My editorship of the *Elementary School Journal* ended June 1, 2008. Gail Hinkel served admirably as the associate editor of the *Elementary School Journal* from 1980–2008.

## 1974: Emergence of a Field

Mick Dunkin and Bruce Biddle created the field of research on teaching in their seminal work *The Study of Teaching* (1974). They noted that thousands of studies of teacher effectiveness were available, but few involved observations of teaching. They argued for a field—the study of teaching—organized around theory and systematic observations and noted deficiencies in research on teaching, such as inadequate theory, the use of inadequate criteria of effectiveness, and a lack of concern for contextual effects.

In 1974, Nate Gage was asked by the U.S. Office of Education to organize a conference to make research on teaching more productive. That 1974 conference was attended by leading scholars in the field, and their reports eventually led to the Institute for Research on Teaching (IRT) at Michigan State University.[3] Under Lee Shulman's leadership (and later Jere Brophy's and Andy Porter's), the IRT not only conducted research on teaching, but it also provided a forum that brought scholars together to discuss research on teaching. Further, the IRT taught a new group of graduate students[4] to become knowledgeable about research on teaching.

Classroom researchers in 1968 had no idea how difficult it would be to relate teaching to student achievement. In the late 1960s, we were moving from an era where researchers primarily used "black box" approaches, which directly linked input variables to outcome variables. Little was known about how those links occurred. For example, black-box studies linked the impact of differential school resources and climates on student achievement (Coleman et al., 1966) and considered teachers more for who they were (Getzels & Jackson, 1963) than what they did.

---

[3]My current dean, Ron Marx, was a graduate student "scribe" for one of the panels.

[4]Mary Rohrkemper (now my wife, Professor Mary McCaslin) was among the initial group of IRT interns!

Observation researchers thought that important discoveries were just around the corner because we were moving systematically *inside* the black-box classroom.

In writing this chapter, I wanted to acknowledge that I have been involved with research on teaching since its inception. I bring some bias to this task. Today, researchers have a greater appreciation of how difficult it is to isolate the classroom—to separate home, societal, community, school, teacher, curriculum, and student variables. Students' achievement is affected by many factors other than what students and teachers do in the classroom; however, what teachers *do* in classrooms is open to influence and remains a critical policy issue.

## The Complexity of Research on Teaching

What do we know from research on teaching that we did not know in 1968? This question would be answered somewhat differently by research on teaching scholars. The answer depends, for example, on how change is defined. Is the criterion for change a mere difference or a distinct improvement? There have been many changes in the research on teaching between now and then; however, I argue that research on teaching has not improved its capacity for theoretically (and empirically) explaining how teachers impact students' subject-matter learning.

### Research in the Social Sciences and Society

While considering research on teaching from 1968 to 2008, I also wondered about the realm of appropriate comparison: Has educational research improved? How about in comparison to other social sciences? For example, have typical hospitals become safer? Is road rage less, or are highways safer? Have employer/employee relationships improved? Have they improved for both groups equally? Has drug dependence lessened? Do we possess and use greater knowledge about how to sustain the environment? Have the poor gotten poorer? Can and do more people read?

Has the use of alternative fuels improved in important ways? Is credit used more appropriately? Answers to these questions likely suggest that societal gains have been less than what we hoped for in 1968. So, too, is the case in research on education.

Some would argue that the goal of educational research is not to improve practice, but rather to generate knowledge relevant to improving practice; similarly, some might argue that the goal of social-science research is not to solve social problems, but to generate concepts that others can apply to problems. I do not assert that changes or the lack thereof in society are comparable to changes or lack thereof in education, but I do challenge the reader to think about what constitutes progress and the role of research in improving practice.

## What Have We Learned?

### Teachers Make a Difference

In the 1960s, many social scientists believed that student achievement was largely due to heredity and home effects and that the impact of teaching was exceedingly small (Coleman et al., 1966; Heath & Nielson, 1974; Jensen, 1973). Over time, researchers have demonstrated that teachers impact student learning in important ways. The initial evidence that teachers make a difference in student achievement was overwhelming (Anderson, Evertson, & Brophy, 1979; Good & Grouws, 1979; Good, Grouws, & Ebmeier, 1983; Stallings, Cory, Fairweather, & Needels, 1978), and this evidence continues to grow (Clotfelter, Ladd, & Vigdor, 2007; Darling-Hammond et al., in press; Mendro, 1998; Miller, Murnane, & Willett, 2008; Nye, Konstantopoulos, & Hedges, 2004; Rivkin, Hanushek, and Kain, 2001, 2005; Rowan, Correnti, & Miller, 2002; Sanders & Horn, 1994; Sanders & Rivers, 1996; Stronge, Ward, Tucker, & Hindman, 2007; Wright, Horn, & Sanders, 1997).

However, since 1986, most large-scale research has returned to black-box studies that do not include observational measures of classroom process, making it impossible to describe how more- and less-effective teachers vary in their instruction. If classroom process was measured, it was to provide information on a small sample of teachers, limiting generalizability. Ironically, as evidence that teachers make a difference in student achievement grows, our ability to explain why and how teachers impact student achievement differentially has not improved substantially (Good, 2008).

**How do teachers make a difference? One research example.** In the 1970s, Doug Grouws and I (1977, 1979) studied how to make mathematics more meaningful and increase students' learning. This research, supported by the National Institute of Education, in time became known as the Missouri Math Project (MMP).

We first assessed teacher effects on students' learning. The MMP began in an era when scholars assumed that individual differences in teachers were unimportant determinants of student learning. Doug and I had no preconceived idea about the desirability of any particular teaching or learning format. In our naturalistic study, there were teachers who used individualized, group, and whole-class formats. Teachers varied both in their effectiveness from year to year in terms of student achievement and in their students' perceptions of classroom climate. We studied teachers whose students had relatively stable and relatively high achievement and those whose students had relatively stable and low achievement. As it turned out, both groups primarily used *whole-class* rather than individualized or group teaching methods. Clearly, whole-class teaching did not predict teacher effectiveness in our correlational study, as both *effective* and *less-effective* teachers used whole-class teaching. We then pursued the question of causality: can the practices associated with effective teachers be taught to other teachers in ways that improve their students' achievement? Our experimental work demonstrated that teachers who used the recommended practices had an important positive effect on student achievement.

In building our training program, we used our correlational work[5] describing how teachers who consistently obtained high student achievement scores taught differently than teachers who obtained lower achievement scores from similar students under similar conditions. We also used a small but powerful set of basic, theoretical studies in mathematics.[6] These studies highlighted the value of the amount of time spent on understanding material and showed in several experiments that student achievement was higher when the ratio of time spent on exploring the meaning of the content was greater than time spent on practice (Dubriel, 1977; Shipp & Deer, 1960; Shuster & Pigge, 1965; Zahn, 1966).[7] These data suggested that providing a rich conceptual base allowed for meaningful practice and increased skill proficiency. Mathematics teachers at that time, however, tended to spend most of their instructional time on practice.

Our study combined information about what effective teachers did and placed those discrete behaviors into a system of instruction. Our experiment demonstrated that teachers generally could implement most aspects of the treatment, *except* they did not focus on development of a rich conceptual base for as long as we wanted before turning to application and practice. However, teachers may have believed (correctly) that they had spent sufficient time on development. Clearly, more work was needed on how teachers can best develop mathematical meaning for students, but we had made some improvement in practice.[8]

---

[5] Our observational instruments were also based on earlier research by Barak Rosenshine, Norma Furst, Jere Brophy, Carolyn Evertson, David Berliner, Nate Gage, and others.

[6] There is a long history in mathematics education of the need to teach mathematics in a meaningful way (Brownell, 1947).

[7] In all cases, development of meaning preceded practice.

[8] We believe, but cannot document, that teachers' attempts to involve students more in discussing the meaning of the mathematics made student seatwork more likely to connect skills and understanding.

The MMP is not an answer to enhancing students' mathematical achievement per se. Howard Ebmeier and I illustrated that teacher and student beliefs mediate the impact of the treatment (Ebmeier & Good, 1979). Classroom composition factors also mediate achievement findings (Beckerman & Good, 1981). Although MMP teachers were able to produce greater student achievement than control teachers, our treatment worked better for some teachers and students than for others.

The MMP provided prima facie experimental evidence that teachers make a difference in student achievement, and it provided some information about how this occurred. Teachers focused on the meaning of the math and presented ideas in a direct, clear, and coherent fashion. They involved students actively in discussing math so that teachers had a good idea that students understood the assigned seatwork, and teachers assessed students' seatwork to assure that homework would be meaningful work for students.

Missouri Math Project teachers knew the mathematics they taught. We provided teachers with a better system to achieve their goals. Despite these important experimental data and the data reported by others, this type of research was largely abandoned. In part, the focus on large-group instruction was seen as a limiting form of instruction. Progressively, teachers were seen and described as coaches or facilitators, minimizing active teaching.

**Proactive management: Another research example.** Kounin's (1970) study of teachers who were more- and less-effective managers revealed a system of proactive management associated with attentive students, including alerting (anticipating what will happen), accountability (following through on announced action), "withitness" (finding ways to show students that the teacher is aware of their behavior), smoothness of transitions (clear communication about how to disengage from one task and begin another), and variety in seatwork. Students had a clear classroom structure in which to navigate and to pursue tasks.

Work by many other scholars has extended these ideas through careful field experiments. Evertson (and her colleagues) have expanded the variables included in classroom management work. Research on the Classroom Organization and Management Program (COMP; see www.comp.org for more details) found that COMP teachers demonstrate desirable changes in both teacher and student behavior in many studies in various contexts, and that COMP training impacts student achievement.

Freiberg, Huzinec, and Lamb (in press) report the effects of their proactive classroom management program on 350 upper elementary students and 350 matched controls. Treatment students outperformed control students in both math and reading. These data provide clear evidence that better management per se can directly enhance student achievement.

However, a "Kounin framework" can be misused. Mary McCaslin (personal communication, July 3, 2008) has noted, for example, that Kounin teachers are not teaching students self-responsibility, and if the teacher does not coregulate management responsibilities with students, over time, their capacity for self-management may be reduced. I have concluded that teachers' accountability actions could convey low expectations (for example, if the same students are always called on at transition points, it might convey "If *you* understand, we can move on"). Further, the model can be implemented in an authoritarian or in a friendly "we are in this together" approach. With recognition (and correction) of these weaknesses, the model has considerable strength.

### Time and Student Achievement

How teachers use time is related to student achievement. One good illustration comes from the Beginning Teacher Evaluation Study (BTES; Berliner, Fisher, Filby, & Marliave, 1978; Fisher, Filby, Marliave, Cahen, & Dishaw, 1980). Data from BTES showed that on average only 58% of allocated time was spent on academic subjects and that 18% of the school day was spent on noninstructional topics. Student achievement was positively associated with time utilization. In some second-grade classrooms students received on average fifteen to twenty minutes of daily math instruction, whereas in other classes students averaged forty-five to fifty minutes of daily math instruction. The discrepancy in allocated time was often compounded by the extent to which students were engaged in instructional activities. In some classes students were engaged about 50% of the time, whereas in other classes they were engaged about 90% of the time. Student success rates varied from class to class. In some classes students frequently coped with tasks that were too hard, yet in other classes this rarely happened. Patterns of relationships between student seatwork success and ultimate achievement varied by grade level and subject matter, but generally better student achievement was more often associated with moderate levels than with high rates of seatwork success (see Burnstein, 1980).

Smith (2000) documented the amount of instructional time that certain Chicago public elementary schools allocated to students. The study involved 300 observations in social studies, math, and language arts classes in seventy teachers' classes at grades 2, 5, and 8. Overall, 23% of time allocated for instruction was used for noninstructional purposes. However, the average amount of noninstructional time of more "effective" teachers was 14% compared with 30% of "less effective" teachers. Smith reasoned that 300 minutes were supposed to be allocated for daily instruction, yet only 280 minutes could really be considered as available for instruction due to various things like school announcements. Using this metric, Smith concluded that less-effective teachers' students received 200 minutes of instruction—two thirds of the intended amount of time.

I argue that not all time should be allocated for "academic" learning, and indeed I have noted the importance of non-subject-matter outcomes in two special issues of the *Elementary School*

*Journal* (1999, 2000). I am against such practices as eliminating school recess and reducing time for youth to exercise (Nichols & Good, 2004). Still, I suggest that teaching is problematic when one-third of the available time for instruction is not used day after day. Clearly some teachers use allocated time unproductively.

## General Principles of Effective Teaching

Jere Brophy summarized what has been learned from observational research about effective teaching. He drew upon a considerable volume of work conducted in the 1990s and 2000s and reached some general conclusions about effective teaching. Brophy's list merits serious consideration. It provides a general heuristic for planning instruction and allows for particulars that vary by context (Good & Brophy, 2008).

1.  **Teacher expectations**—Teachers who obtain good achievement gains accept responsibility for teaching their students. If students do not understand entirely, teachers are willing to reteach in a different way. They fully convey the belief that students can learn.

2.  **Proactive and supportive classrooms**—Students learn best in supportive classrooms that offer a caring community in which academic and social goals are clear. Supportive classrooms allow students to take intellectual risks. In supportive classrooms, the focus is placed on learning, not simply on "knowing" or on right and wrong answers.

3.  **Opportunity to learn**—Opportunity to learn is a big variable in countries like the United States where there is no common curriculum (Porter & Polikoff, 2009). In countries with a national curriculum, opportunity to learn is not a major variable as students largely receive a known curriculum. However, in the United States, fourth-grade students in one class may receive a "facts" curriculum while students across the hall receive a "problem solving" curriculum. In America, teaching effects are a product of curricula as well as what teachers do.

4. **Curriculum alignment**—In effective instruction, content is aligned to create a visible and coherent plan for achieving curriculum goals. Teachers carefully differentiate between more- and less-important content and allocate time accordingly.

5. **Coherent content**—In effective instruction, content is organized and explained in sufficient depth to allow students to learn meaningfully. More important concepts need greater consideration, and major points should not be cluttered with inappropriate details. Good teachers achieve coherence both within and across lessons.

6. **Thoughtful discourse**—Thoughtful discourse allows for the voicing of various opinions and the exploration of alternative explanations. Thoughtful discussion goes beyond defining what "is" to explaining why, solving problems, and considering future implications. Thoughtful discourse can occur in both teacher-led and student-led activities.

7. **Scaffolding students' ideas and task involvement**—Teachers actively support student learning activities and strive to help students understand concepts more fully. In many classrooms, discussions focus mainly on what is known or just found. Good student scaffolding can help learners move from their present knowledge to future knowledge, just as teacher scaffolding can help students to understand at a higher level.

8. **Practice/application**—Students need ample opportunity to practice concepts, and once they have firmly acquired the learning, they need opportunities to apply concepts in new contexts. Periodic review is needed to enhance students' ability to apply key concepts.

9. **Goal-oriented assessments**—Tests, quizzes, and papers need to focus on important curricular goals. Such assessments help students to focus upon important content.

Students need to know that their daily activities are important. These activities serve as learning objectives for showing what knowledge teachers think is important and how students can best display that knowledge.

## So What Do We Know?

Many may see these findings as simplistic. If so, they should consider the potential impact of simple ideas. Consider, for example, what we know about preventative medicine. The recommendations "wash your hands frequently" and "cover your mouth when coughing or sneezing" are common ones. These simple points were powerfully reinforced for me during a recent trip to the International Red Cross Museum in Geneva. During my tour, I learned that Florence Nightingale was able to drop mortality rates by 75 percent during the Crimean war by implementing a good hygiene policy. This is nothing to sneeze at! But getting people to change their habits is surprisingly hard.[9]

## What Have We Learned?

Teachers who possess subject-matter content, focus on meaning, present with clarity and warmth, use positive and proactive management systems, and teach in large-group settings are more likely to impact student achievement than teachers who do not teach in these ways. Is this the best way to teach? Probably not. Are there better models for teaching? Probably yes. My claim—and it is an important one—is that this system is research based and flows from evidence and not assertion.

---

[9] Dr. Val Curtis, the director of the Hygiene Center at the London School of Hygiene & Tropical Medicine, spent years trying to persuade people in the developing world to wash their hands habitually with soap. Studies indicate that disease and disorders caused by dirty hands kill a child somewhere in the world about every fifteen seconds, and about half of those deaths could be prevented with the regular use of soap. To overcome this hurdle, Dr. Curtis called on three top consumer goods companies to find out how to sell hand-washing the same way they sell Speed Stick deodorant and Pringles potato chips (Duhigg, 2008).

Further, it is a model useful for certain types of learning, and good use of this model can lay the foundation and provide the time needed for the use of other instructional models. Perhaps researchers outside the United States have found better models.

### Cross-National Research

Does poor student learning in the United States equal poor teaching? International comparisons are problematic. For example, Stevenson and Stigler (1992) have shown that children in Japan know much more math when they enter kindergarten than do American students. There are differences in teacher pay. Pay in countries that perform well in mathematics is often higher than in the United States, making it likely that teachers elsewhere will not have to moonlight with a second or third job. And there are striking differences in curricula and cultural support for learning (Hess & Azuma, 1991). With these considerations in mind, cross-national research may yield interesting hypotheses about improving math teaching in America.

Stigler, Lee, and Stevenson (1987) collected observational data in Japanese and Taiwanese classrooms (countries whose students routinely outperform American students) and compared teaching in those countries with that in the United States. Teachers in Japan and China spent more time working with the whole class (86% and 77%, respectively) than in America (46%). Teachers in America spent less time imparting mathematical information to children (25%) compared to China (63% of the time) and in Japan (33%). Student engagement rates also varied by country. First graders' engagement in learning was 69.8% in America, 85.1% in China, and 79.2% in Japan. The corresponding engagement rates at the fifth-grade level were marked: 64.5%, 91.5%, and 87.4%. The authors concluded the following:

> American children fail to receive sufficient instruction. They spend less time each year in school, less time each day in classes, less time in the school day in mathematics

classes, and less time in each class receiving instruction. The classes were organized so that American children were frequently left to work alone at their seats on material in mathematics that they apparently did not understand well, they engaged in many irrelevant activities, and they spent large amounts of time in transition from one activity to another. (pp. 1284–1285)

Hiebert et al. (2005) reviewed the third Trends in International Mathematics and Science Study, which examined eighth-grade mathematics teaching in six high-achieving countries and in the United States. They found that eighth-grade math lessons in the United States involved considerable review and that teaching typically focused on procedures and unchallenging tasks. Not surprisingly, the authors recommended a better integration of procedural and conceptual orientation, less review,[10] and increasing the coherence of lessons. They argue that these changes are dependent upon creating a system of teaching. "It is not enough to simply include a new feature, such as presenting more challenging problems or spending more time on new material" (Hiebert et al., 2005, p. 128).

I do not want to over argue the similarities between teaching math in high-achieving Asian countries and in the United States, as there are documented differences. Asian teachers are more likely to push students and to let them struggle at times, and whole-class teaching lessons in Asian classes focus more on problem solving than in U.S. classrooms. Mathematics educators have recently stressed the distinction between teaching for skill efficiency and teaching for conceptual understanding (Grouws & McNaught, 2009; Hiebert & Grouws, 2007). American educators typically equate whole-group instruction with the development of skill efficiency; however, international research has shown

---

[10]This is of course what we tried to do in the Missouri Math Project (Good, Grouws, & Ebmeier, 1983).

that teachers can use whole-group instruction when teaching for conceptual understanding.

Ironically, American educators have recommended minimizing whole-class teaching. However, Asian teachers—the gold standard—spend more time teaching students in large groups and more successfully engage students in learning than do American teachers. Although this literature offers some suggestions for adjusting instruction in American classrooms, it generally supports conclusions about good practice presented earlier in this chapter. So good teachers here and abroad present well-organized, coherent content in well-managed classrooms and use allocated time for instruction. They focus on meaning, present with clarity and enthusiasm, and provide a supportive learning climate.

## Value-Added Research

Large-scale studies of classroom process diminished considerably in the 1990s. Stronge et al. (2007) lament the dirge of studies linking classroom process and student achievement: "The last forty years of reform efforts have focused primarily on the development of curriculum standards, assessments to measure student achievement, and school-level reporting mechanisms to publicly explain results" (p. 184). Recently, researchers have conducted several value-added studies that are notably similar to process-product studies (such as the MMP discussed earlier). Although the dependent measures used to describe student achievement are more sophisticated in value-added studies now than in earlier work, the problems of their use for evaluating teachers (Miller & Chait, 2008) remain highly similar to those raised by David Berliner (1979) and other process-product researchers of that time. Stronge et al. (2007) report that teachers who added more value to student achievement scores in comparison to less-effective teachers placed a greater emphasis on meaning than memorization, used a variety of materials, collected student assessment information frequently, utilized better management procedures, expressed higher expectations for student learning, and exhibited fairness to and respect for students. Do these findings sound familiar?

Linda Darling-Hammond and colleagues (in press) describe a large value-added study (using many process measures of teaching) that reassesses the old question, How do teachers who obtain good student achievement differ from those who do not? Darling-Hammond et al. studied teachers who demonstrated marked capacity for increasing student achievement. Their findings support the conclusion that teachers *teach* (and are more than coaches):

> The highly effective teachers consistently engaged the students in mathematical sense-making activities, provided opportunities to explore and formalize mathematical patterns, continually assessed students' understanding through questioning, conversation and observations. (Darling-Hammond et al., in press, p. 28)

These two modern studies largely confirm what previous process-product researchers noted some time ago. Importantly these new value-added studies were presented without reference to earlier process-product work and findings (Brophy & Good, 1986). For whatever reason, these researchers present their findings as "new" and independent of any intellectual heritage. This is a good example of the failure to integrate research findings.

## Normative Curriculum and Normative Instruction

### Normative Practice

The normative (typical) instructional activities in grades 3 through 5 are now reasonably well established by research, especially in mathematics. There can be wide variation in how teachers enact normative instruction (some teachers average three periods a week on drill/practice and others allocate only one-and-a-half periods). Still, the components of instruction generally vary around the same set of practices and range of content. We have long known the normative curriculum, and we continue to confirm it (Berliner, 1979; Fisher et al., 1980; Fisher & Berliner, 1985; Freeman et al., 1983; Freeman & Porter, 1989; Pianta, Belsky, Houts, Morrison, & NICHD Early Child Care Research Network, 2007; McCaslin et al., 2006; McNaught, Tarr, & Grouws, 2008; NICHD, 2003, 2004, 2005; Porter, 1989; Porter et al., 1988).

Typically, classrooms focus on drill/practice, have limited time for conceptual development, focus on basic skills and concepts, and provide limited time for application and even less so for problem solving. The affective climate is generally supportive, and students' answers are typically correct. Most instruction is in whole-class or large-group settings. Students ask few questions, make few choices, and get few, if any, rewards (McCaslin et al., 2006). Yet importantly, the enactment—the quality—of this basic faire shows marked variation, as some teachers working with similar students under similar conditions obtain significantly more achievement from their students than do other teachers.

As we know from our own experience, a chicken dinner with salad, wine, and apple pie can be a completely *different* experience as we move from restaurant to restaurant or eat at different homes. Please understand that I would like to add to this repertoire of choices: I say yes to better wine, and I support good appetizers and even organic vegetables. However, understand that the literature on effective teaching is not established on evidence showing that effective teachers bring in new components or better ingredients. Rather, the literature indicates that some teachers work with basic ingredients better than do other teachers. The typical math curriculum in grades 3 through 5 is well established, and there is much to like and support, and, of course, there are things to change.

### Changing Normative Practice

Certain teaching practices have endured for over a century (Cuban, 1984). Why? Reformers have failed for various reasons but the most basic is that teachers favor teacher-centered instruction as a frequent lesson format and teacher educators do not. Also, reform recommendations are too sweeping and call for radical changes like moving from traditional classrooms to open classrooms or rejecting one form of instruction for another. Thus, reading, math, and other change wars wax and wane (Hargreaves & Fullan, 2009), but in the end teacher-centered instruction endures.

Many are not happy with teacher-centered instruction. Lefstein (2008) laments teachers' unwillingness to embrace reform: "Teachers ignore, resist, subvert, misinterpret, selectively adopt, or otherwise distort reformers' intentions. Changes tend to be superficial, seldom penetrating the core of instructional practice" (p. 701). I do not suggest that Lefstein's beliefs are held by typical teacher educators, but they do point to tension between teacher educators and teachers.

Teacher resistance to reform is often reasonable. Teachers may find aspects of a reform attractive, but they may also believe that the scope of required changes and the speed with which they are expected to be enacted will not be more effective than their current practices. Some teachers likely reject the new reform because it arrives on the basis of *assertion,* not *evidence.*

Historically, reformers have erred by attempting to do too much too soon. Changing normative practice can better be seen as a series of small steps that allow for major progress over time. And these changes must occur with teacher support, and the reform process must encourage teacher thought and innovation—not just simple compliance (Randi & Corno, 1997). It is better to implement needed and accepted small reforms over time than to urge radical reform that will be rejected.

Mary McCaslin and I (Good & McCaslin, 2008; McCaslin & Good, 2008; McCaslin et al., 2006) have hypothesized that many comprehensive school reform (CSR) classrooms could be enhanced with more opportunities for students to apply knowledge and to elaborate on facts, concepts, and skills intended to sharpen their understanding of the content they study. I believe these same issues apply in many other grade 3 through 5 classes as well. More opportunities for student choice also seem important so that students can learn how to make choices, develop their interests, and meet the responsibilities that come with choice. Expectations for student understanding and responsibility can be too high as well as too low, and achieving the appropriate balance between breadth and depth, and other- and self-direction is not easy. Teachers involved in these research and development efforts should know that they are involved in the search for *balance* (McCaslin et al., 2006). The degree of balance is to be determined through cooperative research with teachers. What constitutes an enabling balance, however, is likely to vary with such factors as teacher knowledge of mathematics; beliefs they hold about teaching math and students' prior knowledge; and beliefs and dispositions that they hold about learning. Balance is also mediated by subject matter, grade level, and the type of learning outcome sought (Ebmeier & Good, 1979; Hiebert & Grouws, 2007; McCaslin & Burross, 2008; Pianta et al., 2007).

More work on students' dispositions seems especially warranted. McCaslin (2008) organizes students' motivational opportunities into three categories: supports, challenges, and threats. Subsequently, survey measures were developed to add a rich and efficient way to understand students' dispositions (as compared to interviews). Other studies applied this framework (Dolan & McCaslin, 2008; Florez & McCaslin, 2008; McCaslin & Burross, 2008). Student reports strongly suggest that interpersonal validation is central to students' achievement and affiliation motivation and that individual differences in student orientations can be linked to student achievement. Importantly, it is clear that most students were working hard and productively engaged in school tasks and interacted with peers and teachers in a civil, supportive, and warm fashion. Apparently, students' motivation is poorly captured by current motivational surveys that emphasize aspects of motivation that appear less central to how students actually feel and what they believe.

## Why Do We Not Know More About How Teachers Enhance Student Achievement?

Why do we not know more about how teachers can facilitate student achievement? I provide several explanations. First, the sheer complexity of teaching militates against identifying clear and strong links between classroom processes and outcomes. Students are prepared for the fourth grade by different combinations of first- through third-grade teachers. Some of these variations are important. Some teachers teach how to divide fractions well; others do not teach it well; some do not teach it at all. Home effects are real and need no explanation except perhaps to note that the effects of poverty on student learning are often underestimated. Because of various community effects, the variation in language and other skills students bring to school is enormous. Cohort effects are real—the average ability level of sixth graders varies from year to year even in the same school. Teachers' lives change over time, and some years leave less energy for teaching.

Although teacher influences on students are complex, many believe that the need for instructional change is obvious. Reformers must realize that the quality of teaching is more important than its format. Reformers call for more small-group instruction, and more project work; however, the enactments of these and other reforms show marked differences. Some small-group projects work, but many fail. The cost and complexity of the research needed to determine the quality of a format are considerable. To establish whether whole-class instruction or student-directed inquiry is of good quality requires careful observation and good measurement. Two visits by a peer teacher or the principal are insufficient to make judgments about the quality of a teaching/learning format. Failure to differentiate quality—say of technology—greatly slows the generation of useful research knowledge. Adding technology may not enhance teaching, and in some instances it may have negative effects. Any variable—even seemingly simple ones like homework or review—can take many forms, and their usefulness always depends on their quality, the instructional context, and the learning goal. Further, no single variable relates to student achievement independent of other instructional variables. Thus, the quality of teaching is necessarily determined by relationships among variables.

In comparison, reform initiatives typically address variables in sequence and isolation. For example, documentation of the effects of a reform typically comes after implementation. Problems of prior practice are noted (low achievement) and the prevailing form of previous instruction is challenged. If formal teaching is normative, then the call for more informal learning and wall-less classrooms is rampant. When schools are seen as supporting too much choice and student autonomy, calls erupt for a common and more rigorous curriculum (Powell, Farrar, & Cohen, 1985). Reactive research follows the proposed solution and shows the uneven effects of the reform, and irrespective of the particular "problem" or its "solution," we commonly discover that today's answer has become tomorrow's problem: too much drill/practice becomes too little review, and so forth. A good example of reactive research is the documentation of the poor effects of zero-tolerance management systems to improve school safety—years after its wide implementation (American Psychological Association Zero Tolerance Task Force, 2008).

We have known about the dangers of reactive research for some time. For example, the Soviets' launching of Sputnik touched off wide reactive reform of the mathematics curriculum without any research evidence. Others have reached similar conclusions:

> In many ways the new math movement has the character of the children's crusade of the middle ages. It is recognized as such by many responsible educators, but it is difficult to stop because of the very large and tightly

knit web of vested interest preying on the mathematical unsophistication of the press, the public and the foundations themselves. Under these circumstances, I urge administrators to forget the prestige of the sponsors and view with restraint and enthusiasm anything which does not really make sense to them, rather than be Sputnik-panicked into the hysterical adoption of new progress. (Mosie, 1961, in Good & Braden, 2000, p. 31)

"New" research on teaching is not additive. For example, the era of process-product paradigm (Brophy & Good, 1986) ended in part by a focus on what the paradigm was not suited to do well. Research on what teachers do was seen as insufficient (understandably) for describing what teachers thought about. When the call for correcting this "problem" was sounded, researchers flocked to studies of teaching thinking without bridging to or building on the important differences that had been documented by careful research. For example, at that time we knew that teachers used time in dramatically different ways and that poor use of time was related to reduced levels of achievement. Thus, it would seem important to know how teachers think about allocating time. Yet perhaps to distinguish themselves from previous researchers, many researchers feel a need to ask different—especially new—questions; thus, research becomes "almost new" and not integrated. In this sense, research becomes something other than the attempt to improve practice:

In a perfect world, there would be a body of research that could be used to answer the "What next?" question. It would be in a form that teachers would find accessible and useable, and it would be factored into discussions in a just-in-time manner. This is not how research works, however. Research gets done on topics that concern researchers, and gets funded by agencies and foundations that in some sense know what the important problems are before they start studying them (and often the answers they will get), based on their own organizational interests at a particular moment in time. Sometimes the knowledge produced through these relationships happens to match the problems that practitioners are dealing with; however, more often than not, the connections are, at best, distant and problematic. (Elmore, 2009, p. 229)

Ironically, because of the ahistorical nature of research on teaching, what is thought to be "new" today has often been explored at an earlier time. For example, in the past decade, the call for increased use of small cooperative groups has been frequent and passionate. This advocacy for small-group instruction has been ahistorical, ignoring earlier foundational research including Deutsch (1949) and Sherif, Harvey, White, Hood, & Sherif (1954/1961). This lack of knowledge was costly because many problems in using small groups had to be rediscovered (such as the need to deal with within-group competition as well as between-group competition). In addition to a lack of respect for earlier research, many reformers continue to undervalue (and sometimes scorn) the wisdom of practice.

Federal government initiatives like No Child Left Behind ignore teacher conceptions of how to evaluate students' performance in favor of state tests made "on the fly" and whose cutoff scores for determining proficiency are typically made on political grounds and not on measurement consideration. The amount of money spent on state-made tests in the last decade is enormous, and the return on this public investment is scant. Teachers receive information too late to use for instructional decision making. Indeed, if we want to improve rather than describe student performance, we would test students in August rather than April (McCaslin et al., 2006). Instead we use tests to rank students' teachers and schools (often poorly), and we label some schools as inadequate, although we do not know how to "fix" the schools proclaimed as failing.

The mistrust of teachers goes beyond policymakers as reformers often ask teachers to radically change their practice even when the reformers have no compelling evidence that the advocated change (which may involve countless hours of teacher effort) will pay off. And when teachers do not change, they are blamed for not implementing ideas that are backed only by assertion.

I believe that teachers will implement recommended reform when they see it as reasonable. And I believe that teachers are more likely to accept change when it modifies current practice rather than replacing it.

Reform, and teacher education to a lesser extent, has become a culture of assertion rather than a culture of evidence. The lack of confidence in teachers' professional decisions is difficult to understand, especially when criticisms are expressed harshly and without evidence. Some scholars have reacted equally harshly to teacher educators because of their many assertions for change without evidence. B.O. Smith (1980) was especially critical:

> What is now required is an about face for faculties of pedagogy. They are accustomed to thinking in terms of what can be done to improve the schools. And professors of pedagogy have been all too ready to have teachers do thus and so, or administrators to introduce this and that remedy. But the time has come for improvements to be at home, for faculties of pedagogy to look at their own programs in light of research knowledge and to create a genuine program of professional education. We can no longer enjoy the luxury of trying to change everything but our own programs. (p. 57)

> When the faculty of pedagogy does not know what it is about, it grabs any and every newfangled idea and purpose that any organization or agency offers, suggests, or insists upon. It will take on the task of providing courses, workshops, or any other device for meeting such

demands as the call for urban education, sex education, drug education, or human relations education, even though the faculty is already falling far short of performing the task it was created to do: to train teachers in the knowledge and skills of classroom work. (p. 87)

Although I think Smith is basically correct, I am more sympathetic to teacher educators, as there are aspects of normative practice that merit reform. However, teacher educators and policymakers who seek to improve practice must understand that much of what many teachers do is reasonable practice within the condition of teaching. Teachers are professionals and need information about practice that they can use to make decisions; they do not need to be told what to do.

So as someone who has studied the effects of teaching for over forty years, I conclude that extant knowledge has moved us to a point where in cooperation with teachers we can conduct "research-findings stimulated" experiments in elementary schools and especially in mathematics. This is because we now know more about what the normative curriculum is, and we have working hypotheses about how to improve it. The effects of our field—research on teaching—are modest but evident and potentially important.

## Acknowledgments

Special thanks to Amanda Bozack for early work on this paper, and special thanks to Alyson Lavigne Dolan for her extensive help in obtaining research and documents and preparing this manuscript through several revisions. Finally, I express my deep gratitude to Mary McCaslin for her extensive suggestions for improving the paper both substantively and editorially.

## References and Resources

American Psychological Association Zero Tolerance Task Force. (2008). Are zero tolerance policies effective in the schools? An evidentiary review and recommendations. *American Psychologist, 63*(9), 852–862.

Anderson, L., Evertson, C., & Brophy, J. (1979). An experimental study of effective teaching in first-grade reading groups. *Elementary School Journal, 79*, 193–223.

Beckerman, T. M., & Good, T. L. (1981). The classroom ratio of high- and low-aptitude students and its effect on achievement. *American Educational Research Journal, 18*(3), 317–327.

Berliner, D. (1979). Tempus educare. In P. Peterson & H. Walberg (Eds.), *Research on teaching: Concepts, findings, and implications*. Berkeley, CA: McCutchan.

Berliner, D., Fisher, C., Filby, N., & Marliave, R. (1978). *Executive summary of Beginning Teacher Evaluation Study*. San Francisco: Far West Laboratory.

Bloom, B. (1968). Learning for mastery. *Evaluation Comment, 1*(2), 1.

Brophy, J. E. (2006). Observational research on generic aspects of classroom teaching. In P. A. Alexander & P. H. Winne (Eds.), *Handbook of educational psychology* (pp. 755–780). Mahwah, NJ: Lawrence Erlbaum Associates.

Brophy, J., & Good, T. (1970). Teachers' communication of differential expectations for children's classroom performance: Some behavioral data. *Journal of Educational Psychology, 61*(5), 365–374.

Brophy, J., & Good, T. (1986). Teacher behavior and student achievement. In M. Wittrock (Ed.), *Third handbook of research on teaching* (pp. 328–375). Chicago: Rand McNally.

Brownell, W. (1947). The place of meaning in the teaching of elementary school arithmetic. *Elementary School Journal, 47*(5), 256–265.

Burnstein, L. (1980). Issues in the aggregation of data. *Review of Research in Education, 8*, 158–233.

Clotfelter, C. T., Ladd, H. F., & Vigdor, J. L. (2007). *Teacher credentials and student achievement in high school: A cross-subject analysis with student fixed effects*. Working Paper No. 13617, National Bureau of Economic Research.

Coleman, J. S., Campbell, E. Q., Hobson, C. J., McPartland, J., Mood, A. M., Weinfeld, F. D., et al. (1966). *Equality of educational opportunity*. Washington, DC: U.S. Office of Education.

Cuban, L. (1984). *How teachers taught: Consistency and change in American classrooms 1890–1980*. New York: Longman.

Darling-Hammond, L., Dieckmann, J., Haertel, E., Lotan, R., Newton, X., Philipose, S., et al. (in press). Studying teacher effectiveness: The challenges of developing valid measures. In G. Walford and E. Tucker (Eds.), *The handbook of measurement: How social scientists generate, modify, and validate indicators and scales*. Thousand Oaks, CA: Sage Publications.

Deutsch, M. (1949). A theory of co-operation and competition. *Human Relations, 2*, 129–152.

Dolan, A. L., & McCaslin, M. (2008). *Student perceptions of teacher support*. Accessed at www.tcrecord.org/content.asp?contentid=15282 on July 16, 2008.

Dubriel, J. B. (1977). *Utilization of class time in first year algebra.* Unpublished doctorial dissertation, University of Missouri-Columbia.

Duhigg, C. (2008, July 13). Warning: Habits may be good for you. *New York Times.* Accessed at http://www.nytimes.com/2008/07/13/business/13habit.html?_r=1 on May 1, 2009.

Dunkin, M., & Biddle, B. (1974). *The study of teaching.* New York: Holt, Rinehart, & Winston.

Ebmeier, H., & Good, T. L. (1979). The effects of instructing teachers about good teaching on the mathematics achievement of fourth-grade students. *American Educational Research Journal, 16,* 1–16.

Elmore, R. F. (2009). Institutions, improvement, and practice. In A. Hargreaves and M. Fullan (Eds.), *Change wars* (pp. 221–236). Bloomington, IN: Solution Tree Press.

Fisher, C. W., & Berliner, D. C. (Eds.) (1985). *Perspectives on instructional time.* New York: Longman.

Fisher, C., Filby, N., Marliave, R., Cahen, L., & Dishaw, M. (1980). Teaching behaviors, academic learning time, and student achievement: An overview. In C. Denham & A. Lieberman (Eds.), *Time to learn.* San Francisco: Far West Laboratory for Educational Research and Development.

Florez, I. R., & McCaslin, M. (2008). Student perceptions of small-group learning. *Teachers College Record, 110*(11), 2438–2451.

Freeman, D., & Porter, A. (1989). Do textbooks dictate the content of mathematics instruction in elementary schools? *American Educational Research Journal, 26,* 403–421.

Freeman, D. J., Kuhs, T. M., Porter, A. C., Floden, R. E., Schmidt, W. H., & Schwille, J. R. (1983). Do textbooks and tests define a national curriculum in elementary school mathematics? *Elementary School Journal, 83,* 501–513.

Freiberg, H. J., Huzinec, C. A., & Lamb, S. M. (in press). Classroom management— A pathway to student achievement. *Elementary School Journal.*

Gage, N. L. (1968). Can science contribute to the art of teaching? *Phi Delta Kappan, 49*(7), 399–403.

Gage, N. L. (1972). *Teacher effectiveness and teacher education: The search for a scientific basis.* Palo Alto, CA: Pacific.

Getzels, J. W., & Jackson, P. W. (1963). The teacher's personality and characteristics. In N. L. Gage (Ed.), *Handbook of research on teaching.* Chicago: Rand McNally.

Good, T. L. (1968). *Student achievement level and differential opportunity for classroom response.* Unpublished doctoral dissertation, Indiana University, Bloomington.

Good, T. L. (1970). Which pupils do teachers call on? *Elementary School Journal, 70*(4), 190–198.

Good, T. L. (1999). Introduction: The purposes of schooling in America. *Elementary School Journal, 99*(5), 383.

Good, T. L. (2000). Introduction. *Elementary School Journal, 100*(5), 405.

Good, T. L. (2008, April 7). Teaching mathematics in grades 3–5 classrooms. *Teachers College Record.* Accessed at www.tcrecord.org/Content.asp?ContentID=15196 on April 8, 2008.

Good, T. L., Biddle, B., & Brophy, J. (1975). *Teachers make a difference.* New York: Holt, Rinehart, & Winston.

Good, T. L., & Braden, J. S. (2000). *The great school debate: Choice, vouchers, and charters.* Mahwah, NJ: Lawrence Erlbaum Associates.

Good, T. L., & Brophy, J. (2008). *Looking in classrooms* (10th ed.). Boston, MA: Allyn & Bacon.

Good, T. L., & Grouws, D. (1977). Teaching effects: A process-product study in fourth grade mathematics classrooms. *Journal of Teacher Education, 28*(3), 49–54.

Good, T. L., & Grouws, D. (1979). The Missouri mathematics effectiveness project: An experimental study in fourth-grade classrooms. *Journal of Educational Psychology, 71*(3), 355–362.

Good, T. L., Grouws, D. A., & Ebmeier, M. (1983). *Active mathematics teaching.* New York: Longman.

Good, T. L., & McCaslin, M. (2008). What we learned about research on school reform: Considerations for practice and policy. *Teachers College Record, 110*(11), 2475–2495.

Grouws, D. A., & McNaught, M. D. (2009). Three pillars of a sound mathematics education: Curriculum, teaching and assessment. In T. L. Good (Ed.), *21st century education: A reference handbook* (Vol. 1, pp. 343–351). Thousand Oaks, CA: Sage.

Hargreaves, A., & Fullan, M. (Eds.). (2009). *Change wars.* Bloomington, IN: Solution Tree Press.

Heath, R. W., & Nielson, M. A. (1974). The research basis for performance-based teacher education. *Review of Educational Research, 44*(4), 463–484.

Hess, R. D., & Azuma, A. (1991). Cultural support for schooling: Contrasts between Japan and the United States. *Educational Researcher, 20*(9), 2–8.

Hiebert, J., & Grouws, D. A. (2007). The effects of classroom mathematics teaching on students' learning. In F. K. Lester (Ed.), *Second handbook of research on mathematics teaching and learning* (pp. 371–404). Greenwich, CT: Information Age.

Hiebert, J., Stigler, J. W., Jacobs, J. K., Givvin, K. B., Garnier, H., Smith, M., et al. (2005). Mathematics teaching in the United States today (and tomorrow): Results from the TIMSS 1999 video study. *Educational Evaluation and Policy Analysis, 27*(2), 111–132.

Jackson, P. (1968). *Life in classrooms.* New York: Holt, Reinhart & Winston.

Jensen, A. (1973). *Educability & Group Differences.* New York: Harper & Row.

Kounin, J. S. (1970). *Discipline and group management in classrooms.* Huntington, NY: R. E. Krieger.

Lefstein, A. (2008). Changing classroom practice through the English National Literacy Strategy: A micro-interactional perspective. *American Educational Research Journal, 45*(3), 701–737.

McCaslin, M. (2008). Learning motivation: The role of opportunity. *Teachers College Record, 110*(11), 2408–2422.

McCaslin, M., & Burross, H. L. (2008). Student motivational dynamics. *Teachers College Record, 110(11),* 2452–2463.

McCaslin, M., & Good, T. L. (2008). A study of Comprehensive School Reform programs in Arizona. *Teachers College Record, 110*(11), 2319–2340.

McCaslin, M., Good, T. L., Nichols, S., Zhang, J., Hummel, C., Bozack, A. R., et al. (2006). Comprehensive school reform: An observation study of teaching in grades 3 to 5. *Elementary School Journal, 106,* 313–331.

McNaught, M. D., Tarr, J. E., & Grouws, D. A. (2008, March). *Assessing curriculum implementation: Insights from the Comparing Options In Secondary Mathematics Project.* Paper presented at the Annual Meeting of the American Education Research Association, New York.

McNergney, R. F., & Imig, S. R. (2006). *Challenges of assessing value added to PK–12 education by teacher education.* Accessed at www.tcrecord.org/PrintContent.asp?ContentID=12814 on December 4, 2006.

Mendro, R. L. (1998). Student achievement and teacher accountability. *Journal of Personnel Evaluation in Education, 12*(3), 257–267.

Merton, R. (1948). The self-fulfilling prophecy. *Antioch Review, 8,* 193–210.

Miller, R., & Chait, R. (2008). *Teacher turnover, tenure, policies, and the distribution of teacher quality: Can high-poverty schools catch a break?* Accessed at www.americanprogress.org/issues/2008/12/pdf/teacher_attrition.pdf on March 30, 2009.

Miller, R. T., Murnane, R. J., & Willett, J. B. (2008). Do teacher absences impact student achievement? Longitudinal evidence from one urban school district. *Educational Evaluation and Policy Analysis, 30*(2), 181–200.

National Institute of Child Health and Human Development. (2004). *Child Development and Behavior Branch (CDBB), NICHD, report to the NACHHD Council.* Washington, DC: U.S. Government Printing Office.

National Institute of Child Health and Human Development Early Child Care Research Network. (2003). Social functioning in first grade: Associations with earlier home and child care predictors and with current classroom experiences. *Child Development, 74,* 1639–1662.

National Institute of Child Health and Human Development Early Child Care Research Network. (2005). A day in third grade: A large-scale study of classroom quality and teacher and student behavior. *Elementary School Journal, 105,* 305–323.

Nichols, S., & Good, T. L. (2004). *America's teenagers—myths and realities: Media images, schooling, and the costs of careless indifference.* Mahwah, NJ: Lawrence Erlbaum Associates.

Nye, B., Konstantopoulos, S., & Hedges, L. V. (2004). How large are teacher effects? *Educational Evaluation and Policy Analysis, 26,* 237–257.

Pianta, R. C., Belsky, J., Houts, R., Morrison, F., & NICHD Early Child Care Research Network (2007). Opportunities to learn in American's elementary classrooms. *Science, 315,* 1795–1796.

Porter, A. C. (1989). A curriculum out of balance: The case of elementary school mathematics. *Educational Researcher, 18*(5), 9–15.

Porter, A. C., & Polikoff, M. S. (2009). National curriculum. In T. L. Good (Ed.), *21st century education: A reference handbook* (Vol. 2., pp. 434–442). Thousand Oaks, CA: Sage.

Porter, A., Floden, R., Freeman, D., Schmidt, W., & Schwille, J. (1988). Content determinants in elementary school mathematics. In D. A. Grouws & T. J. Cooney (Eds.), *Perspectives on research on effective mathematical teaching* (pp. 96–113). Hillsdale, NJ: Lawrence Erlbaum.

Powell, A. G., Farrar, E., & Cohen, D. K. (1985). *The shopping mall high school: Winners and losers in the educational marketplace.* Boston: Houghton Mifflin.

Randi, T., & Corno, L. (1997). Teachers as innovators. In B. J. Biddle, T. L. Good, & I. F. Goodson (Eds.), *International handbook of teachers and teaching* (pp. 1163–1221). Dordrecht, The Netherlands: Kluwer Academic Publishers.

Rivkin, S. G., Hanushek, E. A., & Kain, J. F. (2001). *Teachers, schools, and academic achievement.* Working Paper No. 6691, National Bureau of Economic Research.

Rivkin, S. G., Hanushek, E. A., & Kain, J. F. (2005). Teachers, students, and academic achievement. *Econometrica, 73*(2), 417–458.

Rosenthal, R., & Jacobson, L. (1968). *Pygmalion in the classroom: Teacher expectation and pupils' intellectual development.* New York: Holt, Rinehart and Winston.

Rowan, B., Correnti, R., & Miller, R. J. (2002). What large-scale, survey research tells us about teacher effects on student achievement: Insights from the prospects study on elementary schools. *Teachers College Record, 104*(8), 1525–1567.

Sanders, W. L., & Horn, S. P. (1994). The Tennessee Value Added Assessment System (TVAAS): Mixed model methodology in educational assessment. *Journal of Personnel Evaluation in Education, 8,* 299–311.

Sanders, W. L., & Rivers, J. C. (1996). *Research project report: Cumulative and residual effects of teachers on future student academic achievement.* Knoxville: University of Tennessee Value-Added Research and Assessment Center.

Sherif, M., Harvey, O. J., White, B. J., Hood, W. R., & Sherif, C. W. (1954/1961). *The robbers cave experiment: Intergroup conflict and cooperation.* Scranton, PA: Wesleyan University Press.

Shipp, D., & Deer, G. (1960). The use of class time in arithmetic. *Arithmetic Teacher, 7*, 117–121.

Shuster, A., & Pigge, F. (1965). Retention efficiency of meaningful teaching. *Arithmetic Teacher, 12*, 24–31.

Smith, B. (2000). Quantity matters: Annual instructional time in an urban school system. *Educational Administration Quarterly, 365*(5), 652–682.

Smith, B. O. (1980). *A design for a school of pedagogy.* Washington, DC: U.S. Department of Education.

Stallings, J., Cory, R., Fairweather, J., & Needels, M. (1978). *A study of basic reading skills taught in secondary schools.* Menlo Park, CA: SRI International.

Stigler, J. W., Lee, S-Y., & Stevenson, H. (1987). Mathematics classrooms in Japan, Taiwan, and the United States. *Child Development, 58*, 1272–1285.

Stevenson, H. W., & Stigler, J. W. (1992). *The learning gap: Why our schools are failing and what we can learn from Japanese and Chinese education.* New York: Simon & Schuster.

Stronge, J. H., Ward, T. J., Tucker, P. D., & Hindman, J. L. (2007). What is the relationship between teacher quality and student achievement? An exploratory study. *Journal of Personnel Evaluation in Education, 20*, 165–184.

Wright, S. P., Horn, S. P., & Sanders, W. L. (1997). Teacher and classroom context effects on student achievement: Implications for teacher evaluation. *Journal of Personnel Evaluation in Education, 11*(1), 57–67.

Zahn, K. G. (1966). Use of class time in eighth grade arithmetic. *Arithmetic Teacher, 13*, 113–120.

# Barrie Bennett

Barrie Bennett, Ph.D., is cross-appointed professor to the undergraduate and graduate programs at the University of Toronto's Ontario Institute for Studies in Education (OISE/UT). Dr. Bennett's current research interest relates to how teachers intersect curriculum, assessment, and instruction, guided by how students learn. He is also working with twelve districts in three countries (Ireland, Australia, and Canada) focused on long-term systemic change related to instruction. He has written three books related to instruction and is completing two other books; one related to graphic organizers, the other a twenty-six-year analysis of instructional change in three districts. In 2007, Phi Delta Kappa awarded him educator of the year for Ontario.

In this chapter, Dr. Bennett explores the concepts of art and science as they relate to the teaching and learning process. He then connects the idea of art and science to the classification of instructional methods and how this classification facilitates thinking and action about intersecting instructional methods and their relationship to assessment. He then focuses on a modification of the Levels of Use (LoU) model and reflects on a key "missing think" in the teaching and learning process.

# Chapter 3

# The Artful Science of Instructional Integration

## Barrie Bennett

In a ten-year study of leadership in three countries, Leithwood, Day, Sammons, Harris, and Hopkins (2007) found that the best predictor of student achievement is improving the instructional practices of teachers. The second most powerful factor, they discovered, is the leadership practice of the principal in facilitating student and teacher learning. Likewise, a four-year case study of five not-so-effective secondary schools by Louis and Miles (1990) found that two of the five schools that were ultimately successful in improving focused on instruction and creating a safe learning environment. Louis and Miles also found that no other type of classroom change causes more conflict than attempting to change the instructional practices of teachers. We can deduce, then, that researching and valuing instruction is one thing; implementing and collectively sustaining it systemically over time is another.

That said, this chapter is not about justifying the "doing" of instruction through an exploration of research. Numerous studies and books (past and present) provide examples of the effects of instructional innovations on student learning (for example,

Friedman & Fisher, 1998; Marzano, 1998, 2003; Waxman & Walberg, 1991; Wittrock, 1986). Rather, this chapter contains practical insights into the delightful complexities and possibilities that exist within the teaching and learning process. In 1978, when I was teaching middle school, I labeled these insights *instructional intelligence*, and I share insights here that are the result of thirty-six years of classroom teaching (Bennett, 2002; Fullan, 2002).

Instructional intelligence, as a process, has evolved; it now merges curriculum, assessment, instruction, knowledge of how students learn, and theories of change and systemic change. Conceptually, in terms of intent, it parallels differentiated instruction. The belief that no one right or best way to teach exists is central to instructional intelligence. Every teacher in the world could be given the same two-week unit to teach, and each teacher could teach it differently with equal effectiveness or ineffectiveness. So, given the time span of a teaching career—say thirty or more years—and all that we know about the teaching and learning process, the possibilities for the design of learning environments are endless.

In this chapter, I explore the idea of teaching as both an art and science and apply this thinking to the classification of instructional methods. I show how this classification facilitates thinking and action about intersecting instructional methods. Importantly, I also address integrating instructional methods and how this impacts student learning and directly relates to assessment. Following that I focus on a modification of the Levels of Use (LoU) model, an innovation from the Concerns-Based Adoption Model (CBAM; Hall & Hord, 2006). I argue that if we fail to attend to the concept of LoU, we are only half right about assessment. The chapter concludes with key "missing thinks" in the teaching and learning process.

As you read this chapter, consider whether or not you think teachers deeply grasp the complexity of instruction—the art and the science. Do they intentionally understand and apply their instructional repertoire, or are they limited to being tacitly or unconsciously skilled? Do they think of their instructional repertoire as a way of integrating multiple processes for academic power?

I argue, as do many others, that teaching is one of the most complex, important, and demanding of all occupations; to be effective as an educator takes years of intense effort and constant reflection and dialogue. In my current work in classrooms, I observe that most teachers work incredibly hard and care deeply about what happens in their classrooms. Nonetheless, for obvious reasons, such as the speed with which innovations come and go, the number of innovations teachers must respond to simultaneously, the funding structure that pushes the chasing of grants for professional development, the range of students at risk in each classroom, the diversity of learning needs, and so on, it is little wonder that teachers are not as intentionally or explicitly skilled about instruction as they must become. And from what I see about myself and other teachers who continue to teach in K–12 classrooms, we are also part of the problem—sort of like Pogo: "We have met the enemy, and he is us" (Kelly, 1953). Our intensity of action about assessing student learning is matched by our inaction about assessing our instructional methods. This means that not only are we less likely to align how we teach with how we assess, but too often we assess the impact of our instructional interventions when we ourselves are naïve users of those interventions.

## The Art and Science of Teaching

Applying art and science to education is an old idea (see Eisner, 2004; Gage, 1977; Marzano, 2007; Rubin, 1985). I used the idea myself in *Beyond Monet: The Artful Science of Instructional Integration* (Bennett & Rolheiser, 2001). In Northrop Frye's *The Educated Imagination* (1964), the author explores the value and uses of literature and its study. He repositions art and science at opposite ends of the same continuum, arguing that they indeed differ but that in certain situations, art and science merge.

In describing the differences between art and science, Frye considers the pursuits of scientists and artists. Whereas scientists pursue the idea of "better" (for example, determining the best methods for heart surgery), Frye suggests, artists do not. Rather, artists communicate from an inherent belief that they do not know the best way to "do" art and that one form of art is not better than another (for example, dancing is not better than sculpting).

How does this relate to education? Most educators have at one time or another discussed whether teaching is more of an art or more of a science. They may ask the questions, (1) Are educators concerned about which methods are better, and (2) Do educators know the best way to teach? Virtually all teachers say yes to question one and no to question two. After further discussion, they usually reach the conclusion that in the teaching and learning process, art and science merge; one informs the other. Like scientists, we are concerned about more effective ways to teach students; like artists, we do not know a best way for all students to learn, but we are aware of the possibilities. Like scientists, we research better ways, we test, we experiment; like artists we communicate, tell our stories, interpret, deconstruct, and reconstruct, keeping an open mind to new possibilities.

This tension between the drive to get better and the lack of a best way creates fertile ground for conflict, and how we deal with that conflict determines our ultimate success. Louis and Miles (1990) found that the ability to confront and resolve conflict is the number-one predictor of whether or not a school becomes and stays effective. They add that no amount of visioning or planning prevents or solves conflict—change and conflict are inseparable. Tangentially, Blumer (1954) presents two types of concepts: *definitive*, which have clarity (for example, the concepts of window, dog, and house), and *sensitizing*, which do not have absolute clarity (for example, the concepts of love, justice, and motivation). Instruction and learning are sensitizing concepts, as no single best way exists to teach or to learn. That lack of clarity results in discussion and dissention; it also reminds us that to get better as a teacher, one must integrate different instructional methods to more effectively meet the diverse needs of students.

When integrating instructional methods, the teacher designs learning experiences by merging or stacking two or more instructional methods. This aligns the focuses of science (a best way) with art (no best way). For example, does having students integrate multiple graphic organizers (such as a mind map, concept map, Venn diagrams, fish-bone diagrams, and ranking ladders) in summarizing a unit of study impact student learning? What if students first work in effectively structured small groups to produce the first draft and then work on their own—would that make more of a difference?

If each instructional method has a certain amount of power to affect learning, then we might assume that by integrating instructional methods, we would increase the power to impact student learning. By increasing our instructional repertoire, we are more likely to become more artful or creative and more scientific or intentional when differentiating our instruction to meet the diverse needs of students. In teaching, the research on effective group work is the science; how often you employ it, and when, where, and with whom you apply it is the art. If we are not wise in the art, then the science will be misinformed.

In the next section, I take a more experiential (that is, *artful*) perspective on the interactive nature of instruction.

## Classifying Instruction

Classifying is an everyday inductive-thinking process of putting things into categories based on common attributes. For example, we classify utensils into knives, forks, and spoons; clothing into pants, shirts, socks, dresses, and so on; transportation into land, sea, air, and space. With the exception of most proper nouns (for example, there is no concept called "Susan" or "San Francisco"), everything else in the world has been classified inductively.

Classifying instructional methods allows us to be more specific when we communicate, when we plan, when we teach, and when we assess the effects of our efforts or those of our students. The idea of classifying instruction is certainly not new. Joyce and Weil's book *Models of Teaching* (2000) engages the learner to explore different instructional methods that serve different purposes—such as impacting memory, creativity, critical thinking, and so on—in the design of learning environments. Their text, *Models of Teaching* is still one of the most important and powerful ways of understanding the more complex models or strategies of teaching. Hunter's (1994) program Instructional Theory Into Practice (ITIP) is a practical, meaningful, and well-researched body of literature that covers the less-complex instructional concepts and skills that effective teachers, regardless of their philosophical bent, employ daily in the design of learning environments. Hunter looks at instruction in terms of four key areas: motivation, retention, rate and degree of learning, and transfer. Interestingly, much of what is promoted today as effective instruction can be found clearly articulated in Hunter's work from the 1970s and 1980s.

We lose these connections to past insights, however, because we tend to unwittingly ignore concept labels or change them— with the effect of losing access to the history of an innovation. For example, the concept of *task analysis* has been swallowed by less precise phrases such as "designing down" or "starting with the end in mind," and *cognitive coaching* has supplanted Goldhammer and Cogan's (1973) work on *clinical supervision,* and we end up blurring the foundation of clinical supervision and peer coaching.

We lose these connections due to the loose way we use certain terms in education—*methods, approaches, models, strategies, tactics, skills, structures, techniques*, and *tools*, to name a few—with little sense that they can have different meanings. When we apply these terms and others with little or no grasp of their foundational constructs and the research behind them, we increase the chances of applying them in less-effective and disconnected ways.

In developing my own classification of instruction, I was encouraged by Bruner's argument (1966) that we do not have a clearly articulated theory of instruction—a way of explaining instruction's interactive nature. Concomitantly, for twenty-six years, I have been developing a practical theory of instructional integration—a way of thinking about what happens when we merge or integrate two or more instructional processes, guided by what we know about how we learn. This theory explains the application of five instructional areas—*skills, tactics, strategies, concepts*, and *organizers*—to situate the research and practices related to instruction and student learning.

### A Practical Theory of Instructional Integration

**Skills.** Instructional *skills* are the specific and relatively simple instructional actions of teachers that enhance learning. Their purpose is to increase the chances that the more complex instructional processes (tactics and strategies) are effectively implemented. Examples of instructional skills include framing questions at different levels of complexity, providing time to think after asking a question, linking to the learner's past experiences, checking to see if students understand, and providing models or visual presentation. In an example from outside of school, such as building a house, the skills would be hammering, sawing, and measuring. Obviously, those skills are necessary for enacting the more complex processes involved in building a house, such as squaring the foundation and completing the blueprint.

Most skills used by teachers in the classroom have not been researched (with the exception of questioning, wait time, and discussing the objective and purpose of the lesson). In fact, most teachers are not aware they are applying instructional skills; they are tacitly or unconsciously skilled and are not able to specifically talk about what they do.

Without skills, we would find it difficult to engage all learners in learning, and the power of instructional tactics and strategies is drastically reduced.

**Tactics.** *Tactic* is a word that is used rather indiscriminately both in education and in the world of business. In this paper, a tactic, in terms of complexity, fits between a skill and a strategy. Instructional *tactics* are actions initially invoked by the teacher (but actions that can also be selected by students as they take more responsibility for their learning). Tactics include Venn diagrams, fish-bone diagrams, ranking ladders, and flow charts, to name a few. Teachers often use tactics to enrich or strengthen the application of instructional strategies. Tactics can be applied in most subjects and grade levels, and may be linked to other instructional tactics and skills in the enactment of a more complex strategy. For example, a student could integrate tactics such as Venn diagrams, fish-bone diagrams, ranking ladders, and flow charts, into the strategy of concept maps. Tactics are not necessarily driven by theory; and interestingly, they also have a limited or nonexistent research base (for example, place mat, four corners, fish-bone diagrams, word webs, and Venn diagrams). A useful resource for a variety of tactics related to small-group cooperative learning is Spencer Kagan's *Cooperative Learning* (1985).

To continue with our example of house building from the previous section, squaring the foundation is a tactic, which involves the skills of hammering, sawing, and measuring. Another helpful example comes from the game of basketball: in basketball, a skill would be passing and catching a ball; a tactic would be a "give and go" or "pick and roll." A basketball coach would be somewhat naïve to expect a player to enact a "give and go" (a tactic) if players could not pass, catch, and shoot a basketball (skills).

Too often teachers attempt to enact more complex processes (strategies) without the skills and tactics to drive them. This makes strategies seem too complex and difficult, and so they stop using them. This is unfortunate, as strategies have the most potential to impact student learning.

**Strategies.** Instructional *strategies* are usually grounded in theory and are designed to have specific effects and a more extensive line of inquiry and research. They involve a sequence of steps (for example, Bruner's Concept Attainment Strategy [1966] has three phases) or a number of related elements (for example, the Johnsons' [2000] five basic elements of effective group work). Like instructional skills and tactics, strategies also have applicability across grade levels and subject areas. Unlike most skills and tactics, they have an intended effect on student learning. For example, they can affect inductive and deductive thinking, social action, critical thinking, and so on. Examples of strategies include Buzan's mind mapping (1993), Novak and Gowin's concept mapping (1984), Taba's concept formation (1967), and Aronson's jigsaw (1978).

In the previous house-building example where hammering and sawing were skills and squaring the foundation a tactic, the blueprint for the house is the strategy. The skills and tactics are necessary parts of the strategy. In the basketball example, passing, catching, and shooting (skills) come together to make a "give and go" (a tactic) which make the strategy of "1-3-1 offense" possible. Skills drive tactics, and skills and tactics drive strategies.

**Concepts.** Instructional *concepts* provide lenses to understand how, when, and where to apply one's instructional repertoire. They increase the chances that a teacher more effectively selects and integrates those instructional skills, tactics, and strategies that will make a difference in learning.

Note that although skills, tactics, and strategies are also concepts, the difference is that some instructional concepts cannot be "done." For example, instructional concepts such as safety, accountability, relevance, authenticity, novelty, and meaning cannot be "done." Rather, these are key concepts that teachers seek to enact through the application of a variety of instructional concepts labeled as skills, tactics, and strategies. For example, one can frame questions employing wait time and think/pair/share to invoke the concepts of safety, accountability, and active participation.

Teachers are often encouraged to "make the lesson a bit more interesting" or try to "make the classroom safer." These comments speak to concepts, and they can be confusing. I worked for six years with teachers who were at risk of losing their jobs, and making suggestions like these to improve teaching through attending to concepts (rather than to skills, tactics, and strategies) is not that helpful. To more precisely learn how teachers teach and how to improve the science of instruction, we must deconstruct lessons so that we attend to instructional concepts, skills, tactics, and strategies. Instructional organizers help us do this.

**Organizers.** In this chapter, instructional *organizers* refer to frameworks or bodies of research that assist teachers in organizing an array of instructional skills, tactics, and strategies into an interrelated yet open-ended pedagogical set. Instructional organizers act as lenses to clarify or enhance communication and thought about instruction. They are not to be confused with graphic organizers such as Venn diagrams and concept maps. Examples of organizers include the research on multiple intelligence, learning styles, Bloom's Taxonomy, children at risk, learning disabilities, gender, and ethnicity. Instructional organizers increase teacher wisdom when it comes to making decisions about the teaching and learning process and allow teachers to make instructional decisions with respect to the needs and inclinations of each individual learner.

### The Goal of Classification

By classifying instructional methods into skills, tactics, strategies, concepts, and organizers, I am attempting to make instruction somewhat more specific and focused so that we are more likely to demonstrate intelligent or expert behavior in the design and assessment of learning environments. If I was you, I would not be overly concerned whether something is a skill or a tactic, or whether it is a tactic or a strategy; gray areas exist. And, importantly, some skills are more powerful than some tactics; for example, the skill of framing questions merged with the skill of wait time is more powerful and in some instances more complex than the tactic of place mat. But place mat has the potential to facilitate a number of powerful tactics and strategies, so it has a lot of potential for greater power.

The key to integrating instruction is understanding how skills, tactics, and strategies are categorized from less complex and powerful to more complex and powerful in terms of their impact on student learning. Teachers must select from a variety of instructional skills, tactics, and strategies to invoke instructional concepts and organizers.

The basketball metaphor sheds light on the classroom application and research connection in education, for example, when a teacher attempts to apply the cooperative learning strategies of jigsaw, group investigation, or academic controversy. When students cannot effectively complete simple cooperative learning tactics such as think/pair/share and four corners because they cannot apply the skills of attentive listening, paraphrasing, suspending judgment, seeking clarification, probing, accepting and extending the ideas of others, disagreeing agreeably, and so on, then how can the process of cooperative learning be effectively applied? If they are not effectively applied, then we are not going to get the intended effects identified in the research. This clearly connects to assessment. The more effectively teachers and their students apply instructional methods, the greater the impact on student learning. In addition, each instructional process has an effect on student learning, by integrating two or more, we get a cumulative effect on student learning. Interestingly, virtually no studies exist on the impact of integrating two or more instructional methods on student learning. Going back to the basketball analogy, imagine researching the impact of the 1-3-1 offense strategy in basketball if the players could not effectively enact a "give and go"; could not pass, catch, or shoot a basketball; and were poor sports who refused to share. Of what value is assessing the 1-3-1 offense in this situation?

### Knowledge as Design

In analyzing instructional methods, it is helpful to employ four questions Perkins asks in *Knowledge as Design* (1991) where he differentiates between having knowledge as *information* and knowledge as *design*. He argues that too often we only have knowledge as information, which is passive and does not allow us to really think with that concept. For example, we all know (have information) that $-2 \times -2$ is 4; however, few of us can provide an example in the real world where a minus times a minus is a plus. *Knowledge as design* means we really deeply grasp a concept, such as the difference between racial discrimination, prejudice, and apartheid. If given a Venn diagram of these three concepts, could you fill in the Venn diagram? If not, you have knowledge as information, not knowledge as design. When attempting to understand knowledge as design, Perkins posits we should be able to answer the following questions:

1. What are the essential attributes of the concept?

2. What is the purpose of the concept?

3. What are model cases of the concept?

4. What is the value of the concept?

For example, the following responses might arise as we try to understand the concept of a mind map:

1. Essential attributes—Mind maps contain a clear defined center, ideas branching out hierarchically as subconcepts from the center, and use color, images, and cross links.

2. Purpose—Mind maps assist students in organizing information.

3. Model cases—Students analyze examples of mind maps.

4. Value—Mind maps increase memory.

By understanding the responses to these questions, we are more able to apply the instructional method appropriately and more able to reflect and assess our efforts. I would argue that having a meaningful conversation about the implementation of an innovation would be difficult if one does not understand the innovation. Hundreds of methods of instruction exist; instructional differentiation really happens when the methods are combined or integrated. Let us consider an example: in the cooperative learning literature, there are approximately 250 group structures. Of these, 240 would be classified as tactics (less complex and less powerful) and about ten as strategies (more complex and more powerful). For example, the category "cooperative learning tactics" would include processes such as think/pair/share, place mat, four corners, and two-three-four person interview. "Cooperative learning strategies" would include team games tournament, jigsaw, student teams achievement division, academic controversy, and group investigation. As stated earlier, few tactics have a research base, but strategies do, and for some strategies the research is quite extensive. Again, if we are using this research to impact student learning, strategies are likely to have a more powerful impact than tactics; that said, what if we merged three tactics simultaneously? Would the combined effect of three or more tactics be more powerful than a strategy applied in isolation? We do not know. Remember, however, that we have not illustrated how the instructional concepts, skills, and organizers connect with those tactics and strategies. How do they connect? This is what the science of teaching proposes to discover. The art is how they play out given what we know about how students learn.

In cooperative learning, if you are asking students to apply or be engaged in a complex strategy, such as academic controversy, and they cannot effectively complete four corners, this is akin to asking someone to run the Boston Marathon when they struggle to run around a city block. This has serious implications for both classroom practice and assessment *of*, *for*, and *as* student learning. If we do not assess the quality of our instructional implementation, we are less likely to be precise in assessing and impacting student learning. When we decide to assess student learning as it relates to the concept of cooperative learning, but we select cooperative learning tactics that are not complex and not that powerful, and then we state that cooperative learning did not have a meaningful effect on student learning, we are making an assessment error in terms of the impact of cooperative learning. In fact, the cooperative learning methods did exactly what they were designed to do—they had a small effect on student learning. Why expect sandpaper to take a lot of wood off a plank? If you want more power, use a table saw, but do not blame the sandpaper—it did exactly what it was designed to do.

### Instructional Integration in Practice

What does instructional integration of skills, tactics, strategies, concepts, and organizers look like in practice? In February 2008, I watched a fourth-grade teacher in the Northern Lights School District in northern Alberta engage her students in completing a mind map (a strategy) that integrated four tactics— Venn diagrams, fish-bone diagrams, timelines, and cross-sectional diagrams—to summarize a unit they had just completed. The students decided what graphic organizers they would employ. Curious that the students were using two and three Venn diagrams, not just one, I asked her, "How many times have your students done Venn diagrams?" She replied, "Do you mean this year?" I said, "Yes." She replied, "About forty, but at least seventy since kindergarten."

The school staff in this school meets at the start of each year to discuss what instructional methods will be introduced at the different grade levels so that students develop an increasing level of skill as they move up through the grades. The teachers also have a common instructional language.

A twelfth-grade English teacher in the York Region District School Board in Ontario had her students work in small cooperative groups using the five basic elements of effective group work (a strategy) to integrate three or more graphic organizers of students' choice to summarize a unit on Julius Caesar. The graphic organizer they had to employ was concept mapping (a strategy); the rest were optional. A secondary math teacher had her students complete a concept map inside a Venn diagram. Most of those students were doing this for the first time. The idea is that they will experience this strategy at progressively more difficult levels and more often as they advance through the grade levels.

These real-life examples illustrate the idea of instructional integration in action. The five areas of instructional methods—skills, tactics, strategies, concepts, and organizers—all interact with one another to more effectively respond to the varying needs of a diverse student population.

## Levels of Use of an Innovation

This section is based on the work of Susan Loucks-Horsley and Gene Hall and Shirley Hord as described in Hall and Hord's *Implementing Change: Patterns, Principles, and Potholes* (2006). Levels of Use (LoU) is one of the components of the Concerns-Based Adoption Model (CBAM). The model is designed to assess how individuals implement new ideas or processes to become integrative users of innovations. In this chapter, *innovations* refers to instructional skills, tactics, and strategies. In this section, I show how we have reworked the idea of an integrative user and refined the idea of a user of an instructional innovation so that they align more specifically with teachers' attempts to refine and extend their instructional practice.

First, teachers must realize it is their responsibility to increase their skill level or "level of use" of innovations in their instructional practice. Second, when we assess the effect of an innovation on student learning, if we fail to first assess the teacher and student's levels of use of that innovation, then our assessment will be invalid.

In research and professional development, we have historically valued the effect of single innovations on student learning; however, we have rarely taken the time to determine whether teachers are effectively implementing those innovations. In a personal conversation with Susan Loucks-Horsley in 1993, she told me that in her research about levels of instructional use, she rarely found teachers even at the mechanical levels of use with most instructional processes. We know from the work of Susan Loucks-Horsley, Gene Hall, and Shirley Hord (Hord & Hall, 2006) that little student benefit comes from teachers who are not at least routine users of innovations. Table 1 describes the levels of use of innovations. Note that in table 1, the level descriptions have been modified from Hall and Hord's work (2006). See Craib's (2006) research for a more in-depth analysis of how we are applying CBAM in our systemic work with instructional intelligence related to measuring the tacit knowledge of teachers.

Table 2 (page 82) illustrates three of the levels of use—mechanical, routine, and refined—based on Johnson and Johnson's (2000) five basic elements of effective group work (individual accountability, promoting face-to-face interaction, teaching a collaborative skill, processing the academic task, and collaborative skill and building in positive interdependence). How many teachers do you think are routine or higher users

**Table 1: Teachers' Levels of Use of an Innovation**

| Nonuser | Not using the innovation, but may have heard of it |
|---|---|
| Orienting | Interested and seeking more information |
| Preparing | Getting ready to apply the innovation for the first time |
| Mechanical | Applying the innovation in the classroom, but application is clunky |
| Routine | Has applied innovation often enough that it is working smoothly |
| Refined | Extending application of the innovation into new areas |
| Integrative | Connecting the innovation to other innovations |
| Refocusing | Searching for other innovations |

of instructional methods? What would it take to get teachers to the routine and refined levels of use?

To put this rubric in perspective, after three years of intensive work related to instruction in Ontario's York Region District School Board (where we paid attention to the research about the conditions under which teachers learn), most teachers were still at the mechanical levels of use of most innovations. More important, however, is that this assessment process is time consuming and expensive. We had no cost-effective and time-efficient method to systemically, meaningfully, and continually provide feedback to teachers on their actions and thinking related to instruction and how it connects to assessment, curriculum knowledge, and how students learn.

Figure 1 (page 83) illustrates the interaction of three continuums for the number of innovations, instructional power, and integration merged with level of use of instructional methods in a classroom. Students and parents most likely hope that over time teachers will shift into the top corner of the right quadrant and maximize the number of instructional innovations

**Table 2: Levels of Use by Teachers of the Five Basic Elements of Effective Group Work**

| Mechanical | Routine | Refined |
|---|---|---|
| Teacher has notes to remind him or her of how and when to apply the basic elements. | Teacher may have a few notes to refer to, but for the most part he or she smoothly uses the five basic elements. | Teacher does not need notes; he or she clearly and effectively applies the five basic elements. |
| Accountability and discussion of the academic goal happens, but it is not as meaningful to students as it could be. | Most students are accountable. The goal is discussed and is, for the most part, meaningful. Some students may still take over and do a bit more work than others. Periodically, one or two students will take over and do more than their share. Students begin to deal with their own conflicts, but may need help at times. Students can work with most students in the class. | Most of the time, all students are accountable and actively involved. Students are clearly skilled at working in groups. They can identify their own collaborative skills needed to complete the academic task. Students skillfully process their academic and collaborative tasks. There are few conflicts. If they occur, students usually deal with them. Students easily work with all students in the class. |
| Students are not very skilled at processing their academic and social task. Not all students are involved and others may be taking over and doing all the work. Students have few skills to confront and resolve conflict. Students struggle working with some students in their class. | | |
| Teacher is not merging the five basic elements with other instructional methods. | Teacher may be bogged down using a limited number of collaborative skills. Teacher is beginning to connect the five basic elements to other instructional methods, but those methods are less complex. | When appropriate, the teacher easily and effectively integrates the five basic elements into other instructional methods, including more complex strategies. |

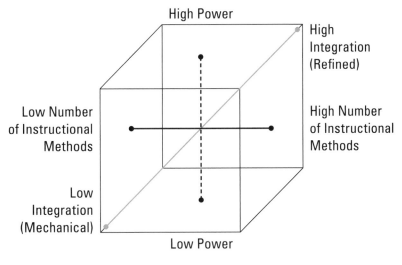

**Figure 1: Merging three continuums.**

they can apply and integrate at a refined level of use. That said, being at the refined level of use with a few innovations would be a wiser start than to be at the mechanical level of use with many. Hall and Hord's research (2006) shows that we will not see much of a difference in student achievement when teachers are at the mechanical levels of use. At this level, they are in the implementation dip and things are somewhat clunky and less smooth. Also, keep in mind that teachers tend to experiment more with tactics than they do with strategies because tactics are easier to implement. Nonetheless, thinking systemically, school staff and administration must consider the best stage (grade) to start certain innovations. Beginning in kindergarten increases the chances students become more skilled as they move up through the grades. For example, in a kindergarten/grade 1 class at Rostrata Elementary School in Perth, Western Australia, I watched grade 1 students teach kindergarten students how to do a Venn diagram. In a conversation with Chris Hall, a secondary math teacher in the Durham Board of Education in Oshawa, Ontario, he stated that his grade 13 students had been working in groups, effectively, since kindergarten. In 1996, that district won a 300,000 dollar award from the Bertelsmann Foundation of Germany as one of the top school districts in the world.

## A "Missing Think"

This chapter has focused on understanding the complex and integrative nature of instruction. But the question I have to ask is, "So what?" What will change because this chapter exists? In this last section, I consider the idea of a "missing think" related to how we too often fail to realize we exist professionally because of students, and tangentially, how often we fail to stop and ask students what they think about the instructional methods we enact. Given we are here for students, why do we fail to ask them what they think and feel about the instructional decisions we make during a lesson? One might think that as educators, we do not have to worry about what students think and how they feel. Yet, without students, there would be no teachers unions, ministries of education, faculties of education, or school districts. All of these institutions exist because of and for students; however, the individuals in those organizations seldom work as a professional learning community—a group collectively focused on working for students (DuFour, DuFour, & Eaker, 2008). Interestingly, most service providers spend a lot of time determining whether or not the service they are providing is valued by and effective for their customers. How often do we ask the students their thoughts and feelings about the instructional methods they experience? Following are two examples of how students think and feel about their experience with different instructional methods—one elementary and one secondary.

Teacher A, a graduate student, as part of an action research project, asked her fifth-grade students to use mind maps and place mats to complete a review at the end of the unit. This was the first time they had done place mat; a few had done mind maps. We can be pretty sure the students are mechanical users of these two instructional innovations, so they are just starting to understand how those innovations work. She asked her students the following questions on a feedback sheet. Questions 1, 2, 3, 4, and 7 relate to their thoughts on how the methods connected to their learning; questions 5 and 6 relate more to the affective effect of those methods.

1.  How did the mind map and/or place mat help you to gather and organize information about Canada's parliamentary system?

2.  How did the mind map or place mat help you to understand the different parts of government being studied and discussed in class?

3.  List three other subject areas where you think the use of a mind map or place mat would help you to understand information presented in class. Explain why.

4.  Explain what you found challenging when creating a mind map.

5.  What did you like best about using the place mat to identify key points about the electoral process in Canada?

6.  Did you enjoy working in a small group to complete the place mat activity? Support your answer with specific examples from your learning experience.

7.  If you were to complete the mind map and place mat activity again, what would you do differently?

She then collected the feedback sheets and discussed the answers with her students. Her summary statement for herself was as follows:

This is helpful in reminding me how students construct knowledge. It allows students to take risks in order to develop and enhance their understanding of concepts. As educators, we need to acknowledge and listen to the messages that students give us about the ways in which they learn best. Only then can we work toward becoming informed practitioners.

Teacher B, in an action research project, taught her secondary students a miniunit, "The Seven Habits of Highly Effective Teens," that focused on leadership skills. In one class, students watched a film, mind mapped individually, and worked in small groups to do a place mat. For most students, this was the first time they had used mind maps and place mat; they had worked in groups for most of the year. She then asked students to reflect on the lesson. Half the class preferred to work alone, and half preferred to work in a group. The first group said that they could do the work faster by themselves, and they did not have to rely on others or compromise. Those who preferred the group work liked the synergy of ideas and the reduction of individual work load. The entire class agreed that viewing the film, then doing the place mat activity and the mind map built on and complemented each other. One student said, "It was a different way of using what you learned. It was much more interesting doing all three together." Another said, "I think this lesson connected together because each activity was fun and relevant with each other."

The teacher then summarized and shared the comments with the class. She said that "gathering the thoughts of the students is extremely powerful for teachers as it can really help you determine what you need to change about your teaching practice and makes you reflect on your lesson and the methods of delivery."

If assessment is so important for learning, why do we so infrequently ask our students their thoughts about how we are designing and implementing our learning environments? Students should be encouraged to ask, Why are we doing a mind map and not a concept map? Why didn't you use concept attainment instead of talking at us for fifteen minutes? Why did you make us work in teacher-selected groups and not friendship groups? Why don't you frame questions so that we all get a chance to think and not just a few? Why do you always say, "Does everyone understand?" Don't you realize we don't but we are not brave enough to put up our hands and admit it publicly? Professionally, our responsibility is to find out what is working and what is not; that is part of our assessment responsibility. Currently, one key issue is the disconnect between assessment and instruction. Until we take the time to care about our students' thinking and feelings related to our instructional decisions, we will not evolve in our level of skill with instructional methods.

Table 3 (page 88) shows a rubric created by one of my preservice students designed to assess how she framed questions (a skill discussed by Millar [1897] and found in Hunter's ITIP program in the 1970s and 1980s). At the University of Toronto's Ontario Institute for Studies in Education, our preservice students in the Doncrest create various types of rubrics to self-assess their thinking and actions as learning.

## Shifting to Being Consciously Competent

The intent of this chapter is to illustrate and clarify why teaching is so delightfully complex —the delight emerging in our creative responses to differentiating our instruction to meet the diverse needs of a diverse group of students. I push the idea of the science of learning, of being more thoughtful about how we understand instruction and realizing that some methods are more powerful than others, that some methods depend on or are enhanced by other methods. I also remind teachers not to expect students to apply more complex methods when they and their students do not have the skills to enact less complex methods. In addition, I argue the importance of realizing that our skill level shifts from being mechanical to routine to refined and integrative. And until we, as teachers, and our students become at least routine users as we enact different instructional methods, we will not get the results we expect. In terms of assessment, I urge readers to more deeply understand how the science of teaching informs the art of teaching, to grasp the complexity of instruction and how we can creatively integrate multiple instructional methods to more thoughtfully align instruction and assessment to meet the differing needs of a diverse body of students.

**Table 3: Preservice Student's Rubric to Assess How She Framed Questions**

| Framing Questions | Level One | Level Two | Level Three | Level Four |
|---|---|---|---|---|
| Are students accountable and involved? | No students are accountable, and few are involved. | Some students are accountable, and a few are involved. | Most students are accountable, and most are involved. | All students are accountable and involved. |
| Do students know how to respond? | Students do not know how to respond. | Students sometimes know how to respond. | Students usually know how to respond. | Students always know how to respond. |
| Do they use variety in framing? | Students use no variety. | Students use some variety. | Students use appropriate variety. | Students use appropriate and effective variety. |
| Do students use wait time? | There is no evidence of wait time. | Wait time occurs sometimes, but it does not match the cognitive demand of the question. | Wait time occurs most of the time and usually matches the cognitive demand of the question. | Wait time always occurs when appropriate and effectively matches the cognitive demand of the question. |

As a colleague of mine, Pauline Lang, once said, "Our goal is to make sure that as educators we become consciously competent and not simply accidentally adequate." Our students are worth the effort.

## References and Resources

Aronson, E., Blaney, N., Stephen, C., Sikes, J., & Snapp, M. (1978). *The jigsaw classroom*. Beverly Hills, CA: Sage.

Bennett, B. (2002). Instructionally intelligent: Socially smart. *Orbit, 32*(4). Accessed at http://www.oise.utoronto.ca/orbit/core5_teach_strat.html on May 15, 2009.

Bennett, B., & Rolheiser, C. (2001). *Beyond Monet: The artful science of instructional integration*. Ajax, ON: Bookation.

Blumer, H. (1954). What is wrong with social theory. *American Sociological Review, 18*, 3–10.

Bruner, J. (1966). *Towards a theory of instruction*. Cambridge, MA: Harvard University Press.

Buzan, T. (1993). *The mind map book*. London: BBC Books.

Collins, M. L. (1978). *The effects of training for enthusiasm on the enthusiasm displayed by preservice elementary teachers*. Unpublished doctoral dissertation, Syracuse University.

Craib, G. (2006). *Measuring tacit knowledge of practicing teachers*. Unpublished doctoral dissertation, Ontario Institute for Studies in Education, University of Toronto.

Dale, E., & Raths, L. E. (1945). Discussion in the secondary school. *Education Research Bulletin, 24*, 1–6.

De Bono, E. (1986). *CoRT thinking*. Oxford, UK: Cavendish Information Products.

DuFour, R., DuFour., R., & Eaker, R. (2008). *Revisiting professional learning communities at work: New insights for improving schools*. Bloomington, IN: Solution Tree.

Earl, L. M. (2003). *Assessing as learning: Using classroom assessment to maximize student learning*. Thousand Oaks, CA: Corwin Press.

Eisner, E. (2004). *Artistry in teaching*. Accessed at http://www.culturalcommmons.org/eisner.htm on December 17, 2008.

Friedman, I., & Fisher, S. P. (1998). *Handbook on effective instructional strategies: Evidence for decision making*. Columbia, NC: The Institute for Evidence-Based Decision-Making in Education.

Frye, N. (1964). *The educated imagination*. Bloomington: Indiana University Press.

Fullan, M. (2002). Socially smart: Instructionally intelligent. *Orbit, 32*(4).

Gage, N. (1977). *The scientific basis of the art of teaching*. New York: Teachers College Press.

Goldhammer, R., & Cogan, M. (1973). *Clinical supervision*. Boston: Houghton-Mifflin.

Goodlad, J. (1984). *A place called school: Prospects for the future*. New York: McGraw-Hill.

Hall, G. E., & Hord, S. M. (2006). *Implementing change: Patterns, principles, and potholes*. New York: Allyn & Bacon.

Hunter, M. (1994). *Enhancing teaching*. Don Mills, ON: Maxwell McMillan.

Johnson, D. W., & Johnson, F. P. (2000). *Joining together: Group theory and group skills*. Boston, MA: Allyn & Bacon.

Joyce, B., & Weil, M. (2000). *Models of teaching*. New York: Allyn & Bacon.

Kagan, S. (1985). *Cooperative learning*. San Juan Capistrano, CA: Resources for Teachers.

Kelly, W. (1953). *The Pogo papers*. New York: Simon & Schuster.

Leithwood, K., Day, C., Sammons, P., Harris, A., & Hopkins, D. (2007). *Seven strong claims about successful school leadership*. Nottingham, UK: National College for School Leadership.

Louis, K. S., & Miles, M. B. (1990). *Improving the urban high school: What works and why*. New York: Teachers College Press.

Marzano, R. (1992). *A different kind of classroom: Teaching with dimensions of learning*. Alexandria, VA: Association for Supervision and Curriculum Development.

Marzano, R. J. (1998). *A theory-based meta-analysis of research on instruction*. Aurora, CO: Mid-continent Regional Educational Laboratory.

Marzano, R. J. (2003). *What works in schools: Translating research into action*. Alexandria, VA: Association for Supervision and Curriculum Development.

Marzano, R. J. (2007). *The art and science of teaching: A comprehensive framework for effective instruction*. Alexandria, VA: Association for Supervision and Curriculum Development.

Mager, R. R. (1962). *Preparing educational objectives: A critical tool in the development of effective instruction*. Belmont, CA: David S. Lake.

Millar, J. (1897). *School management*. Toronto, ON: William Briggs.

Novak, J., & Gowin, D. (1984). *Learning how to learn*. New York: Cambridge University Press.

Perkins, K. (1991). *Knowledge as design*. Hillsdale, NJ: Lawrence Erlbaum.

Rubin, L. (1985). *Artistry in teaching*. New York: Random House.

Taba, H. (1967). *Teacher's handbook for elementary school social studies*. Reading, MA: Addison-Wesley.

Tomlinson, C. (2001). *How to differentiate instruction in mixed-ability classrooms* (2nd ed). Alexandria, VA: Association for Supervision and Curriculum Development.

Waxman, H. C., & Walberg, H. J. (1991). *Effective teaching: Current research.* Berkeley, CA: McCutchan.

Wittrock, M. C. (1986). *Handbook of research on teaching* (3rd ed). New York: Macmillan.

# Richard E. Mayer

Richard E. Mayer, Ph.D., is professor of psychology at the University of California, Santa Barbara. His research interests are in educational and cognitive psychology. His current research involves the intersection of cognition, instruction, and technology with a special focus on multimedia learning and computer-supported learning. He is past president of the Division of Educational Psychology of the American Psychological Association, former editor of the *Educational Psychologist,* former coeditor of *Instructional Science*, and former chair of the UCSB Department of Psychology. He is the year 2000 recipient of the E. L. Thorndike Award for career achievement in educational psychology, and the winner of the 2008 Distinguished Contribution of Applications of Psychology to Education and Training Award from the American Psychological Association. Currently, he is vice president for Division C (Learning and Instruction) of the American Educational Research Association. He serves on the editorial boards of fourteen journals, mainly in educational psychology. He is the author of nearly four hundred publications, including twenty-three books.

In this chapter, Dr. Mayer first examines the science of learning and the science of instruction. He then shares some highlights of research on the psychology of school subjects in order to demonstrate what the science of learning has to contribute to improving instruction in schools.

## Chapter 4

# Applying the Science of Learning to Instruction in School Subjects

### Richard E. Mayer

How should educators decide how to teach in the classroom? Which instructional methods are best for helping students learn how to read, how to comprehend text, how to write essays, how to solve math problems, and how to think scientifically? Such decisions can be made on the basis of fads, opinions, or expert advice, but in this chapter I suggest another approach: classroom practice should be informed by a research-based theory of how people learn (the science of learning) and by research evidence concerning how to help people learn (the science of instruction). This simple call for applying the science of learning to classroom instruction has a long history in education and psychology dating back to William James' classic *Talks to Teachers* (1899) and E. L. Thorndike's *Principles of Teaching Based on Psychology* (1906). Yet as we enter the twenty-first century, there is still a need to renew this one-hundred-year-old call to base classroom practice on research in learning and instruction.

Learning is at the center of education because the primary goal of education is to promote appropriate learning in students. Since the 1980s, much progress has been made in understanding how learning works, and in particular, understanding how learning works in subject matter areas such as reading, writing, math, and science (Bransford, Brown, & Cocking, 1999; Mayer, 2008a). Researchers have referred to this field as *psychologies of school subjects* (Mayer, 2004; Shulman & Quinlan, 1996). In this chapter, after examining the science of learning and the science of instruction, I share some highlights of research on the psychology of school subjects in order to demonstrate what the science of learning has to contribute to improving instruction in schools.

## The Relationship Between Psychology and Education

The *science of learning* is the scientific study of how people learn. The goal is to produce a research-based model of how learning works. The *science of instruction* is the scientific study of how to help people learn. The goal is to produce research-based principles indicating which instructional methods work best for teaching—which kinds of knowledge to which kinds of learners.

What should be the relationship between psychology, which focuses on theoretical issues concerning how learning works, and education, which focuses on practical questions concerning which instructional methods work? In the early 1900s, there was optimism that this relationship could be a one-way street where basic researchers created the science of learning and practitioners applied it. The problem with this approach was that even if researchers could have figured out how learning works, this finding could not have translated directly into effective instructional methods. By the mid-1900s, the relationship between psychology and education had become a dead-end street where psychologists ignored the challenges of education by basing learning theory mainly on how rats learned to perform contrived tasks in sterile lab environments, and educators ignored learning theory when choosing instructional methods. Finally, by the late 1900s, a reciprocal relationship developed between psychology and education—a two-way street. On a two-way street, learning researchers are challenged to study learning in authentic educational contexts, and instructional researchers test instructional principles that are grounded in theory. The transition from the one-way street to the dead-end street to the two-way street is a promising progression that encourages us to consider how to apply the science of learning (Mayer, 1992).

What should be the relationship between basic research on the science of learning and practical research on the science of instruction? Figure 1 (page 96) suggests four possible relationships between basic and applied research, inspired by Stokes (1997). The upper-left quadrant represents research that is not intended to contribute to theory or practice, so it is of little value to anyone. The upper-right quadrant represents research that addresses a practical instructional issue but is not based on learning theory. This can be called *pure applied research*. The problem with pure applied research is that even if we can determine which instructional method works best, we do not know how it works, and, thus, we do not know much about the conditions under which it will work. The lower-left quadrant represents basic research on learning that is not relevant to practical educational problems. This is called *pure basic research*. The problem with pure basic research is its lack of relevance for authentic learning environments. Finally, the lower-right quadrant represents research that has two overlapping goals: to contribute to the science of learning by developing a theory of how learning works and to contribute to the science of instruction by discovering principles for effective instruction. Stokes (1997) refers to this kind of research as "use-inspired basic research" and Mayer (2008b) calls it "basic research on practical problems."

As you can see, instead of viewing basic and applied research as two opposing poles on a dimension, it is more fruitful to view them as two possible research goals that can overlap. The research presented in this chapter comes from this fourth quadrant of

| | No SOI: Addresses a contrived learning situation | SOI: Addresses an authentic learning situation |
|---|---|---|
| **No SOL: Does not test learning theory** | | SOI only: Pure applied research |
| **SOL: Tests learning theory** | SOL only: Pure basic research | SOL and SOI: Basic research on applied problems |

Figure 1: The overlap between practical (science of instruction, or SOI) and theoretical (science of learning, or SOL) research.

overlapping research goals—that is, studying how learning works in authentic contexts that are relevant to improving instruction.

## The Science of Learning: How Do People Learn?

The science of learning seeks to determine how people learn. Learning is a change in the learner's knowledge attributable to the learner's experience (Mayer, 2008a). This definition of learning consists of three elements: learning is a change, what is changed is what the learner knows, and the cause of the change is some interaction with the environment that primes appropriate cognitive processing in the learner. This definition is broad enough to include learning to read the word *dog*, learning to understand a paragraph, learning to write an essay, learning to solve an arithmetic word problem, or learning a scientific theory.

Figure 2 (page 98) shows an information-processing framework for how learning works. The boxes represent memory stores and the arrows indicate cognitive processes. First, spoken words enter the learner's cognitive system through the ears and are briefly held in auditory sensory memory. Similarly, printed words and pictures enter the learner's cognitive system through the eyes and are briefly held in visual sensory memory. If the learner pays attention to the incoming information (indicated by the "selecting words" and "selecting images" arrows), some is transferred into working memory and held as sounds or images. If the learner mentally organizes the material in working memory (indicated by the "organizing words" and "organizing images" arrows), the learner can construct a verbal model and pictorial model in working memory. Finally, the learner can activate relevant prior knowledge from working memory and integrate it with knowledge in working memory, as well as integrate the verbal and pictorial models in working memory (indicated by the "integrating" arrows).

According to this cognitive theory of learning, meaningful learning occurs when learners engage in appropriate cognitive processing during learning. These processes include *selecting*—paying attention to the relevant incoming material; *organizing*—mentally constructing coherent mental representations of the selected material; and *integrating*—connecting the new mental representations with each other and with relevant prior knowledge.

## The Science of Instruction: How Can We Help People Learn?

The science of instruction seeks to determine how to help people learn. Instruction is the teacher's manipulation of the learner's environment in order to foster learning (Mayer, 2008a). This definition has two parts: (1) instruction involves creating a learning experience for the learner, and (2) the goal of instruction is to foster a change in the learner's knowledge. This definition is broad enough to include a book chapter such as this one, a live PowerPoint presentation, or an interactive online simulation game.

An important first step in designing instruction is to specify the *learning objective*. A learning objective is a description of the intended change in the learner's knowledge. For example, one objective of this chapter is to help you develop a belief that research in the science of learning is relevant to classroom practice.

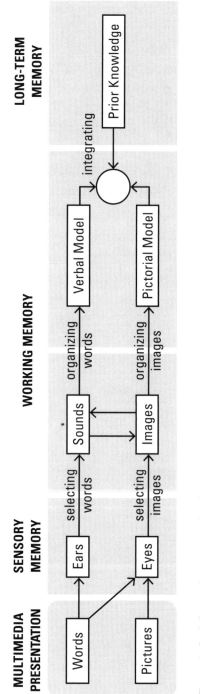

**Figure 2: An information-processing framework for how learning works. Adapted from Mayer (2008b). Reprinted with permission.**

How do we know what someone has learned? Knowing what students know is the central challenge of educational assessment (Pellegrino, Chudowsky, & Glaser, 2001). Learning outcomes are typically evaluated using *retention tests*, which measure the student's ability to remember what was presented in a lesson, and *transfer tests*, which measure the student's ability to use the material in new situations. For example, asking you to state the definitions of *retention* and *transfer* would be an example of a retention test, whereas asking you to generate a question based on this section of the chapter would be an example of a transfer test.

Table 1 lists three kinds of learning outcomes: *no learning*, which is reflected in poor retention and poor transfer performance; *rote learning*, which is reflected in good retention and poor transfer performance; and *meaningful learning*, which is reflected in good retention and good transfer performance (Mayer, 2008a). Much of school-based instruction is intended to promote meaningful learning, so tests of transfer are particularly important in assessing what was learned.

**Table 1: Three Kinds of Learning Outcomes**

| Learning Outcome | Cognitive Description | Retention Test Score | Transfer Test Score |
|---|---|---|---|
| No learning | No knowledge | Poor | Poor |
| Rote learning | Fragmented knowledge | Good | Poor |
| Meaningful learning | Integrated knowledge | Good | Good |

In specifying learning objectives, it is important to indicate which kind(s) of knowledge the learner is intended to learn. Table 2 (page 100) lists five kinds of knowledge: facts, concepts, procedures, strategies, and beliefs. Each type of knowledge may require a different kind of instructional method, and most complex tasks—such as solving a word problem or comprehending a passage—require learning to coordinate several kinds of knowledge (Anderson et al., 2001).

**Table 2: Five Kinds of Knowledge**

| Kinds of Knowledge | Definition | Example |
|---|---|---|
| Facts | Factual knowledge of the world | There are 100 cents in a dollar. |
| Concepts | Categories, schemas, models, principles | In the number 25, the 2 refers to the number of tens. |
| Procedures | A step-by-step process | Multiplying 212 x 54 |
| Strategies | A general method | Breaking a problem into parts |
| Beliefs | Thoughts about learning | Thinking, "I am not good at solving math problems." |

In specifying learning objectives, it is also important to be sensitive to the characteristics of the learner. Perhaps the single most important individual-differences characteristic is the learner's prior knowledge. If you could know only one thing about a learner, you would want to know what the learner already knows about the to-be-learned material. Research on individual differences shows that instructional methods that are effective for low-knowledge learners may not be effective for high-knowledge learners and vice versa. Kalyuga (2005) refers to this finding as the *expertise reversal effect*. Importantly, most students in K–12 schools do not possess high amounts of prior knowledge, so I focus mainly on instructional methods for beginners in this chapter.

In the remainder of this chapter, I explore examples of contributions of the science of learning to instruction in five school subject areas: reading, reading comprehension, writing, mathematics, and science, as summarized in table 3.

## Applying the Science of Learning to Reading Instruction

Learning to read is perhaps the single most important educational goal of schools in the primary grades. In particular,

**Table 3: Five Examples of Applying the Science of Learning to Instruction in School Subjects**

| Subject | Example of Learning |
|---|---|
| Reading | Phonological awareness |
| Reading Comprehension | Knowledge of prose structure |
| Writing | Planning strategies |
| Mathematics | Mental number line |
| Science | Recognition of misconceptions |

one crucial aspect of learning to read involves developing skill in *decoding*—being able to make the sound that corresponds to printed letters. For example, decoding involves being able to say /dog/ when you see the printed letters d-o-g. For hundreds of years, educators have debated how to teach reading, including whether to use a phonics-based approach or a whole-word approach (Adams, 1990; Chall, 2000). Decisions about reading instruction often have been based on opinions and fads, swinging back and forth every generation or so without clear rationale.

Where does the science of learning come in? One of the most important discoveries from reading researchers concerns an indispensable piece of knowledge that is required for learning how to decode words. That piece of knowledge is called *phonological awareness*: knowledge of the sound units (called phonemes) of one's language, including the ability to hear and produce each sound unit (or phoneme). In English, there are approximately forty-four sounds, so students need to be able to make each sound and to distinguish each sound in other people's utterances. For example, children who have phonological awareness are able to perform tasks such as substitution of first phoneme: "Say /ball/. Instead of /b/ begin the new word with /k/." (Answer: "call.")

Since the 1980s, reading researchers have shown that phonological awareness is a readiness skill for learning to read. Two important pieces of evidence are (1) students who do not develop phonological awareness have difficulty in learning to read (Bradley & Bryant, 1978; Juel, Griffith, & Gough, 1986), and (2) teaching students to recognize phonemes improves their ability to learn to read (Bradley & Bryant, 1983; Fuchs et al., 2001).

As shown in the top line of table 3 on page 101, the implications for instruction are clear: if students do not develop phonological awareness on their own (while their cohort does), then we should provide them with phonological awareness training; that is, we should provide training in how to recognize and produce sound units. For example, Bradley and Bryant (1983) provided phonological awareness instruction to five- and six-year-olds in forty ten-minute sessions. In one session, they were given a set of picture cards and asked to select the picture that started with a different sound than the others. Students who received phonological training showed a large improvement on tests of phonological awareness whereas a control group did not. More importantly, the phonological training group scored much higher than the control group on subsequent tests of reading, even five years later. These results—and those of dozens of other similar studies—provide clear evidence that "successful training in phonological awareness helps children learn to read" (Goswami & Bryant, 1992, p. 49). Thus, an important contribution of the science of learning to early reading instruction is evidence showing that phonological awareness is "a skill essential to becoming a proficient reader" (Blachman, 2000, p. 495).

## Applying the Science of Learning to Reading Comprehension Instruction

Learning to say the words printed on a page (learning to read) is an important step, but starting in about the fourth grade, readers are also expected to be able to comprehend the text they are reading (reading to learn). Research on reading comprehension shows that early readers may be able to read every word in a passage, but they have difficulty in determining what is important and what is not. For example, when third graders were asked to rate the importance of each idea unit in a story, they rated the unimportant material at the same level as the important material (Brown & Smiley, 1977). In contrast, college students gave high importance ratings to the important material and low importance ratings to the unimportant material (Brown & Smiley, 1977).

What do skilled readers know that less-skilled readers do not know? One important difference concerns knowledge of prose structure. Any story or prose passage can be organized into an outline in which some material is at the highest level, some at the next level, and so on. For example, research on rhetorical structures (Chambliss & Calfee, 1998; Cook & Mayer, 1988) shows that prose passages may be organized in structures such as compare/contrast (comparing two or more items across several dimensions as in a matrix), classification (relating concepts to each other with set-subset relations as in a hierarchy), sequence (presenting a cause-and-effect chain in correspondence with a flowchart), enumeration (presenting a list), or generalization (presenting a main point and supporting points). Interestingly, most students, even students entering college, are not aware of rhetorical structures, and therefore have difficulty judging what is important in a textbook passage (Cook & Mayer, 1988). In short, research in the science of learning pinpoints a specific kind of knowledge—knowledge of prose structure—that is crucial for reading comprehension but lacking in many students.

What are the instructional implications? As shown in the second line of table 3 (page 101), students who lack knowledge of prose structure need systematic training in how to recognize the structure of the text they are reading and outline the text based on its structure. For example, for a compare/contrast text, students should be able to determine the items being compared, the dimensions they are being compared on, and the value of each item for each dimension. Cook and Mayer (1988) trained community college students in the names, definitions, and examples of each type of prose structure, and gave them practice in sorting paragraphs based on their prose structure and outlining them based on templates for each type of prose structure. Students who received the training showed much greater improvements in their note taking as compared to control students, and more importantly showed much greater improvements in their reading comprehension scores for new material. Again, this work provides an example of how the science of learning can make useful contributions to classroom teaching in a subject area.

## Applying the Science of Learning to Writing Instruction

Another important instructional goal is that students should be able to express themselves in writing, such as being able to write a persuasive essay. Classic writing instruction focuses on the mechanics of writing—legibility, spelling, grammar, and paragraph structure—which, of course, are important skills. However, research in the science of learning indicates that proficiency in writing also involves other important cognitive strategies. For example, Hayes and Flower (1980) found that writers need to engage in three intertwined cognitive processes— planning (generating, evaluating, and organizing information), translating (generating written text), and reviewing (detecting and correcting errors).

Let us focus on just one important cognitive process in writing: planning. Writing researchers have found that most students spend almost no time engaged in global planning—that is, developing a writing plan before they start writing (Gould, 1980). Instead, they engage in local planning—pausing at the end of a sentence or clause to plan out the next five or six words they wish to write (Scardamalia, Bereiter, & Goelman, 1982). However, experienced writers are more likely than inexperienced writers to generate, evaluate, and organize their ideas before they start writing (Pianko, 1979). In short, the science of learning has pinpointed planning as a crucial cognitive process in writing.

The implications for instruction are that students who do not naturally engage in planning should be taught planning strategies, as summarized in the third line of table 3 (page 101). For example, when high school students are asked to write a persuasive essay, they do not engage in much planning and they produce an essay that is rated mediocre (about six on a ten-point scale) by writing experts (Kellogg, 1994). However, when high school students are required to produce an outline before they begin writing—thus forcing them to generate, evaluate, and organize information—they write higher-quality essays rated as between nine and ten on a ten-point scale (Kellogg, 1994). Research on planning in writing provides yet another example of how the science of learning can contribute to improving classroom practice.

## Applying the Science of Learning to Mathematics Instruction

Being able to solve arithmetic problems, such as $2 + 4 =$ _____, is a major goal of schools in the primary grades. What is the best way to teach arithmetic to students? For more than a century, drill and practice has been a popular instructional method for arithmetic instruction. For example, suppose a student sits at a computer and sees "$2 + 4 =$ _____" on the screen. If the student presses the "6" button, a happy face appears on the screen and the student gets points added to her score. If the student presses the wrong answer, a frowning face appears on the screen and the student gets points subtracted from her score.

Drill-and-practice methods such as this one can be effective for helping students sharpen their procedural skills, but may result in students learning procedural knowledge (such as how to add) that is isolated from conceptual knowledge (such as what a number is). A major contribution of the science of learning is that a particular kind of conceptual knowledge—the mental number line—is a prerequisite for mastering basic arithmetic. A mental number line (or number sense) refers to a coherent conception of counting numbers, such as indicated by being able to move a token five spaces ahead or three spaces backwards along a path on a board game. Students who have acquired the mental number line are able to answer correctly on tasks such as the following: What comes after 4? Which is smaller, 6 or 4? Count backwards from 8. Two important pieces of evidence are (1) students who do not develop number sense have difficulty in learning arithmetic (Aunola, Leskinen, Lerkkanen, & Nurmi, 2004; Griffin & Case, 1996) and (2) teaching students about number sense improves their ability to learn arithmetic (Arnold, Fisher, Doctoroff, & Dobbs, 2002; Griffin & Case, 1996).

The instructional implications are summarized in the fourth line of table 3 (page 101). If students have not developed number sense by the early primary grades, they should receive training in number sense, such as with the mental number line. For example, the RightStart Mathematics program (Griffin & Case, 1996) consists of forty thirty-minute sessions in which students learn about the number line through playing board games. Students roll a die, determine who has the highest number, and move a token along a number-line path on a game board. When low-performing first graders were given this training, they showed a large improvement on tests of number-line knowledge, whereas a control group did not. Importantly, the number-line trained students were much more successful in learning arithmetic—simple addition and subtraction—than were students who received standard mathematics instruction. Similar results have been reported in other experiments (for example, Aunola et al., 2004).

Again, research on the mental number line represents another example of a contribution of the science of learning to instruction in a school subject. Without understanding the concept of the mental number line, students are not able to understand how arithmetic works and thus have difficulty in learning how to add and subtract. Bruer (1993) eloquently summarizes this point: "For mathematics to be meaningful, conceptual knowledge and procedural skills have to be interrelated in instruction" (p. 90).

## Applying the Science of Learning to Science Instruction

Finally, consider an aspect of the science curriculum: learning how scientific systems work. For example, in physics, students are expected to learn Newton's laws of motion, such as the idea that an object in motion stays in motion unless some force acts on it. Research shows that many students who take a physics course can perform well in defining and using Newton's laws of motion within the course, yet when given basic tests of their knowledge of motion, they opt for an incorrect theory of motion in which an object in motion requires a force to keep it in motion (Clement, 1982). McCloskey (1983) provides overwhelming evidence of students' misconceptions of how the physics of motion works. For example, what happens when a person who is running along at a constant rate drops a heavy ball? The correct answer, based on Newton's laws of motion, is that the ball will continue moving forward and will move downward, striking the ground at exactly the same point as the runner. However, the majority of students believe the ball will fall straight down, landing behind the runner—a view consistent with the idea that to continue in forward motion the ball would need a force to act on it.

Overall, research on the science of learning shows that students often learn scientific principles in a compartmentalized way. They enter the science classroom with what can be called *intuitive physics*—a theory of how motion works based on their own experiences. They can learn to give school answers about motion when in school, but they rely on their own intuitive physics when outside of school. How can we help students learn scientific principles more deeply? An important approach to the problem of learner misconceptions (or preconceptions) is based on the conceptual change theory of learning. The main idea in conceptual change theory is that students need to recognize that their existing theory does not work before they are willing to replace it with a new theory.

An instructional implication of the conceptual change approach is that students need experience in seeing that their preexisting conceptions are incorrect—that is, they must recognize an anomaly between what their theory predicts and what really happens. For example, White (1993; White & Frederiksen, 1998) developed a computer-simulation game in which students were asked to make objects move along a path. As shown in the left side of figure 3, students can use a controller to give the ball any number of kicks in a given direction (up, down, right, or left). To move the ball, a student might press the right arrow and then press the hit button three times, starting the ball in motion to the right. When the ball reaches the corner, the student might press the up arrow and press the hit button three times, expecting the ball to make a left turn and now move upward. Instead the ball travels at the forty-five-degree angle to the right and upward, moving outside the pathway as shown in the right side of figure 3. Based on experiences like these, students are asked to explain what happened and to generate rules that describe how objects move in the game. Through generating these explanations, students learn to change their conception of motion, and thereby are better able to succeed in a physics course. Chi (2000) has also shown that this process of conceptual change can be fostered by asking students to engage in self-explanation as they read a text passage—that is, when they are asked to explain how the system works to themselves.

Overall, research on conceptual change shows that students can learn to recognize anomalies between their existing mental model and actual evidence, thereby paving the way to learn a new theory more deeply. Again, research on conceptual change suggests another productive way of applying the science of learning to classroom instruction.

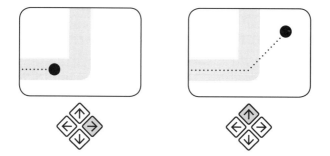

**Figure 3: An interactive physics simulation.**

## A Worthwhile Contribution

My goal in this chapter is to interest you in the idea that the science of learning has something worthwhile to contribute to designing effective instruction for classroom practice. I began with the idea from the science of learning that meaningful learning depends on the learner's active cognitive processing during learning, and the idea from the science of instruction concerning the need to specify the knowledge that we expect students to learn. Next, I provided examples of how the science of learning can contribute to improving instruction in subject matter areas: learning to read, learning to comprehend text, learning to write, learning to think mathematically, and learning to think scientifically. From my vantage point, these are exciting times, because researchers in learning and instruction actually have something useful to contribute to educational practice. My hope is that this chapter gives a useful glimpse of these potential contributions.

## References

Adams, M. J. (1990). *Beginning to read*. Cambridge, MA: MIT Press.

Anderson, L. W., Krathwohl, D. R., Airasian, P. W., Cruikshank, K. A., Mayer, R. E., Pintrich, P. R., et al. (2001). *A taxonomy for learning, teaching, and assessing*. New York: Longman.

Aunola, K., Leskinen, E., Lerkkanen, M., & Nurmi, J. (2004). Developmental dynamics of math performance from preschool to grade 2. *Journal of Educational Psychology, 96*, 699–713.

Arnold, D. H., Fisher, P. H., Doctoroff, G. L., & Dobbs, J. (2002). Accelerating math development in Head Start classes. *Journal of Educational Psychology, 94*, 762–770.

Blachman, B. A. (2000). Phonological awareness. In M. L. Kamil, P. B. Mosenthal, P. D. Pearson, & R. Barr (Eds.), *Handbook of reading research* (Vol. 3, pp. 483–502). Mahwah, NJ: Erlbaum.

Bradley, L., & Bryant, P. (1978). Difficulties in auditory organization as a possible cuase of reading backwardness. *Nature, 271*, 746–747.

Bradley, L., & Bryant, P. (1983). Categorizing sounds and learning to read—a cause connection. *Nature, 301*, 419–421.

Bransford, J. D., Brown, A. L., & Cocking, R. (Eds.). (1999). *How people learn*. Washington, DC: National Academies Press.

Brown, A. L., & Smiley, S. S. (1977). Rating the importance of structural units of prose passages: A problem of metacognitive development. *Child Development, 48,* 1–8.

Bruer, J. T. (1993). *Schools for thought.* Cambridge, MA: MIT Press.

Chall, J. S. (2000). *The academic achievement challenge: What really works in the classroom.* New York: Guilford Press.

Chambliss, M. J., & Calfee, R. C. (1998). *Textbooks for learning.* Oxford, England: Blackwell.

Chi, M. T. H. (2000). Self explaining: The dual processes of generating inferences and repairing mental models. In R. Glaser (Ed.), *Advances in instructional psychology* (Vol. 5, pp. 161–238). Hillsdale, NJ: Erlbaum.

Clement, J. (1982). Students' preconceptions in elementary mechanics. *American Journal of Physics, 50,* 66–71.

Cook, L. K., & Mayer, R. E. (1988). Teaching readers about the structure of scientific text. *Journal of Educational Psychology, 80,* 448–456.

Fuchs, D., Fuchs, L. S., Thompson, A., Al-Otaiba, S., Yen, L., Yang, N. J., et al. (2001). Is reading important in reading readiness programs? A randomized field trial with teachers as program implementers. *Journal of Educational Psychology, 93*(2), 251–267.

Gould, J. D. (1980). Experiments on composing letters: Some facts, some myths, and some observations. In L. W. Gregg & E. R. Steinberg (Eds.), *Cognitive processes in writing* (pp. 97–128). Hillsdale, NJ: Erlbaum.

Goswami, U., & Bryant, P. (1992). Rhyme, analogy, and children's reading. In P. B. Gough, L. C. Ehri, & R. Treiman (Eds.), *Reading acquisition.* Hillsdale, NJ: Erlbaum.

Griffin, S., & Case, R. (1996). Evaluating the breadth and depth of training effects when central conceptual structures are taught. In R. Case & Y. Okamoto (Eds.), The role of central conceptual structures in the development of children's thought (pp. 83–102). *Monographs of the Society for Research in Child Development, 61*(1 & 2, Serial No. 246).

Hayes, J. R., & Flower, L. S. (1980). Identifying the organization of writing processes. In L. W. Gregg & E. R. Steinberg (Eds.), *Cognitive processes in writing* (pp. 3–30). Hillsdale, NJ: Erlbaum.

James, W. (1899/1958). *Talks to teachers.* New York: Norton.

Juel, C., Griffith, P. L., & Gough, P. B. (1986). Acquisition of literacy: A longitudinal study of children in first and second grade. *Journal of Educational Psychology, 78,* 243–255.

Kalyuga, S. (2005). The prior knowledge principle in multimedia learning. In R. E. Mayer (Ed.), *The Cambridge handbook of multimedia learning* (pp. 325–339). New York: Cambridge University Press.

Kellogg, R. T. (1994). *The psychology of writing.* New York: Oxford University Press.

Mayer, R. E. (1992). Cognition and instruction: Their historic meeting within educational psychology. *Journal of Educational Psychology, 84*(4), 405–412.

Mayer, R. E. (2004). Teaching of subject matter. In S. T. Fiske, D. L. Schacter, & C. Zahn-Waxler (Eds.), *Annual review of psychology* (Vol. 55, pp. 715–744). Palo Alto, CA: Annual Reviews.

Mayer, R. E. (2008a). *Learning and instruction: Second edition.* Upper Saddle River, NJ: Pearson Merrill Prentice Hall.

Mayer, R. E. (2008b). Applying the science of learning: Evidence-based principles for the design of multimedia instruction. *American Psychologist, 63*(8), 760–769.

McCloskey, M. (1983). Intuitive physics. *Scientific American, 248*(4), 122–130.

Pellegrino, J. W., Chudowsky, N., & Glaser, R. (Eds.). (2001). *Knowing what students know: The science and design of educational measurement.* Washington, DC: National Academies Press.

Pianko, S. (1979). A description of the composing process of college freshman writers. *Research in Teaching of English, 13*(1), 5–22.

Scardamalia, M., Bereiter, C., & Goelman, H. (1982). The role of production factors in writing ability. In M. Nystrant (Ed.), *What writers know.* New York: Academic Press.

Shulman, L. S., & Quinlan, K. M. (1996). The comparative psychology of school subjects. In D. Berliner & R. Calfee (Eds.), *Handbook of educational psychology* (pp. 399–422). New York: Macmillan.

Stokes, D. E. (1997). *Pasteur's quadrant: Basic science and technological innovation.* Washington, DC: Brookings Institution Press.

Thorndike, E. L. (1906). *Principles of teaching based on psychology.* New York: Seiler.

White, B. Y. (1993). ThinkerTools: Causal models, conceptual change, and science education. *Cognition & Instruction, 10*(1), 1–100.

White, B. Y., & Frederiksen, J. R. (1998). Inquiry, modeling, and metacognition: Making science accessible to all students. *Cognition & Instruction, 16*(1), 3–118.

# David C. Berliner

David C. Berliner, Ph.D., is a Regents' Professor in the Mary Lou Fulton Institute and Graduate School of Education at Arizona State University. His books include *Educational Psychology* (sixth edition, with N. L. Gage), *The Manufactured Crisis* (with B. J. Biddle), and *The Handbook of Educational Psychology* (edited with R. L. Calfee). He has served as president of the American Educational Research Association and president of the Educational Psychology Division of the American Psychological Association. Berliner is a fellow of the Center for Advanced Study in the Behavioral Sciences and a member of the National Academy of Education.

In this chapter, Dr. Berliner raises the question of whether the high-stakes testing requirements built into the No Child Left Behind accountability system can ever help us achieve the many and diverse goals that professional educators, parents, the business community, and politicians want for students of the twenty-first century.

## Chapter 5

# The Incompatibility of High-Stakes Testing and the Development of Skills for the Twenty-First Century

David C. Berliner

In a May 12, 1780, letter to his wife, Abigail, John Adams wrote:

> I must study politics and war that my sons may have liberty to study mathematics and philosophy. My sons ought to study mathematics and philosophy, geography, natural history, naval architecture, navigation, commerce and agriculture in order to give their children a right to study painting, poetry, music, architecture, statuary, tapestry, and porcelain.

These are the perfect words to begin a discussion of curriculum in American schools at the start of the twenty-first century. For Adams, a former schoolteacher, the ultimate goal of education in a free society was to foster the arts. War was a necessity so that his children had freedom—freedom that would generate wealth through commercial and agricultural skills in a nation independent of European powers. Adams knew, however, that the ultimate goal of education for a free person was the opportunity to appreciate and participate in the arts.

This view of the importance of what is more broadly called the liberal arts is derived from our Greek heritage. The root of *liberal* as used in the term *liberal arts* actually has little to do with the term *liberal* as used in the political realm. Instead, the root of liberal when referring to the arts is in *liberty*, indicating that art, music, government, rhetoric, philosophy, and the like are the arts of free men and women. Benjamin Barber (1994) contrasted the liberal arts against the servile arts: business and law enforcement, food preparation and medicine, mechanics and technology. The servile arts encompass the knowledge and skills needed to run a country—exactly what the Greeks wanted their slaves and servants to do while they engaged in the grand kind of political and philosophical thinking that gave the Western world its intellectual heritage.

America, being a practical country, the land of Yankee ingenuity, and eventually a land dominated by the interests of business, never was in awe of the liberal arts or the humanities. There never was a golden age in America in which the liberal arts and humanities flourished while the servile arts were looked down upon. There always was resistance as intellectuals and artists fought the dominant theme of American culture, namely, that business was the business of the USA. But the practical was always foremost. This can be seen in the expansion of the agricultural and mechanical state universities (Texas A&M, Alabama A&M, and Florida A&M, for example) during the late nineteenth century. In particular, many of these schools were schools for newly freed blacks, who were helped to prosper in schools that were committed to the practical and the servile arts and denied access to schools that focused more on the liberal arts and humanities. That unfortunate history may be repeating itself, as today's schools for the poor, particularly poor minorities, are too easily compared to the schools in an apartheid system, as was once in effect in South Africa and America's Deep South (Kozol, 2005).

We find today, as has been true since the founding of the public schools a century and a half ago, that America's students are primarily enrolled in courses Adams understood were needed for his children. Our youth are not enrolled in great numbers, and never have been, in the courses he wanted for his grandchildren. The theme of this chapter is that the curriculum balance, long in favor of the practical and the servile arts, has tipped even further in that direction, particularly in schools serving poor and minority children. The disruption in what was already an uneven distribution of access to the arts and humanities in the curriculum is due to the use of high-stakes testing that has become normalized throughout the fifty states as a function of the No Child Left Behind Act (NCLB) that went into effect in 2002.

The decrease in exposure to certain curricula is of concern as we contemplate what the twenty-first century might have in store for our youth. Certainly, it is not easy to discern that future, and a good deal of the speculation about twenty-first century skills seems a bit like fortune telling; that is, it is notoriously vague and likely invalid. Nevertheless, it also seems clear that certain knowledge and skills that might be desirable in the future or are wanted by parents for their children are getting dropped from the curriculum. These are the issues discussed in what follows.

## Changing Curriculum Time and Content

Survey research and anecdotal evidence document a shift in both the amount of time spent by students in various subjects and the content of some subjects. The Center on Education Policy (2008), a nonpartisan monitor of the effects of NCLB, reports data on this issue from a nationally representative sample.

## The Curriculum in Language Arts and Mathematics

As shown in table 1, increases in time for the teaching of reading and mathematics in elementary schools were quite dramatic between 2002 and 2007. The time allocated to reading has been increased, on average, over two and a third hours a week, while mathematics time has been increased, on average, about an hour and a half a week. It should be noted when interpreting this table, however, that the "average" masks relevant information. It is likely that many school districts increased time in these subjects a lot more than the average, because the average includes districts serving high-income children, who typically score well on the tests used to satisfy NCLB requirements. Those districts probably changed their time allocations very little.

Of course, such changes are not all bad. It is highly desirable that students read and do mathematics well. We might normally welcome such changes unless there is reason to believe that the increased time is used poorly and is having either no effect or detrimental effects on students. There is evidence that this

**Table 1: Changes Since 2001–2002 in Instructional Time for Elementary School English Language Arts and Mathematics in Districts Reporting Increases (Center on Education Policy, 2008)**

| Subject | Average Total Instructional Time Pre-NCLB (Minutes per Week) | Average Total Instructional Time Post-NCLB (Minutes per Week) | Average Increase (Minutes per Week) | Average Increase as a Percentage of Total Instructional Time |
|---|---|---|---|---|
| English Language Arts | 378 | 520 | 141 | 47% |
| Mathematics | 264 | 352 | 89 | 37% |
| Either/Both Subject(s) | 513 | 699 | 186 | 43% |

may indeed be the case. If reading or English language arts consists of too much phonics practice, too much drill and test preparation, too many worksheets for practicing reading skills, not enough writing to express thoughts, not enough reading for enjoyment, and not enough reading of academic material to increase vocabulary for aiding comprehension, then the increased time fosters the goal of basic literacy and not literacy for its pleasure or for its value in exploring science or the arts and humanities. We are learning that reading that is more critical and emancipatory is not stressed as frequently when tests are highly consequential for schools. Instead, drills on test formats and items suspiciously like those on the test constitutes too much of the reading curriculum (Nichols & Berliner, 2007).

The evidence shows that the schools with the poorest children, and therefore the schools with the greatest likelihood of being sanctioned under NCLB, are those where reading of the most functional type is learned. Mathematics, while rarely taught as well as the experts would like it to be taught (see Ball, Lubienski, & Mewborn, 2001; Lampert, 2001) can be even more boring and inadequately taught than ever before under the threat of sanctions. Mathematics, then, like reading, can be turned from a subject that is a rich source of discourse and debate, of conjecture and the testing of ideas, and even an important contributor to democratic practices (Ball & Bass, 2008) when taught correctly, into a drill-oriented, teacher-dominated subject in which the increased time spent results in increased boredom and dislike of the subject.

The programs of reading and mathematics instruction, especially for the poor or for the students in many of the schools that have failed to make adequate yearly progress (AYP), are designed so that test scores will rise. And they do, at least on the state tests from which AYP is judged under NCLB. This is the evidence defenders of NCLB within the federal government and throughout the states use to justify the kind of curricula now being used extensively in the schools that serve the poor.

Although the narrow focus on drill-like activities to increase state test scores in reading and mathematics appears to work, gains on audit tests (a different test covering much of the same curriculum area) are found not to be nearly as large or consistent. And the gap between wealthier and poorer students on the best audit test America has, the National Assessment of Educational Progress (NAEP), has not been closing at all (Lee, 2008). This suggests that something is wrong. Increases in allocated time *ought* to result in increased learning. But if the increased time for learning reading and mathematics results in a less interesting curriculum for teachers to teach and for students to learn, then the results make sense. Under those conditions, results on the "trained-for tests" (a state's own tests) will show large gains and the tests that have not been trained for will not show such gains. Perhaps this is the reason that gains in reading and mathematics in the years *before* NCLB were more pronounced than in the years *after* NCLB (M. Smith, personal communication, October 10, 2007). Table 2 and table 3 (page 120) show this odd trend. They display the gains made and the rate of gain per year on the fourth- and eighth-grade NAEP tests in reading and mathematics for various time periods before and after the introduction of NCLB. Oddly, in almost all cases, gains were greater before the increases in time allocations were made to produce scores to satisfy the NCLB requirements.

Table 4 (page 120) shows a similar phenomenon. It presents the number of states making progress on the NAEP, or more accurately, failing to make progress on the NAEP reading test at the eighth-grade level during the same years that NCLB was triggering a movement for increased time to be spent in reading. The anticipated consequences of more time for learning reading have not materialized.

England faced similar problems when trying to reform its schools through heavily test-oriented accountability plans. For the first time since IQ tracking was started, IQs appear to be

**Table 2: Fourth- and Eighth-Grade Reading Gains and Rate of Gains Before and After Enactment of NCLB in 2002 (Adapted from M. Smith, personal communication, October 10, 2007)**

| | Student Race or Ethnicity | | |
| --- | --- | --- | --- |
| | **White** | **Black** | **Hispanic** |
| Fourth-Grade Reading NAEP Gains (and Rates of Gain) in the Years 1998–2002 (Before NCLB) | 4<br><br>(1 point per year) | 6<br><br>(1.5 points per year) | 7<br><br>(1.75 points per year) |
| Fourth-Grade Reading NAEP Gains (and Rates of Gain) in the Years 2002–2007 (After NCLB) | 3<br><br>(.6 points per year) | 5<br><br>(1 point per year) | 5<br><br>(1 point per year) |
| Eighth-Grade Reading NAEP Gains (and Rates of Gain) in the Years 1998–2002 (Before NCLB) | 3<br><br>(.75 points per year) | 2<br><br>(.50 points per year) | 4<br><br>(1 point per year) |
| Eighth-Grade Reading NAEP Gains (and Rates of Gain) in the Years 2002–2007 (After NCLB) | −1<br><br>(−.20 points per year) | 0<br><br>(0 points per year) | 1<br><br>(.20 points per year) |

declining quite dramatically in UK middle grades, and in a relatively short amount of time (Flynn, 2009). No one currently has a good explanation for this effect. But at least one reason given is that the UK has become a test-oriented culture and this has stunted the intellectual growth of its students. Research in primary schools in England reveals that there are few opportunities for expressing anything that resembles creative reasoning (Galton, 2007). Following up his own research of the 1970s, the investigator found that teacher-centered pedagogy, characterized by interactions of a very low cognitive level, managerial in their intent, had actually *increased* between 1976 and 1996. Pupils had fewer opportunities to question or to explore new ideas after the tests became the primary instrument that government used

**Table 3: Fourth- and Eighth-Grade Math Gains and Rate of Gains Before and After Enactment of NCLB in 2002 (Adapted from M. Smith, personal communication, October 10, 2007)**

|  | Student Race or Ethnicity | | |
|---|---|---|---|
|  | **White** | **Black** | **Hispanic** |
| Fourth-Grade Math NAEP Gains (and Rates of Gain) in the Years 1996–2003 (Before NCLB) | 12 (1.7 points per year) | 18 (2.6 points per year) | 14 (2.0 points per year) |
| Fourth-Grade Math NAEP Gains (and Rates of Gain) in the Years 2003–2007 (After NCLB) | 5 (1.25 points per year) | 6 (1.5 points per year) | 6 (1.5 points per year) |
| Eighth-Grade Math NAEP Gains (and Rates of Gain) in the Years 1996–2003 (Before NCLB) | 8 (1.14 points per year) | 13 (1.9 points per year) | 9 (1.3 points per year) |
| Eighth-Grade Math NAEP Gains (and Rates of Gain) in the Years 2003–2007 (After NCLB) | 3 (.75 points per year) | 7 (1.75 points per year) | 6 (1.5 points per year) |

**Table 4: Status of the States on Various Measures of Reading Proficiency After Enactment of NCLB (Barton & Coley, 2008)**

| Grade-Eight Reading Changes, 2002–2007 | | | |
|---|---|---|---|
|  | **States Improving** | **States Unchanged** | **States Worse** |
| Average Score | 0 | 31 | 12 |
| Percent Proficient | 0 | 40 | 3 |
| Top Quartile Score* | 5 | 27 | 11 |
| Bottom Quartile Score* | 5 | 24 | 14 |

Note: Includes those states participating in both the 2002 and 2007 assessments, as well as the District of Columbia and Department of Defense schools.
*Quartile score is calculated as the average score of students in the quartile.

to change the schools (Galton, 2007). The British curriculum, never exemplary in its nurturance of broad intellectual skills, had narrowed even more over time. This also corresponds to what happened to curricula in Chicago and Texas as a function of high-stakes testing (Hong & Youngs, 2008). In Chicago, the researchers found that high-stakes testing seemed to narrow the curriculum and make it harder for students to acquire higher order thinking, writing, and problem-solving skills. In Texas, it was found that schooling changed in ways that emphasized rote learning, not broad intellectual skills (Hong & Youngs, 2008; McNeil, 2000).

In summary, data presented in tables 2, 3, and 4 all show that after the enactment of NCLB, smaller gains were made on NAEP reading tests than were made before, and that most states showed no change in reading performance at all, while many showed a decrease in scores after NCLB was passed. In England, the testing culture is at least as strong as in the United States, and as it grew in importance, so did evidence of intellectual decline. In Chicago and Texas, curricula became limited as each adopted stronger accountability programs.

Test-oriented accountability cultures value convergent thought and mimetic processes, but these are styles of teaching and learning not likely to increase measured achievement and intelligence much, if at all. So these data only make sense if the surge in time and the narrowing of the curriculum were used to overprepare students for passing their state and national tests, and in so doing, missed affecting the constructs that were the real goals of the assessments—the measurement of reading proficiency and mathematical understanding.

In mathematics, however, in the United States, the situation is a bit different than it is for reading. It appears that drill-and-test preparation in mathematics works better than in reading, perhaps because mathematics tests are more predictable than reading tests. Perhaps it is because math is less dependent on background knowledge than is reading. Perhaps the underlying construct to be measured, mathematical understanding, may be easier to assess than reading with the multiple-choice test items that make up the majority of the questions on all these tests. In any case, the curriculum in mathematics may be no more exciting than that of reading, but the extra time spent in math instruction does seem more related to increased scores on the NAEP tests.

### The Rest of the Curriculum

Time added for reading and math in the typical 6½-hour school day and the typical 180-day school year needs to come from somewhere else in the curriculum. Table 5 makes clear that the increased time for reading and mathematics has come from other parts of the school curriculum. Again, it is important when interpreting this table to remember that the average masks the bigger cuts that some districts have made in these subjects; indeed, some districts—those with children doing well on the tests—probably made fewer changes to their curriculum. With this caveat in mind, we see that the teaching of social studies, intended always to be part of youth development for responsible citizenship, is down, on average, over an hour a week. Yet Americans of all political persuasions ask that the schools help to develop citizenship. So this trend in curriculum is in opposition to the aspiration Americans have for their school curriculum.

Time spent on science, a field that probably will be even more important in the twenty-first century than in the previous two centuries, is down, on average, over an hour a week as well. Although science is now one of the areas tested under the NCLB act, scores on the science tests do not count toward AYP. Thus, lack of progress in science and/or low performance on science tests can safely be ignored by schools and districts since no sanctions attach to the test. Science, therefore, has been robbed of minutes to expand time for reading and mathematics. Curriculum that might help ensure American economic competitiveness in the future has been sacrificed.

Table 5 also documents that time for physical education is down, despite the fact that our youth are quite overweight and more sedentary than they should be, and type 2 diabetes is becoming more common. Thus, physical education is more important today than ever before, and it is sacrificed for the possibility of a few more points on state tests that have to rise continuously to satisfy the requirements of NCLB.

**Table 5: Decreases in Instructional Time for Various Curriculum Areas to Accommodate Increases in Time for English Language Arts and Mathematics (Center on Education Policy, 2008)**

| Subject or Period | Average Total Instructional Time Pre-NCLB (Minutes per Week) | Average Total Instructional Time Post-NCLB (Minutes per Week) | Average Decrease (Minutes per Week) | Average Decrease as a Percentage of Total Instructional Time |
|---|---|---|---|---|
| Social Studies | 239 | 164 | 76 | 32% |
| Science | 226 | 152 | 75 | 33% |
| Art and Music | 154 | 100 | 57 | 35% |
| Physical Education | 115 | 75 | 40 | 35% |
| Recess | 184 | 144 | 50 | 28% |
| Lunch | * | * | * | * |
| One or More Subjects Listed | 461 | 318 | 145 | 32% |

Data from those districts reporting an increase in instructional time for English/language arts and/or math *and* a decrease in instructional time for one or more of the subjects listed.

*Not enough data

Not enough data were obtained to make conclusions in the study about the time allocation for lunch. But lunch is obviously wasted time for those who feel the pressure of testing under NCLB. Anecdotally, therefore, it was not surprising that a teacher at a Massachusetts district reported her concern that lunch at her elementary school was less than fifteen minutes on many days "so that more time could be put in on the rigorous curriculum areas" (Nichols & Berliner, 2007, p. 133). "Rigorous curriculum areas" is code for "areas that are tested." Anything else (social studies, history, government, art, music, physical education) has been defined in her school as a nonrigorous subject. The teacher's school had actually abandoned traditional luncheon meals and started serving finger food—wraps and chicken nuggets—to get the students in and out of the cafeteria faster (Nichols & Berliner, 2007).

As seen in table 5 (page 123), time spent on recess was found to be down, on average, about an hour a week. News reports document how a Massachusetts district did this: it cut one day a week of recess for elementary students so they could put in preparation time for the high-stakes testing required by NCLB. Some neighboring districts did away with recess at the elementary grades completely ("Class Requirements Cut Into Recess Time," 2004). The news reports also document how educators around St. Louis have cut back on recess and done away with physical education as well (Aguilar, 2004). At one low-performing elementary school in Texas where the pressure to raise test scores is incessant, teachers have also been taking away recess from students:

> We only have recess one day a week for 15 minutes. You can't be caught out there. Oooo—I'm not sure what would happen. These people [legislators/the state department of education] don't understand child development. I wonder if they ever went to college. Where are they getting their ideas from? They think we shouldn't have recess because we should focus on academics. This year I said, forget it, there's no way I can teach these kids if

they don't have a break, so I've been taking them out. (Booher-Jennings, 2005, p. 255)

Nationally, time spent on art and music instruction is down an average of an hour a week. This is particularly troublesome because the United States never spent a lot of time in these subjects to begin with. Since the 1980s, their place in the curriculum has suffered because of budgetary problems. After NCLB was passed, these courses were cut even further. California, where the arts provide a large source of employment for the state and a great deal of wealth for the nation (through huge overseas earnings that help our trade imbalance), should be a place that countered this trend. Yet 89 percent of California K–12 schools fail to offer a standards-based course of study in all four disciplines—music, visual arts, theatre, and dance—and thus fall short of the state's own goals for arts education. At the elementary level, arts instruction is often left to regular classroom teachers, who rarely have adequate training. In fact, 61 percent of California schools do not have even one full-time-equivalent arts specialist. Secondary schools are much more likely than elementary schools to employ such specialists, but even when they do, participation rates in secondary arts subjects are low (Woodworth, Gallagher, & Guha, 2007).

A defense of the arts can be made on many grounds, but one stands out in terms of twenty-first century needs: the arts are alternative ways to represent reality. Ideas expressed through the visual arts, dance, and music are not presented in the more ordinary verbal or mathematical symbol systems in everyday use. So by cutting the arts, we limit the ways our students can represent the world in which they live and about which they want to comment. A diminution in curriculum for learning the arts, therefore, restricts our students' ways of thinking. It limits the possibility for creativity. Yet it is creativity that seems to be the key to economic survival in the twenty-first century. The pundits say that creativity is the magic bullet for economic prosperity (Friedman, 2006). We want our students to be literate, numerate, and in possession of scientific knowledge, and in addition we want our students to be creative problem solvers. The arts provide such creativity by encouraging ways to think differently about the world. And so a defense of the arts can be based on economic and cognitive psychological reasons as well as the need to have an outlet for the natural expression of our humanity that sometimes results in the creation of works of indescribable beauty.

### The Curriculum for the Poor

The California study also makes clear that the arts are rationed; they are taught primarily to the wealthy and not the poor, as shown by the data in figure 1. Close to twice as many students in schools that serve the wealthy (low-poverty schools) receive instruction in the arts as do the students in schools that serve the poor (high-poverty schools). This an example of the apartheid system of schooling to which Kozol (2005) refers.

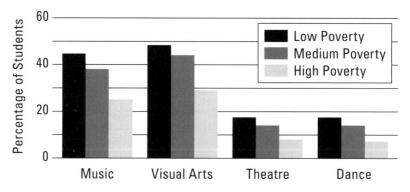

**Figure 1: Percent of California students receiving instruction in various areas of the arts, by poverty level of the school they attend (Woodworth et al., 2007).**

Wealthier students, if they are lucky, will be exposed to a wider range of the arts and humanities in their high schools because the breadth of curriculum offerings in high-achieving schools has not needed to be cut back. Students in these schools are usually passing their state tests, their schools usually make

AYP, and their parents have the political power and resources to maintain a broader curriculum. These wealthier students, even were they to miss some exposure to the arts and humanities in the public schools, have parents who can pay to provide them with extracurricular activities (such as music lessons, drama club, and sports opportunities), and they are much more likely to encounter the arts and humanities in their colleges. But poorer public school students may not be exposed to the ways of thinking embedded in the arts and humanities at all, and since their college attendance rates are low and declining at the most prestigious institutions of higher education (Gerald & Haycock, 2006), poorer students may never get adequate education in the arts and humanities.

Even Chester Finn and Diane Ravitch (2007), once ardent supporters of NCLB, have seen how the focus on only one or two goals of education distorts the entire curriculum. They recently concluded that, if NCLB continues:

> Rich kids will study philosophy and art, music and history, while their poor peers fill in bubbles on test sheets. The lucky few will spawn the next generation of tycoons, political leaders, inventors, authors, artists and entrepreneurs. The less lucky masses will see narrower opportunities. Some will find no opportunities at all [and] frustration will tempt them to prey upon the fortunate, who in turn will retreat into gated communities, exclusive clubs, and private this-and-that's, thereby widening domestic rifts and worsening our prospects for social cohesion and civility. (para. 17)

Poor people can change their lives enormously through exposure to a rich curriculum in moral philosophy, art history, logic, poetry, and American history at the level they might encounter at a first-rate university (Shorris, 2000). But they rarely are exposed to such a curriculum. And under NCLB, their exposure to such a curriculum is even less likely. Not only is there unfairness in a system that is clearly running separate curriculum tracks for the wealthy and the poor, but as Barber has noted (1994), by failing to expose our students to a good portion of the humanities and the arts, we may be endangering our democracy as well.

### Teachers' Views on Curriculum Time and Content

Surveys of teachers reveal how the NCLB high-stakes testing culture affects the content of their courses. One Colorado teacher stated the following (Taylor, Shepard, Kinner, & Rosenthal, 2003):

> We only teach to the test even at 2nd grade, and have stopped teaching science and social studies. We don't have assemblies, take few field trips, or have musical productions at grade levels. We even hesitate to ever show a video. Our 2nd graders have no recess except for 20 minutes at lunch. (p. 31)

Florida teachers, echoing those in Colorado, show the problem to be national in scope. One Florida teacher stated the following (Jones & Egley, 2004):

> Before [the Florida state test] I was a better teacher. I was exposing my children to a wide range of science and social studies experiences. I taught using themes that really immersed the children into learning about a topic using their reading, writing, math, and technology skills. Now I'm basically afraid to NOT teach to the test. I know that the way I was teaching was building a better foundation for my kids as well as a love of learning. Now each year I can't wait until March is over so I can spend the last two and a half months of school teaching the way I want to teach, the way I know students will be excited about. (p. 15)

In Arizona, a teacher of English language learners talks about the test-oriented curriculum and why she might leave the field (Wright & Choi, 2006):

I'm going to get hired by another district to see if it's like this everywhere, because I haven't been teaching really all that long, and if it is like this everywhere, with just nothing but teach-to-the-test type stuff, and to heck with what the kids want to know, then, . . . I'm not going to stay in the classroom because it just breaks my heart. There are things the kids just want to learn about. You teach them a little bit in these programs, but it's so structured that you don't have time to deviate from the program. I mean, we aren't allowed to have parties, they don't have recess. There is no time during the day where I am allowed to just have fun with my kids and just learn something that is just for fun. And it's really depressing. (p. 38)

The point about learning for fun is perhaps the most important part of this teacher's lament. The ability for students to learn in areas that are of interest to them seems almost unlimited. But in this era of high-stakes testing, students cannot be allowed time in school to follow their interests. The standards define what students should know at different grade levels, and deviation from that plan is considered dangerous because it might result in missing some items on the state high-stakes accountability test. Of course schools never allowed much time for individualized work, but now even the teachers that made some use of problem-based or project-based learning, forms of instruction that could ignite students' interests through a curriculum more personally tailored for an individual, are not allowed to do so. One size of the curriculum is supposed to fit all students, yet we are reasonably sure that the twenty-first century economy will require from our workforce a broad set of skills, not a narrow one. Thus, diversity in the outcomes of the educational system ought to be a goal of American education, not sameness.

Increasingly we live in a "VUCA" world—a world of volatility, uncertainty, complexity, and ambiguity (Johansen, 2007). Education for a VUCA world would seem to demand breadth of talent among members of society so at least some of those talents would be appropriate to whatever the world brings our way. It is like evolution: if characteristics of the niche one inhabits change, only organisms that are adaptive will survive. This means that in changeable times, variation in talents, like variation in genes, is needed. Identical skills, like identical genes, may prove of no value for survival. The VUCA world of the twenty-first century, more than ever before in our history, requires breadth of talent so that we might posses an adaptable workforce, much like it was throughout the twentieth century. High-stakes testing works against that goal.

### Teachers, Administrators, and High-Stakes Tests

There is some evidence that many teachers and administrators support NCLB (Wright, 2007). Apparently, some teachers make use of the pressure the bill provides to motivate students to achieve more, while some administrators use the bill to control teachers and for the clarity of the guidance the act provides for curriculum. Many of these professional educators also see test scores going up on state assessments and this makes them proud of their success as teachers and administrators. So teachers' feelings about NCLB are not as one sided as it may seem, although the majority of teachers do feel much like the teachers from Colorado, Florida, and Arizona whose words appeared in the previous section. Their professional practice has been seriously altered. They do not believe they are teaching better. They do not believe their students are really learning more, a point of view validated by the NAEP tests, though not by their own state tests.

The Council for Basic Education (Zastrow & Janc, 2004) did research that supports the teachers who worry about the changed and narrower curriculum. That group looked at school curricula in the post-NCLB world and reported that the liberal arts in contemporary America have atrophied. Most of the areas the council has been concerned about (history, social studies, civics, geography, art and music, and foreign language) are not usually the focus of high-stakes testing. Therefore, under pressure to succeed on the high-stakes tests in reading and mathematics, these courses have been abridged or dropped all across the nation. The loss of these courses was found to be greatest in minority communities, thus providing another report supportive of the repellent conclusion that the system of education practiced in the United States can be described as apartheid.

## What Is the Desired Curriculum?

Americans have always wanted a broader curriculum than that which is emphasized now. Rothstein, Jacobsen, and Wilder (2008), for example, point out that our founding fathers had a broader vision of schooling than that promoted in NCLB. Benjamin Franklin wanted history emphasized because it forced the young to think about issues of right and wrong, and about the nature of justice and injustice. He also wanted more emphasis on physical fitness. Those who recognize the contemporary obesity problems of our youth will echo Franklin's call.

George Washington wanted public support of schools to help unify divergent social groups. Today, this would be a call for multicultural education. He thought schools were most needed to understand oppression and to teach citizens their rights. Thomas Jefferson, while recognizing the need for vocationally relevant school curricula, also saw schools as serving to improve morality and to help youth learn their rights and their obligations to both their neighbors and their country.

John Adams, as evidenced in the opening quote of this chapter, saw the arts as the fulfillment of the American dream of liberty. For other founders of the nation, morality and citizenship ranked highest. These curriculum aspirations are noticeably absent from the NCLB legislation. Our founding fathers saw the basic skills merely as tools, as means to an end, with that end being a virtuous life. Basic skills were not considered as ends in themselves, which tests in mathematics and reading have become under NCLB.

Each state has to make decisions about how much time physical education, history, or algebra will be allotted out of the available time schools have budgeted to provide public education. If teachers and schools are to be judged by their performance in one of these fields and not another, it should be no surprise to find that the curriculum has been distorted. Subject matter that is tested and consequential will be emphasized, while other subject matter is likely to be ignored.

### Surveying Stakeholders About Curriculum

Rothstein et al. (2008) did a study to see if school administrators, school board members, and the general public still prize such goals for our schools. They asked members of each group to rank eight goals. Remarkably, all three groups performed almost identically, indicating that the educators and board members thought about the goals of schooling much as the general public did. Highest ratings went to basic skills mastery. All Americans agree that this is an important curriculum goal. It is the goal that NCLB focuses on with utmost clarity.

**Developing critical thinking.** Not far behind basic skills in the ratings was critical thinking. NCLB pays lip service to this goal, but in a high-stakes testing environment with predominantly decontextualized multiple-choice measures used to assess what has been learned, there appears to be no place in the curriculum to teach—and no way to assess—critical thinking. Thus, a major curriculum goal in the minds of citizens and education professionals is perhaps never taught well and is less likely to be included in the school curriculum. The pundits also say critical thinking is a necessary twenty-first century skill and it is too bad that no one knows how to teach it well, though some have made positive attempts (Ennis, 1996; Ennis, 2002; Nickerson, Perkins, & Smith, 1985; Perkins, Tishman, & Jay, 1995). But what we probably do know is how *not* to teach critical thinking. Unfortunately, we seem to have designed such a system and it is in use now. We also know that testing critical thinking is harder to do in multiple-choice format than in other ways. The problem is that valid assessments of critical thinking are often significantly more expensive to score and Americans are against paying much more for schooling than they do now.

If we simply start out trying to define what we mean by critical thinking, we see the problem with teaching, learning, and assessing this important curriculum goal. Nickerson (1987) offered this set of ideas for thinking about the behavior and characteristics a critical thinker would display:

- Use evidence skillfully and impartially.

- Organize thoughts and articulate them concisely and coherently.

- Distinguish between logically valid and invalid inferences.

- Suspend judgment in the absence of sufficient evidence to support a decision.

- Understand the difference between reasoning and rationalizing.

- Attempt to anticipate the probable consequences of alternative actions.

- Understand the idea of degrees of belief.

- See similarities and analogies that are not superficially apparent.

- Learn independently and have an abiding interest in doing so.

- Apply problem-solving techniques in domains other than those in which they were learned.

- Structure informally represented problems in such a way that formal techniques, such as mathematics, can be used to solve them.

- Strip a verbal argument of irrelevancies and phrase it in its essential terms.

- Habitually question one's own views and attempt to understand both the assumptions that are critical to those views and the implications of the views.

- Be sensitive to the difference between the validity of a belief and the intensity with which it is held.

- Be aware of the fact that one's understanding is always limited, often much more so than would be apparent to one with a noninquiring attitude.

- Recognize the fallibility of one's own opinions, the probability of bias in those opinions, and the danger of weighting evidence according to personal preferences.

There never were many teachers (or others) who modeled these behaviors, and few classes that systematically taught these skills. But today it is even worse because a curriculum driven by high-stakes testing is not conducive to the development of the characteristics that define a critical thinker. Although it is a high-priority goal for our schools, and is considered a "must" for success in the twenty-first century economy, we may have developed a curriculum framework that is less conducive to development of these skills than ever before.

Are there ways to give the public and the pundits what they want? One of the simplest ways to do that is to change the tests used for school accountability under NCLB. Since tests that have high stakes attached to them drive curriculum and instruction, we must develop tests that measure critical thinking. Then the United States would truly have tests worth teaching to. By building tests the way we do now, student performance can be scored reliably, fast, and cheaply, but with disregard to what society and our political leaders all say we need: a generation of citizens who can think critically about the issues our nation and our industries will face in the future.

The study by Rothstein et al. (2008) identified six other areas that were nearly tied for third place as desirable curriculum goals.

**Developing social skills.** Large percentages of the respondents to the survey wanted to be sure that schools teach social skills. Parents and educators want to be sure that children can get along with others. This is not only quite reasonable, but it has become an even more important goal of education because such skills are predicted to be in greater demand in the future. In knowledge-based businesses in particular (such as in Silicon Valley and on Wall Street), but even in contemporary service- or manufacturing-based businesses, employees are expected to have the social skills necessary for collaborative and cooperative work groups. But project-based, inquiry-based, and problem-based cooperative work groups are rarely seen in public schools, where individual efforts are expected and rewarded, despite what we know about the modern workplace.

A twenty-first century workplace is likely to value such social skills as active and tolerant listening, helping to define problems and suggesting courses of action, giving and receiving constructive criticism, and managing disagreements. But in today's high-stakes education climate, collaborative work is seen even less frequently than ever before because such work always means a loss of time that could be used for preparation to take the tests required by NCLB (Nichols & Berliner, 2007). And there is an additional problem: cooperative forms of instruction ask teachers and their students to make dramatic—not small—changes in the roles that they play. This could explain why these kinds of instructional techniques are evaluated, often found promising, and yet rarely institutionalized. Cohen and Spillane (1992), citing numerous examples of the failure of schools to insert reforms that rely on group work into classroom instruction, say this:

> Classroom roles would have to change radically. Teachers would have to rely on students to produce much more instruction, and students would have to think and act in ways they rarely do. Teachers would have to become coaches or conductors and abandon more familiar and didactic roles in which they "tell knowledge" to students.

Researchers have studied only a few efforts at such change, but they report unusual difficulty, for teachers must manage very complex interactions about very complex ideas in rapid-fire fashion. The uncertainties of teaching multiply phenomenally, as does teachers' vulnerability. (pp. 30–31)

The unpredictability of group work, the changed roles of teachers and students, particularly the potential loss of teacher power in the instructional setting, all conspire to keep these kinds of group learning activities to a minimum in most classes, despite the fact that these are exactly the kinds of social learning activities that parents and educational professionals want schools to foster, and business claims it needs.

**Developing a work ethic.** The public also wants schools to develop a work ethic in youth. This is harder to do with some students than others, especially poor and minority students who do not have the social and intellectual capital of their middle-class peers. Poor children come to school academically behind (Hart & Risley, 1995; Lee & Burkam, 2002). On top of that, they lose academic ground in the summer while their middle-class peers gain ground academically (Alexander, Entwisle, & Olson, 2007). In a high-stakes testing environment, these poor and minority students quickly learn they are a liability to the schools that they attend, that they do not have the "right stuff," and that schools are about winners and losers. In such a setting, instead of developing a healthy work ethic, many of these students develop despair, disengage themselves from schoolwork, and leave school before they graduate. An emphasis on test scores as the predominant way to demonstrate school success has been found to increase dropout rates (Amrein & Berliner, 2002; McNeil, Coppola, Radigan, & Vazquez Heilig, 2008). And those having trouble with tests are not the only students who drop out; high-achieving students make up a substantial number of school dropouts. Forty-seven percent of the dropouts in one study left school because the classes were uninteresting to them (Bridgeland, Dilulio, & Morison, 2006). Perhaps classes in schools in the United States have always been dull, but the amount of drill and the amount of practice test taking, day after day, has clearly made schooling duller (Nichols & Berliner, 2007). The data are hard to gather, but about 30 percent of the children that start high school do not finish. Whites may have a rate of finishing of about 75 percent, while African Americans, Hispanics, and American Indians may have completion rates closer to 50 percent. These are often the students who have the lower test scores and thus are made to feel the most unwelcome in a high-stakes testing environment (Nichols & Berliner, 2007). Almost 70 percent of the dropouts surveyed by Bridgeland et al. (2006) reported there was nothing in their schools to motivate them to work hard. Developing their work ethic with the standard curriculum offered to them is not likely to happen. Students need alternatives to the ordinary curriculum that is assessed by means of high-stakes testing to show that they have valuable talents. If success in the twenty-first century depends on a racially and ethnically diverse, highly motivated and highly educated work force with a wide range of talents, then the emphasis on high-stakes testing may only serve to restrict the United States' economic future.

Other curriculum goals desired by the professional educators and parents surveyed in the study by Rothstein et al. (2008) included students' ability to use computers and communication technologies to develop knowledge. Respondents expressed desire to develop in students' personal responsibility, an ability to get along well with others—especially others from different backgrounds. Youth were thought to need knowledge of how government works and of how to participate in civic activities like voting, volunteering, and becoming active in communities. The respondents believed our students should receive vocational, career, and technical education that could qualify them for skilled employment that does *not* require a college degree.

In the area of emotional well being, our students were thought to need tools to develop self-confidence, respect for others, and the ability to resist peer pressure to engage in irresponsible personal behavior. And as already noted, and not surprisingly, these respondents wanted the schools to (1) provide a foundation for lifelong physical health, including good habits of exercise and nutrition, and (2) develop in students a love of literature and the capacity to participate in and appreciate the musical, visual, and performing arts (Rothstein et al., 2008). School testing programs and the amount of time available make these goals hard to achieve in the current climate.

## How Can We Achieve Our Goals?

The question this chapter raises is whether the high-stakes testing requirements built into the NCLB accountability system can ever help us achieve the many and diverse goals that professional educators, parents, the business community, and politicians want. Rather, does this accountability system foster only the development of basic competencies, boring most teachers and students alike, perhaps even reducing gains in achievement over time?

We know from the research that high-stakes tests and the curriculum goals for students of the twenty-first century are incompatible. High-stakes testing may actually limit the kinds of achievement our youth attain, and thus high-stakes testing may limit the United States' ability to compete well in the twenty-first century. The media-smart youth of today find it quite ordinary to communicate, share, buy and sell, exchange, create, meet, coordinate, evaluate, play games to learn, socialize, fantasize whole new lives through avatars, search, analyze, report, program digital devices, and grow up as remarkably well-connected, fantasy-using, action-oriented kids. But they attend schools that look as if they exist in the nineteenth century—not the twenty-first century. It is not all the fault of testing, but it does appear there is a relationship.

No one really knows what twenty-first century skills are needed to foster success for individuals and nations. But school personnel must think ahead and try to see the future, while attempting to develop reasonably high levels of literacy, numeracy, and scientific knowledge in a broad cross-section of youth. What might some of the skills be that are needed? They might include problem identification, critical thinking, creativity, problem solving, media literacy, ability to sort facts from fiction in a knowledge-rich world, Bayesian and probabilistic estimation, systems thinking, collaborative work skills, and many more. These kinds of intellectual skills seem to be more necessary to students' futures than the kinds of things now being taught and learned in most of our schools, and especially in schools that serve the poor.

This out-of-sync curriculum seems to be well recognized by the Ministry of Education in Singapore. Educators in Singapore are proud of their high test performance but acknowledge that their students are ill prepared for the twenty-first century since the teachers and the schools only prepare their students to answer test items like those on international tests. Singaporeans understand how high-stakes testing can limit national talent, and they are trying to change their entire school system to the demands that they think will be placed on them in the new century. The United States does not seem to get it, and may be going backwards, building school systems for the previous century and not for the future.

Some ideas about what we can do quickly to reverse the trend include expanding the school day, week, and year. Otherwise we cannot accomplish all that is desired of the schools. That is quite clear. Of course this would cost more money, but it would allow for the time needed to expose students to a full and diverse curriculum and still allow some time for test preparation, were that necessary.

We could also reduce the time spent in reading and mathematics, reallocating it to other important curriculum areas that include reading and writing and mathematics across the curriculum. Failure to do this is very shortsighted in terms of what students need for general comprehension, practical numeracy, and for enhancing their learning in social studies, science, and other subjects.

More importantly, we should stop forcing high school students into courses they do not want and replace those with courses that are both good for society and constitute learning experiences that they do want. Expending energy controlling students in courses they do not want to be in is silly. We must tap their remarkable motivation to learn through courses and experiences that they do want. A good deal of physics can be taught in photography. A good deal of mathematics and engineering can be taught in auto shop. Neighborhood and family history can be taught well through projects in social studies, and those personal histories can be linked to broader themes in American and world history. Creative teachers and schools do this now. More teachers and schools should learn from them.

We should also find ways to increase the amount of time spent in problem-based and collaborative learning projects. These forms of instruction have the ability to hold students' interests for long periods of time. And the quality of the work that comes from them is quite remarkable when well-trained teachers have a chance to help highly motivated students.

Finally, and perhaps most important, we need to learn how to design and evaluate the information obtained from multiple measures of learning. The paper and pencil multiple-choice test is not the only way to assess learning. It is a limited way to gain insight into what some students know and are able to do. Open-ended questions, performance assessments, portfolios, and other ways to obtain information should be used for assessing students, teachers, and schools. Every student, every teacher, and every school has a right to be assessed in ways that might best show off their abilities, as well as in ways that obtain information for feedback about how they might improve. That requirement calls for more than one kind of assessment instrument.

We are heading the wrong way with our current accountability practices. The same politicians and business persons that want high-stakes testing to be the cornerstone of a school accountability system also want students to develop twenty-first century skills. They cannot have it both ways. These goals are incompatible, and students and our society suffer because of it.

## References

Adams, J. (1780). *Letter from John Adams to his wife from Paris.* Accessed at http://www.quotationspage.com/quote/33545.html on January 10, 2009.

Alexander, K. L., Entwisle, D. R., & Olson, L. S. (2007). Lasting consequences of the summer learning gap. *American Sociological Review, 72*, 167–180.

Amrein, A. L., & Berliner, D. C. (2002, March 28). High-stakes testing, uncertainty, and student learning. *Education Policy Analysis Archives, 10*(18). Accessed at http://epaa.asu.edu/epaa/v10n18/ on January 13, 2009.

Aguilar, A. (2004, September 29). Many Illinois districts opt out of PE requirement, *St. Louis Post-Dispatch.*

Ball, D. L., Lubienski, S., & Mewborn, D. (2001). Research on teaching mathematics: The unsolved problem of teachers' mathematical knowledge. In V. Richardson (Ed.), *Handbook of research on teaching* (4th ed.). New York: Macmillan.

Ball, D. L., & Bass, H. (2008). The role of mathematics in education for democracy. In G. Fenstermacher, D. Coulter, & J. Wiens (Eds.), *Yearbook of the National Society for the Study of Education: Vol. 107(1). Why do we educate in a democratic society?* (pp. 171–184). Malden, MA: Blackwell Publishing.

Barber, B. (1994). *An aristocracy of everyone: The politics of education and the future of America.* New York: Oxford University Press.

Barton, P. E., & Coley, R. J. (2008, April). *Windows on achievement and inequality.* Princeton, NJ: Policy Information Center, Educational Testing Service. Accessed at http://www.ets.org/portal/site/ets/menuitem.c988ba0e5dd572 bada20bc47c3921509/?vgnextoid=6b0c8bc441d79110VgnVCM10000022f95190 RCRD&vgnextchannel=5c75be3a864f4010VgnVCM10000022f95190RCRD on January 12, 2009.

Booher-Jennings, J. (2005). Below the bubble: "Educational triage" and the Texas accountability system. *American Educational Research Journal, 42*(2), 231–268.

Bridgeland, J. M., Dilulio, J. J., Jr., & Morison, K. B. (2006). *The silent epidemic: Perspectives of high school dropouts.* Washington, DC: Civic Enterprises.

Center on Education Policy. (2008, February). *Instructional time in elementary school subjects. A closer look at changes for specific subjects.* Washington, DC: Author. Accessed at http://www.cepdc.org/index.cfm?fuseaction=Page .viewPage&pageId=500&parentID=481 on January 15, 2009.

Class requirements cut into recess time. (2004, February 27). *Waltham Daily News Tribune.*

Cohen, D. K., & Spillane, J. P. (1992). Policy and practice: The relations between governance and instruction. *Review of Research in Education, 1,* 3–49. Accessed at www.jstor.org/pss/1167296 on January 10, 2009.

Ennis, R. H. (1996). *Critical thinking.* Upper Saddle River, NJ: Prentice Hall.

Ennis, R. H. (2002). Goals for a critical thinking curriculum and its assessment. In Arthur L. Costa (Ed.), *Developing minds* (3rd ed.) (pp. 44–46). Alexandria, VA: Association for Supervision and Curriculum Development.

Finn, C. E., & Ravitch, D. (2007). Not by geeks alone. *The Education Gadfly, 7*(30). Accessed at http://www.edexcellence.net/gadfly/index.cfm?issue=302 on December 15, 2007.

Flynn, J. R. (2009). Requiem for nutrition as the cause of IQ gains: Raven's gains in Britain 1938 to 2008. *Economics and Human Biology, 7,* 18–27. Accessed at http:// www.sciencedirect.com/science?_ob=ArticleURL&_udi=B73DX-4VHGC2H -1&_user=10&_coverDate=03%2F31%2F2009&_rdoc=4&_fmt=high&_orig= browse&_srch=doc-info(%23toc%2311482%232009%23999929998%231016081 %23FLA%23display%23Volume)&_cdi=11482&_sort=d&_docanchor=&_ct =19&_acct=C000050221&_version=1&_urlVersion=0&_userid=10&md5=0 4339d6af6574fb38024800376ad8115 on January 13, 2009.

Friedman, T. L. (2006). *The world is flat: A brief history of the twenty-first century.* New York: Farrar, Straus, and Giroux.

Galton, M. (2007). *Learning and teaching in the primary classroom.* London, UK: Paul Chapman Publishing.

Gerald, D., & Haycock, K. (2006). *Engines of inequality: Diminishing equity in the nation's premier public universities.* Washington, DC: The Education Trust.

Hart, B., & Risley, T. R. (1995). *Meaningful differences in the everyday experience of young American children.* Baltimore, MD: Brooks.

Hong, W.-P., & Youngs, P. (2008). Does high-stakes testing increase cultural capital among low-income and racial minority students? *Education Policy Analysis Archives, 16*(6). Accessed at http://epaa.asu.edu/epaa/v16n6/ on January 14, 2009.

Johansen, B. (2007). *Get there early: Using foresight to provoke strategy and innovation.* San Francisco: Berrett-Koehler.

Jones, B., & Egley, R. (2004). Voices from the frontlines: Teachers' perceptions of high-stakes testing, *Education Policy Analysis Archives, 12*(39). Accessed at http://epaa.asu.edu/epaa/v12n39/ on December 15, 2007.

Kozol J., (2005). *The shame of the nation: The restoration of apartheid schooling in America.* New York: Random House.

Lampert, M. (2001). *Teaching problems and the problems of teaching.* New Haven, CT: Yale University Press.

Lee, J. (2008). Is test driven accountability effective? Synthesizing the evidence from cross-state causal-comparative and correlational studies. *Review of Educational Research, 78*(30), 608–644.

Lee, V., & Burkam, D. (2002). *Inequality at the starting gate: Social background differences in achievement as children begin school.* Washington, DC: Economic Policy Institute.

McNeil, L. (2000). *Contradictions of school reform: Educational costs of standardized testing.* New York: Routledge.

McNeil, L., Coppola, E., Radigan, J., & Vasquez Heilig, J. (2008). Avoidable losses: High-stakes accountability and the dropout crisis. *Education Policy Analysis Archives, 16*(3). Accessed at http://epaa.asu.edu/epaa/v16n3/ on May 15, 2008.

Nichols, S. L., & Berliner, D. C. (2007). *Collateral damage: How high-stakes testing corrupts American education.* Cambridge, MA: Harvard Education Press.

Nickerson, R. S. (1987). Why teach thinking? In J. B. Baron and R. J. Sternberg (Eds.), *Teaching thinking skills: Theory and practice* (pp. 27–37). New York: W. H. Freeman.

Nickerson, R. S., Perkins, D. N., & Smith, E. E. (1985). *The teaching of thinking.* Hillsdale, NJ: Erlbaum.

Perkins, D. N., Tishman, S., & Jay, E. (1995). *The thinking classroom: Learning and teaching in a culture of thinking.* Boston: Allyn & Bacon.

Rothstein, R., Jacobsen, R., & Wilder, T. (2008). *Grading education: Getting accountability right.* New York: Teachers College Press.

Shorris, E. (2000). *Riches for the poor: The Clemente course in the humanities.* New York: W. W. Norton.

Taylor, G., Shepard, L., Kinner, F., & Rosenthal, J. (2003). *A survey of teachers' perspectives on high-stakes testing in Colorado: What gets taught, what gets lost.* CSE Technical Report 588. Los Angeles: University of California.

Woodworth, K. R., Gallagher, H. A., & Guha, R. (2007). *An unfinished canvas. Arts education in California: Taking stock of policies and practices. Summary Report.* Menlo Park, CA: SRI International. Accessed at http://policyweb.sri.com/cep/publications/AnUnfinishedCanvasSummaryReport.pdf on January 14, 2009.

Wright, W. E. (2007, April). *Impact of high-stakes testing policies on English language learners in Arizona.* Paper presented at the meetings of the American Education Research Association, Chicago, IL

Wright, W. E., & Choi, D. (2006). The impact of language and high-stakes testing policies on elementary school English language learners in Arizona. *Education Policy Analysis Archives, 14*(13). Accessed at http://epaa.asu.edu/epaa/v14n13/ on July 19, 2009.

Zastrow, C., & Janc, H. (2004). *The condition of the liberal arts in America's public schools: A report to the Carnegie Corporation of New York.* Washington, DC: Council on Basic Education.

# Debra Pickering

Debra Pickering, Ph.D., consults with schools and districts nationally and internationally as vice president of field services for Marzano Research Laboratory. Throughout her educational career, Dr. Pickering has gained practical experience as a classroom teacher, building leader, and district administrator. For many years, she has used this experience to provide training and support to K–12 teachers and administrators as they seek to continually improve student learning.

In addition to her work with schools, Dr. Pickering has coauthored (with Dr. Robert Marzano) educational books and manuals, including *Dimensions of Learning*, *Classroom Instruction That Works*, *Classroom Management That Works*, and *Building Academic Vocabulary*.

In this chapter, Dr. Pickering advocates *teaching the thinking skills we expect*. She proposes that educators recommit to thinking skills, learn from the past, and then take the steps necessary to move beyond the rhetoric. She presents a series of recommendations for schools: narrow the focus, agree to directly teach thinking skills, challenge the perceived barriers to the direct teaching of thinking skills, identify and teach the thinking skills that higher-order classroom tasks demand, and identify and teach the thinking skills that higher-order life tasks demand.

# Chapter 6

# Teaching the Thinking Skills That Higher-Order Tasks Demand

### Debra Pickering

In 1983, the Association for Supervision and Curriculum Development (ASCD) hosted a conference at the Wingspread Conference Center in Racine, Wisconsin. It is considered by many to be the event that launched the thinking skills movement in the United States. Throughout the remainder of the 1980s and into the 1990s, leaders in this movement, including Arthur Costa, Robert Marzano, Lauren Resnick, Robert Sternberg, Richard Paul, Barry Beyer, and David Perkins, dominated the literature. But, as with most movements, interest gradually waned as other topics rose to the forefront in the educational literature and at conferences in the new century.

So here we are today. The "movement" is over, but the topic is still salient. Virtually every state standards document highlights the importance of critical thinking and problem solving. The rhetoric around the identification of twenty-first century skills is rife with references to critical and creative thinking. Even Barack Obama, during his presidential campaign, expressed a strong commitment to thinking skills. In his *Plan for American*

*Leadership in Space* (2008), specifics of his position on K–12 education included the following language:

> Science assessments . . . need to use a range of measures to test inquiry and higher-order thinking skills including inference, logic, data analysis and interpretation, forming questions, and communication. (para. 12)

Gene Carter (2008), the executive director of ASCD, is only one of many educational leaders who challenges American leaders to work with President Obama to make thinking skills a priority:

> If federal lawmakers can work together to bail out the nation's financial institutions, why can't they work together to ensure that our children acquire the critical-thinking and problem-solving skills they need to succeed in the 21st century? (para. 2)

Clearly, the rhetoric reflects a commitment to thinking skills. But rhetoric is not enough.

## Getting Beyond the Rhetoric

Despite the speeches and programs, and even though many educators have worked for years to make thinking skills a focus in education, there is ample evidence that, in general, teachers are not teaching and students are not demonstrating higher-order thinking. In 1989, six years into the thinking skills movement, an *Education Week* headline read, "NAEP Finds Basic Skills Up, Higher Order Skills Lacking" (Snider, 1989). More recently, in a 2006 study, when employers around the United States were asked to describe their perceptions of the high school graduates who were entering the workforce, almost 70 percent of the respondents rated these new employees' critical thinking and problem solving as "deficient" (Casner-Lotto & Barrington, 2006).

Why do we not see evidence of improved thinking skills? The reasons are multiple and complex, and there is no easy fix, but we can learn from our past mistakes. We must acknowledge, for example, that setting high expectations for students' thinking is not enough. Simply asking higher-order questions and then expecting higher-order answers is naïve. Cuing students to think hard—really, really hard—and expecting new insights and discoveries is fruitless. Scolding students for their lack of thinking and then expecting these reprimands to motivate them to reach new levels is unfair.

So, what should we do instead? *Teach the thinking skills we expect.*

The proposal here is that we recommit to thinking skills, learn from the past, and then take the steps necessary to move beyond the rhetoric. What follows is a series of recommendations, all leading to the final two that assert that we must identify and directly teach the thinking skills that we value. Specifically, schools can do the following:

- Narrow the focus.
- Agree to directly teach thinking skills.
- Challenge the perceived barriers to the direct teaching of thinking skills.
- Identify and teach the thinking skills that higher-order *classroom* tasks demand.
- Identify and teach the thinking skills that higher-order *life* tasks demand.

## Narrow the Focus

In order to move beyond rhetoric and begin to take action, we have to acknowledge that terms like *higher-order thinking skills* and *critical thinking skills*, while they sound good in speeches and documents, cover such a broad range of skills and dispositions that it is sometimes difficult to know where to begin. In fact, perhaps one reason there is little evidence of lasting effects from the thinking skills movement is that it encompassed so much. Examine, for example, one of the powerful culminating publications of that movement: *Developing Minds: A Resource Book for Teaching Thinking* (Costa, 2001). This tome contains eighty-five chapters made up of more than five hundred pages of definitions and perspectives—all insightful, but overwhelming in its diversity.

Some would rightfully argue that a movement to emphasize an expansive topic like thinking skills had to include these diverse perspectives. But it might also explain why many educators, seduced by the topic but confused about where to begin, have defaulted to Bloom's Taxonomy to define higher-order thinking. Bloom's Taxonomy, familiar to so many educators, is organized as six levels of cognition: knowledge, comprehension, application, analysis, synthesis, and evaluation. Although this taxonomy provides a manageable framework for teaching thinking skills, the results of relying on Bloom's Taxonomy have been mixed.

Bloom's Taxonomy has helped to define thinking skills, but the way it is often used in the classroom can do a disservice to the complex nature of higher-order thinking. This happens when teachers are simply encouraged to begin questions and tasks with specific verbs assigned to each of Bloom's levels (see table 1), implying that students will then be able to engage in the thinking associated with that level. Starting a question with a particular verb certainly does not mean that the question meets the criteria for that level of the taxonomy. And asking a question from a particular level might stimulate thinking, but it also might ask students to engage in thinking they have not yet learned to do. Prompting students to *compare* or *formulate* or *justify* does not mean that students have these skills. Because Bloom's Taxonomy has been so often used in this way, and for several additional reasons explained later, a different, relatively new taxonomy will be used here to narrow the scope of the recommendations for teaching higher-order thinking skills.

In *The New Taxonomy of Educational Objectives*, Marzano and Kendall (2007) offer a two-dimensional model. One dimension

**Table 1: Bloom's Taxonomy and the Verbs Aligned With Each Level**

| Bloom's Taxonomy Levels | Verbs Aligned With Each Level |
|---|---|
| Knowledge | Count, define, describe, draw, find, identify, label, match, name, quote, recall, recite, sequence, tell |
| Comprehension | Conclude, demonstrate, discuss, explain, identify, illustrate, paraphrase, predict, report, restate, review, summarize |
| Application | Administer, change, choose, compute, dramatize, interview, prepare, produce, role play, select, solve, transfer, use |
| Analysis | Classify, compare, contrast, debate, deduce, diagram, differentiate, discriminate, distinguish, examine, outline, relate, research, separate |
| Synthesis | Compose, construct, create, design, develop, integrate, invent, make, formulate, organize, perform, plan, produce, propose, rewrite |
| Evaluation | Appraise, argue, assess, choose, conclude, critique, decide, evaluate, judge, justify, predict, prioritize, prove, rank, rate, select |

of the taxonomy describes the three domains of knowledge: psychomotor procedures, mental procedures, and information. The second dimension identifies three systems of thought: the self-system, the metacognitive system, and the cognitive system. The cognitive system is further divided into four tiers: retrieval, comprehension, analysis, and knowledge utilization.

Although Marzano and Kendall (2007) do not specifically label the levels as higher order, the descriptions of two of the levels in the cognitive system—analysis and knowledge utilization—match what many educators describe as higher order. Analysis "involves the reasoned extension of knowledge" and asks the learner to go beyond comprehension by guiding them toward the "generation of new information not already possessed" (p. 44). Tasks that require knowledge utilization, according to Marzano and Kendall, ask the learner to apply the knowledge and, as a result, generate new products and ideas.

One reason for using Marzano and Kendall's taxonomy to define higher-order thinking is that it identifies and defines specific reasoning processes. This serves to narrow the focus while also emphasizing specific processes that need to be learned at each level, as follows:

- **Analysis**—matching, classifying, analyzing errors, generalizing, and specifying

- **Knowledge utilization**—decision making, problem solving, experimenting, investigating

Another impetus for using this new taxonomy to define higher-order thinking is the caution offered long ago by Lauren Resnick, a major leader in the thinking skills movement. In her book *Education and Learning to Think* (1987), Resnick expresses concern that the term *higher order* might imply that there are lower-order skills that need to be learned first and "implicitly, at least, it justifies long years of drill on the 'basics' before thinking and problem solving are demanded" (p. 7). Her fear is that using the label *higher order* for thinking skills will result in these skills being taught only to the academically elite or only at upper levels of schooling.

Marzano and Kendall's two-dimensional taxonomy addresses Resnick's concerns in that it explicitly illustrates how the higher-order thinking skills from the cognitive domains can and should be applied to all types of knowledge, even to skills and details that many educators would consider to be basic.

For these reasons, the focus of the recommendations here will be on the processes in Marzano and Kendall's cognitive levels of analysis and knowledge utilization. While it is true that higher-order thinking is typically defined, and probably should be defined, in much broader terms, the reality is that starting with a small but powerful list of specific thinking processes can increase the likelihood that they will be taught. It is not important for all educators to agree that Marzano and Kendall's list of processes defines higher order, but it is important for schools and districts to understand that if they decide to follow the recommendations in this chapter, their definition of *higher order* needs to contain a list of powerful, robust processes that can be taught explicitly to students K–12.

## Agree to Directly Teach Thinking Skills

After identifying higher-order thinking skills, educators must make decisions about how and when to teach them. There are at least two schools of thought on this issue: some educators support the creation of a separate thinking-skills curriculum, even separate thinking-skills courses. In contrast, others believe that thinking skills should only be taught as part of discipline-specific curricula. Although these different perspectives might create interesting debates, most educators from both sides tend to agree on a key point: whether as a separate curriculum or within the discipline, thinking skills should be directly taught. Although there are those who would disagree with this point, the plethora of literature supporting the direct teaching of thinking skills is persuasive (Beyer, 1991, 2001; Bransford & Stein, 1993; Perkins, 1995; Pogrow, 2005; Polya, 1957; Swartz, 1991, 2001).

In addition to the arguments coming from leaders in the thinking-skills literature, there is one other compelling argument in support of directly teaching thinking skills. The research on the teaching of any mental procedure has long provided clear guidelines for teachers. Madeline Hunter (1994) reflects this research when she teaches us that teaching any skill should include modeling, guided practice, and independent practice. Similarly, Marzano (1992), after examining the research, recommends helping students construct models, shape, and internalize when they are learning skills. With different terms, both of these researchers make it clear that to learn a skill, students need carefully designed, explicit teaching. This research, when applied to the teaching of thinking skills, further strengthens the case for directly teaching thinking skills.

## Challenge the Perceived Barriers to the Direct Teaching of Thinking Skills

The reasoning behind the major barriers to teaching thinking skills goes something like this:

> There are so many standards in state and district documents that it is impossible to cover all the content that we have now. We certainly do not need to add thinking-skills standards. Besides, states give lip service to thinking skills that they say are embedded within the content standards, but the tests do not really assess higher-order thinking. And, if districts decided to step up and emphasize the teaching of thinking, doing so would distract from preparing students for the tests.

First, it is true that many educators believe that state standards documents contain too much content. Examination of these documents would likely result in the same conclusion that Marzano (Marzano & Kendall, 1999) reached when looking at national standards. After counting benchmarks and calculating instructional time, Marzano concludes that "educators would have to increase the amount of instructional time by about seventy-one percent in order to cover all of the benchmarks" (p. 104). This means, he asserts, that schooling would have to expand from K–12 to K–21 (Marzano & Kendall, 1999). So the assertion that there are too many standards might be valid.

Second, it is also true that states' tests are often criticized for assessing lower-order thinking. A 2003 newsletter from the American Educational Research Association highlights several studies that validate this criticism. It quotes from one study done by Achieve, Inc., a Washington-based organization, that examined five state tests and concluded:

The most challenging standards and objectives are the ones that are undersampled or omitted entirely . . . [and those] that call for high-level reasoning are often omitted in favor of much simpler cognitive processes. (p. 3)

Perhaps, then, some of the reasoning behind the barriers to directly teaching thinking skills is based on accurate perceptions. But even if we accept the arguments that state standards are too large and that state tests do not assess higher-order thinking, it does not follow that districts should de-emphasize higher-order thinking if they want their students to perform well on standardized tests.

There is plenty of evidence that if higher-order thinking skills are taught directly, even traditional standardized test scores will be fine. Newmann, Bryk, and Nagaoka (2001) found this in a project with Chicago public school teachers. They explain that teachers in the study required higher-order thinking skills and in-depth understanding, and asked for applications to content knowledge but also in situations outside of school. They found the following:

> This study of Chicago teachers' assignments in mathematics and writing in grades 3, 6, and 8 shows that students who received assignments requiring more challenging intellectual work also achieved greater than average gains on the Iowa Test of Basic Skills in reading and mathematics, and demonstrated higher performance in reading, mathematics, and writing on the Illinois Goals Assessment Program. . . .

> The results suggest that, if teachers, administrators, policymakers, and the public at-large place more emphasis on authentic intellectual work in classrooms, yearly gains on standardized tests in Chicago could surpass national norms. (p. 2)

Doug Reeves (2000) cites evidence from a number of districts that emphasized higher-order thinking through informational writing and saw academic gains even on multiple-choice tests. After considering this evidence, Reeves makes his position clear:

> These model districts make it clear that reasoning, thinking, and communications—not mindless test drills—are the keys to improved student achievement. . . .
>
> The administrators who demand test preparation are wrong; the standards critics who assert that only terrible teaching practices will lead to higher multiple-choice test scores are also wrong. (p. 9)

Stanley Pogrow (2005), creator of Higher Order Thinking Skills (HOTS), reports the following dramatic results of his program that directly teaches and reinforces thinking skills as a separate curriculum:

> In a series of evaluations, some conducted by me and some done independently by school districts, HOTS students' scores generally increased twice as much as those of comparison groups in overall reading and about three times as much in reading comprehension. The students also made substantial growth in math. In some cases, the gains were extraordinary. . . .
>
> The relative advantage and the large gains found on nationally normed tests have also carried over to state tests and NCLB criteria. For example, research compiled by the Cleveland County (North Carolina) Schools found that schools using HOTS not only exceeded state expected growth targets, but also exceeded exemplary growth targets, while the non-HOTS schools were on average below even the expected growth targets. (para. 15, 16)

All of this evidence exposes the flaws in the reasoning underlying the barriers to teaching thinking skills. Even with bloated state standards documents and state tests that fail to assess higher-order thinking, thinking skills can still become a major priority for districts.

Any district that espouses to value higher-order thinking skills must conclude that the way is clear for them to proceed. With the major barriers removed, they can take the next steps.

## Identify and Teach the Thinking Skills That Higher-Order Classroom Tasks Demand

Imagine a hypothetical social studies classroom that has been studying the decade of the 1960s with a focus on increasing students' understanding of how individuals have significantly influenced history. The teacher builds the unit on a decision-making task that asks the students to do the following:

> It is 1969. You are on the board of *Time* magazine. Your task is to identify a "person of the decade" for the 1960s.

> Use what you understand about the people, events, and issues of the decade to make your selection. Be ready to identify the people you considered, the criteria you used for your selection, and how each potential candidate met your criteria.

Imagine a student, one who is accustomed to being successful in the classroom, takes on this task in a way that has probably worked in the past. The student simply selects a person from the 1960s to be person of the decade, such as Martin Luther King, Jr. She then prepares a report on his life and accomplishments. The report might begin like this:

> Martin Luther King, Jr., lost his life trying to better the lives of African American people. He was the greatest American Civil Rights leader of the 1960s. He should be person of the decade.

> He was born in 1929 in the city of Atlanta, Georgia. His father was a minister at the Ebenezer Baptist Church in Atlanta. At fifteen, Martin Luther King, Jr., was enrolled at Moorehouse College. He graduated from there in 1948. . . .

For extra credit points, the student embellishes the project with an attractive cover for the paper, an audiotape of the "I Have a Dream" speech, and a poster with pictures depicting key events in King's life.

The student has actually done quite a lot of work for this assignment. The problem is that the higher-order thinking skill—in this case, decision making—was bypassed. The student made a decision and generated a product, but the student did not engage in a process of decision making in a manner that could have expanded and deepened an understanding of the complex issues and individuals from the decade of the 1960s.

Many opportunities such as this one are missed—not because students are unwilling to work hard, but because they have not learned how to engage in, and have not been held accountable for, the thinking skills these tasks require. In fact, students who do these types of projects have probably been reinforced with good grades. So what can schools and districts do to refocus the classroom on the teaching of thinking skills?

First, districts need to identify the thinking processes that students are to learn. Starting with a small, but powerful set of thinking processes like those identified in Marzano and Kendall's taxonomy (2007) makes the task of teaching these skills feasible. Again, the two sets of processes are as follows:

- **Analysis**—matching, classifying, analyzing errors, generalizing, and specifying

- **Knowledge utilization**—decision making, problem solving, experimenting, investigating

(There are other challenging levels identified in the taxonomy, but the focus here is on these two sets of reasoning processes.)

Next, the identified thinking skills must be organized into standards and benchmarks across grade levels, similar to what is done with content standards. Figure 1 is an example of a set of benchmarks to be addressed at each grade-level band for the

**Grade K–2 Benchmarks**

- Identifies decisions that people make daily
- Understands that a decision is made when you select from among alternatives

**Grade 3–5 Benchmarks**

- Examines decisions to identify the alternatives and the criteria that were considered, such as in social studies, science, literature, and daily life
- Understands and uses terms associated with decision making, such as *alternatives*, *criteria*, and *weighing priorities*
- Generates and applies criteria to alternatives to make simple decisions

**Grade 6–8 Benchmarks**

- Generates criteria for student-structured and teacher-structured decision-making tasks, such as from social studies, science, literature, and daily life
- Accesses and evaluates information relevant to determining how well alternatives meet criteria
- Understands how different criteria lead to different decisions in the same situation and that decisions require examining and reexamining alternatives, criteria, and the interaction of alternatives and criteria
- Uses a process and organizer to make or examine decisions, such as from social studies, science, literature, and daily life

**Grade 9–12 Benchmarks**

- Makes and analyzes decisions with multiple alternatives and with subjective and objective criteria, such as from history, science, politics, literature, and daily life
- Uses a variety of tools, such as balance sheets, matrices, and graphs, to determine the extent to which alternatives meet criteria
- Explains decisions in terms of alternatives, priorities, context, and so on

**Figure 1: Example of sets of benchmarks for each grade-level band for the process of decision making.**

process of decision making. These guidelines are general enough to allow for addressing the thinking skill across content areas but specific enough to provide direction for teachers.

After identifying essential thinking skills and designating when they should be learned, districts need to provide teachers with resources to support their teaching of the skills. These resources should include clear explanations and examples of each process, specific recommendations for teaching the processes, and criteria to use when providing students with feedback when they are using the processes.

As an example, refer back to the social studies decision-making task at the beginning of this section. In addition to teaching students about the decade of the 1960s, a teacher who is committed to the process of decision making and armed with resources like those described earlier, could help students increase their understanding of, and ability to use, the process. This means the teacher would perhaps present and demonstrate a model or heuristic that would guide students in the process of decision making, such as the following:

- Clearly identify the goal for the decision, and identify and examine the alternatives you are considering.

- Develop a set of criteria that the final selection should meet.

- Determine the extent to which each of your alternatives meets each criterion.

- Identify the alternative that most closely meets your criteria.

- Reexamine your criteria and your assessment of how the alternatives meet those criteria until you are satisfied that you have made the best selection.

Figure 2 is an example of a matrix students could use as they follow this model. If this matrix were used for the person of the decade task described previously, the student would use what he

|  | Alternative 1 | Alternative 2 | Alternative 3 |
|---|---|---|---|
| Criterion 1 | 4 | 2 | 2 |
| Criterion 2 | 2 | 3 | 2 |
| Criterion 3 | 4 | 3 | 2 |
| Criterion 4 | 4 | 1 | 4 |
| Totals | 14 | 9 | 10 |

Each alternative is rated on a scale of 0–4 (4 is highest) according to the extent to which the alternative meets that criterion. The alternative with the highest number of points is seemingly the best decision.

**Figure 2: Example of a matrix used for the process of decision making.**

or she knows about the 1960s to generate a list of leaders from that era, such as Martin Luther King, Jr., and John F. Kennedy. Next, the student would generate criteria that reflect the characteristics of a leader from that era, such as contributed to civil rights or had a positive influence on world conflicts. Finally, each criterion would be applied to each leader to identify who best met the criteria. Because this is a reflective process and not just a set of steps, the student might, after learning more and thinking about the era, repeat the process multiple times with additional, or different, leaders and criteria.

Providing a model like this one does not imply that decision making, or any thinking skill, should follow a strict set of steps. But much like teaching writing, providing a general model can guide students as they begin to engage in the type of thinking required by the task. It creates a common language (*decision, alternatives, criteria*) that teachers can use to provide consistent feedback to students using the process. It can also help students develop an understanding of the thinking skills (for example, "I realize that good decisions require careful examination and reexamination of the interaction between criteria and alternatives"). Equally important, students are using higher-order thinking to deepen their understanding of the content knowledge. The value of the report, tape, and poster produced by the student in the 1960s social studies example pales in comparison to the value of what could be produced by a student who engages in a rigorous process of decision making.

It makes sense, then, to teach students a process when they are given a task that requires a thinking skill so clearly labeled (such as in the model and the rubric in fig. 2); however, there are many classroom tasks that require specific thinking skills not so clearly labeled. Many challenging questions and tasks, especially in science and math, require what is commonly labeled *deductive reasoning*—what Marzano and Kendall's taxonomy (2007) refers to as *specifying*. This thinking skill is needed when students are asked, for example, to observe a phenomenon and use a scientific principle to predict what will happen, or when they are asked to use their understanding of math principles to determine how to solve a problem. Do students who are challenged with these types of tasks only need to understand the math or science principles, or would they also benefit from direct instruction in the thinking skill itself? Matthew Lipman's experiences with his program Philosophy for Children (P4C) provide evidence to answer this question (Lipman, 1988).

In P4C, students learn the rules of logic, among other thinking skills, through a specially designed set of student and teacher materials. The core student novel, *Harry Stottlemeier's Discovery*, develops students' syllogistic reasoning and continues throughout the novel to help students explore and use complex reasoning processes, largely deductive in nature. After experiencing this separate thinking skills curriculum, students involved in the program showed significant increases in reading and math, even though there were no changes made in the classrooms' reading and math materials (Perkins, 1995).

Like teaching decision making, students can be taught a process for applying a general principle to a new specific situation. Marzano and Kendall (2007, p. 50) offer the following critical attributes for this process of specifying:

- Identifying the generalizations or principles that apply to a specific situation

- Making sure that the specific situation meets the conditions that have to be in place for the generalizations or principles to apply

- If the generalizations or principles do apply, identifying what conclusions can be drawn or what predictions can be made

If students were explicitly taught these attributes, they would begin to develop an understanding of critical terms like *principles* and *conditions*. With practice and feedback, they could also become comfortable with the recursive nature of such a process; that is, they would know that they might have to loop through the process many times before reaching a conclusion that can be supported.

Recommending that students are explicitly taught thinking skills as illustrated in the two examples does not suggest that students will then be good critical thinkers. Obviously, in order to apply the thinking, students would need to develop in-depth understanding of the content knowledge. Further, learning a thinking process through explicit instruction does not mean that when students are faced with new tasks, they will spontaneously recognize the need for and use the appropriate process. Content area teachers will still need to help students identify what type of thinking is required for particular tasks and will need to guide students as they apply the processes to specific content.

In order to deliver the initial instruction in thinking skills and to provide the necessary ongoing support to students described in these recommendations, it is important to reiterate that teachers will need multiple professional resources. They will need examples of the thinking skills applied to specific content standards, time to collaborate with colleagues, and access to professional development opportunities.

In summary, there are a number of small steps districts need to take to ensure that students are learning the thinking skills that challenging tasks demand. They must identify the thinking skills that students need to learn and designate when and where the thinking skills will be taught. They then need to provide teachers with the resources—materials, time, professional development—needed to take on the challenges they will face as they help students to develop higher-order thinking skills.

Whether the plan is for all teachers to be involved in explicitly teaching designated higher-order thinking skills, or a plan where a few teachers take the responsibility for teaching thinking skills to all students, there needs to be a plan. If there is not, even if students are given elegantly designed, cognitively challenging tasks, many of them will default to producing lower-level products, like the student choosing the person of the decade in the decision-making task presented earlier. Or students will attempt the thinking, but they will not be able to achieve higher levels. Or, sadly, they will avoid trying at all.

### Identify and Teach the Thinking Skills That Higher-Order Life Tasks Demand

Educators place a high value on preparing students for success in life, not just for success in school. It is hard to imagine anything more important than the ability to think clearly in diverse situations. There are references to thinking skills in virtually every discussion that focuses on how to help students be productive citizens in the twenty-first century. I have presented the case for the explicit teaching of thinking skills that students need for cognitively challenging classroom tasks; the case becomes even stronger when considering the arguments for teaching the thinking skills students need to be successful in life beyond school.

Consider again the example of the student who is challenged with a decision-making task of choosing a person of the decade for the 1960s. With the explicit teaching of the decision-making process, there is much greater potential for this task to take students to a deeper level of understanding of the content as well as to further develop students' capacity to apply decision making in increasingly complex classroom tasks. Now imagine how empowering it would be if students were able to face life's challenges with the same understanding of, and ability to engage strategically in, the process of decision making.

Of course, in many of life's situations, people do not sit down and create a decision-making matrix. However, imagine what would happen if more people understood that careful consideration of criteria is critical to a good decision and that making the best decision might require examining and then reexamining the interaction of criteria and alternatives. When we consider the myriad of decisions people make throughout their lives—related to personal finances, career paths, health care, ethical behavior, and so on—it is easy to see why teaching decision making is a way of providing students with a life skill.

Similarly, all of the thinking skills included in the upper levels of Marzano and Kendall's taxonomy (2007) can be valuable to students as they tackle higher-order classroom tasks, and can then arm them with critical understandings and skills as they tackle life's challenges. For example, one of the processes identified at the analysis level in the taxonomy is the process of analyzing errors. When applied to information, this process involves examining logic and reasons in claims, assertions, generalizations, and principles. A general set of guidelines for the explicit teaching of this process might include the following:

- Identify what information is being offered to support an assertion or claim.

- Examine the major arguments to look for flawed reasoning or conflicting information.

- If there are flaws or conflicts, seek additional information or clarification.

- Determine if the assertion or claim has valid support.

Ideally, students learning to engage in this process would develop the language and the understanding related to logical fallacies and rhetorical appeals. Let us say that students learning this process of analyzing errors are developing the ability to recognize when arguments and assertions contain any of the following (adapted from Marzano & Pickering, 1997):

- **Arguing against the person**—attacking the person instead of attacking the ideas

- **Accidents**—making an argument by offering a single example as if it were the rule instead of an exception to the rule

- **Citing sources that lack credibility**—using points that come from a source that is not necessarily an informed or expert source for the topic, such as a tabloid newspaper

- **Appealing to emotion**—telling a "sob story" or citing another type of emotional appeal as a valid reason for supporting an assertion or position

- **Appealing through rhetoric**—persuading through masterful use of language in speech making

It is apparent that if students develop an understanding of these types of persuasive techniques, they would then be able to recognize and expose weak arguments related to issues they are studying in school. But it is equally apparent that studying errors in reasoning would equip students to evaluate the overwhelming quantity of information they encounter—and will continue to encounter—in daily life, information that is intended to influence how they vote, what they purchase, who they follow, how they live, and so on.

The recommendations presented here would, admittedly, be challenging for districts to implement. But teaching thinking skills is even more important than some of the content area procedures that tend to get more attention. Is it, for example, a higher priority that students learn how to write a story than it is for them to learn how to deflect artful but flawed arguments designed to influence their values and beliefs? Is it more important for them to construct a Punnett square in biology than to generate and carefully apply thoughtful criteria during decision making?

Ideally, we should not have to make these choices, but in reality, we must. We cannot teach everything. Just as we must identify and commit to the direct teaching of essential content-specific procedures, we must also identify and commit to directly teaching essential thinking skills.

## References

American Educational Research Association. (2003, Spring). Standards and tests: Keeping them aligned. *Research Points, 1*(1), 4. Accessed at www.aera.net/uploadedFiles/Journals_and_Publications/Research_Points/RP_Spring03.pdf on December 18, 2008.

Beyer, B. K. (1991). Practical strategies for the direct teaching of thinking skills. In A. Costa, *Developing minds: A resource book for teaching thinking* (rev. ed., Vol. 1, pp. 274–279). Alexandria, VA: Association for Supervision and Curriculum Development.

Beyer, B. K. (2001). What research says about teaching thinking skills. In A. Costa, *Developing minds: A resource book for teaching thinking* (3rd ed., pp. 275–282). Alexandria, VA: Association for Supervision and Curriculum Development.

Bransford, J. D., & Stein, B. S. (1993). *The ideal problem solver: A guide for improving thinking, learning, and creativity* (2nd ed.). New York: W. H. Freeman & Company.

Carter, G. R. (2008, November). *Is it good for the kids? Is education too big to fail?* Accessed at www.ascd.org/news_media/Is_It_Good_for_the_Kids_Editorials/IIGFTK-11-08.aspx on December 18, 2008.

Casner-Lotto, J., & Barrington, L. (2006). *Are they really ready to work? Employers' perspectives on the basic knowledge and applied skills of new entrants to the 21st century U.S. workforce.* Danbury, CT: The Conference Board, Incorporated.

Costa, A. L. (Ed.). (2001). *Developing minds: A resource book for teaching thinking.* (3rd ed.) Alexandria, VA: Association for Supervision and Curriculum Development.

Hunter, M. C. (1994). *Mastery teaching: Increasing instructional effectiveness in elementary and secondary schools, colleges, and universities.* Thousand Oaks, CA: Corwin Press.

Lipman, M. (1988). *Philosophy goes to school.* New York: Temple University Press.

Marzano, R. J. (1992). *A different kind of classroom: Teaching with dimensions of learning.* Alexandria, VA: Association for Supervision and Curriculum Development.

Marzano, R. J., & Kendall, J. S. (1999). *Essential knowledge: The debate over what American students should know.* Aurora, CO: McREL Institute.

Marzano, R. J., & Kendall, J. S. (2007). *The new taxonomy of educational objectives* (2nd ed.). Thousand Oaks, CA: Corwin Press.

Marzano, R. J., & Pickering, D. J. (1997). *Dimensions of learning: Teacher's manual* (2nd ed.). Alexandria, VA: Association for Supervision and Curriculum Development.

Newmann, F. M., Bryk, A. S., & Nagaoka, J. K. (2001, January). *Authentic intellectual work and standardized tests: Conflict or coexistence?* Accessed at http://ccsr.uchicago.edu/publications/p0a02.pdf on December 18, 2008.

Obama, B. (2008). *Barack Obama's plan for American leadership in space.* Accessed at www.spaceref.com/news/viewsr.html?pid=26647 on December 18, 2008.

Perkins, D. (1995). *Outsmarting IQ: The emerging science of learnable intelligence.* New York: Free Press.

Pogrow, S. (2005, February). HOTS revisited: A thinking development approach to reducing the learning gap after grade 3. *Phi Delta Kappan, 87*(1). Accessed at www.pdkintl.org/kappan/k_v87/k0509pog.htm on December 18, 2008.

Polya, G. (1957). *How to solve it* (2nd ed.). Garden City, NY: Doubleday & Company.

Reeves, D. B. (2000). Standards are not enough: Essential transformations for school success. *NASSP Bulletin, 84*(620), 5–19.

Resnick, L. B. (1987). *Education and learning to think.* New York: National Academies Press.

Snider, W. (1989, February 22). NAEP Finds Basic Skills Up, Higher-Order Skills Lacking. *Education Week.* Accessed at http://www.edweek.org/ew/articles/1989/02/22/08180031.h08.html?r=993497671 on December 20, 2008.

Swartz, R. J. (1991). Infusing the teaching of critical thinking in content instruction. In A. Costa (Ed.)., *Developing minds: A resource book for teaching thinking* (rev. ed., Vol. 1, pp. 177–184). Alexandria, VA: Association for Supervision and Curriculum Development.

Swartz, R. J. (2001). Infusing critical and creative thinking in content instruction. In A. Costa (Ed.)., *Developing minds: A resource book for teaching thinking* (3rd ed., pp. 266–274). Alexandria, VA: Association for Supervision and Curriculum Development.

# Lynn Erickson

Lynn Erickson, Ed.D., is an internationally recognized presenter, author, and consultant in the area of concept-based curriculum and instruction and standards alignment. She has served as a teacher, principal, curriculum director, adjunct professor, and independent consultant over her forty-year career. Appointed by the governor of Washington, Dr. Erickson served as chair of the Washington State History Standards at their inception.

Dr. Erickson is the author of three best-selling books, and several published video programs focus on her work with teachers. She was born and raised in Fairbanks, Alaska. She and Ken Erickson enjoy rollerblading and motorcycling. They now live in the Seattle area and have two children and two grandchildren who stir their heart and soul.

In this chapter, Dr. Erickson addresses three critical issues for improving education: (1) teacher education; (2) support for concept-based curriculum designs that address what students must know factually, understand conceptually, and be able to do in skills and processes; and (3) instruction that develops conceptual thinking along with critical, creative, and reflective thinking.

## Chapter 7

# Conceptual Designs for Curriculum and Higher-Order Instruction

### Lynn Erickson

We all know of master teachers—those passionate, caring, and intuitively sensitive individuals who integrate their intellect and emotions to create student-centered learning environments. These are thinking teachers, lifelong learners themselves, who draw on research and best practice, a keen understanding of children, and a fiery commitment to helping each student succeed. They realize that their job as educators is to help all students learn to use their minds well as they strive to meet the requisite academic standards. These skills are particularly crucial in light of the current intense focus on academic standards that has led to significant pressure to improve classroom instruction.

The United States' model for increasing student achievement has revolved around (1) mandating academic standards; (2) high-stakes testing to ensure the standards are met in each state; and (3) encouraging competition between schools to theoretically challenge low-performing schools to improve. The development of academic standards was a positive step because it provided a basic blueprint of what students must know and be able to do as productive citizens of a democratic society. However, the focus on high-stakes testing has been controversial, with mixed effects on classroom instruction. Some school districts invested heavily in staff development to prepare teachers for the higher expectations. But too many schools and school districts focused on raising test scores without adequately addressing teacher preparation and classroom instruction. This emphasis has had predictable results: teaching to the test; the elimination of subjects not tested at the state level, such as social studies, art, and physical education; and unfortunately, isolated instances of cheating to meet the mandates of No Child Left Behind (NCLB).

Additionally, the puzzling call to create competition between schools as a way to challenge lower-performing schools appears antithetical to the basic premise of academic standards. If the purpose of standards is to raise all children up to high performance levels, then why would we want to encourage competition, which by its very nature implies winners and losers? We need to raise *all* schools—even high-achieving schools—up and beyond where they are currently by focusing on the design and implementation of quality curriculum, instruction, and assessment.

This chapter addresses three critical issues for improving education:

1. Teacher education

2. Support for concept-based curriculum designs that address what students must know factually, understand conceptually, and be able to do in skills and processes

3. Instruction that develops conceptual thinking along with critical, creative, and reflective thinking

## Teacher Education

My work with elementary and secondary teachers for three decades affirms that the majority of educators want to do the best job possible and aspire to be those master teachers that everyone admires. But that goal requires continual staff development because educators today are working in more complex environments with far greater challenges than teachers in years past. As we strive to help all children become the best they can be, we have to be concerned about helping all teachers be the best they can be. We owe it to the teachers—and we also owe it to the children.

Linda Darling-Hammond (2009) reviewed the research related to teacher training and student achievement and found that the nations that score the highest academically, such as Finland and Singapore, invest heavily in teacher education. In Finland, the nation with the highest literacy scores internationally, recent teacher preparation has focused on teaching for higher-order thinking skills such as problem solving and critical thinking. Similarly, Singapore prepares teachers to implement a curriculum focused on inquiry and critical thinking.

A significant finding in Darling-Hammond's review is that teachers in most high-achieving countries have fifteen to twenty hours per week to work with colleagues on lesson planning, book studies, research groups, and seminars to extend their expertise in teaching and learning. This model encourages the thoughtful, reflective practice of professionals. Contrast these high-achieving nations who invest heavily in the training of their teachers to raise academic standards with the United States, a country that emphasizes test scores over teacher development. Teacher education is critical to quality instruction, and so is quality curriculum design.

## The Current State of Curriculum Design

In 1956, Benjamin Bloom and his colleagues developed the Taxonomy of Educational Objectives, which offered a hierarchy of verbs correlated to different cognitive levels. Addressing a variety of cognitive levels advanced curriculum design. These verb-driven objectives became, and remain today, the staple of curriculum guides and frameworks.

Through the decades since the publication of Bloom's Taxonomy, there have been attempts to ensure deeper understanding of disciplinary concepts and principles in curriculum designs. One of the most famous of these researchers and curriculum leaders in the 1950s and 1960s was Hilda Taba. She believed that curricula should use the factual content to develop understanding of the concepts and main ideas. These main ideas were actually universal generalizations that could be applied in different times and places. She realized that one cannot teach every fact, so it is important to be selective of content and teach students to understand the bigger ideas that can transfer to other situations.

There have been other attempts to work toward conceptual understanding through the years: concept attainment (Bruner, 1973; Joyce & Weil, 1986), Bruner's social studies curriculum of the 1960s—*Man: A Course of Study*, science curricula such as Science Curriculum Improvement Study (SCIS), and Biological Science Curriculum Study (BSCS). All of these programs, innovations, or curricular philosophies valued deeper conceptual understanding, but they became involved in political controversies because the pedagogy and curriculum designs were not well understood. Concept-based curriculums of the past were difficult for teachers to implement. Curriculum writers assumed that teachers would have the requisite conceptual background to understand the pedagogy and program goals. We now realize that we cannot make this assumption. Teacher education on the benefits, structure, and pedagogy of concept-based curricula is mandatory for successful implementation.

More recently, Anderson and Krathwohl (2001) updated Bloom's Taxonomy and stated that knowledge is not just factual and procedural; rather, there are actually four general types of knowledge: factual, conceptual, procedural, and metacognitive. They proposed that "by separating *factual knowledge* from *conceptual knowledge*, we highlight the need for educators to teach for deep understanding of *conceptual knowledge*, not just for remembering isolated and small bits of *factual knowledge*" (p. 42, italics added). Conceptually designed curricula help teachers differentiate the original two levels of knowledge and support higher-order instruction in both inter- and intradisciplinary contexts.

Marzano and Kendall's *Designing and Assessing Educational Objectives: Applying the New Taxonomy* (2008) provides a clear and helpful model for understanding and designing curriculum frameworks for the twenty-first century. The authors extend the work of previous taxonomies by clearly explaining and differentiating with apt examples the different levels, kinds, and uses of knowledge, as well as the domains of mental and psychomotor processes and skills. Academic standards developed using previous taxonomies fail to clearly differentiate between factual, conceptual, and process/skill benchmarks. The definitions and examples in Marzano and Kendall actually *teach* teachers the meaning and language of curriculum—a first step in designing quality units and lessons for instruction. One would think that teachers already know this information, but when they have been trained to teach mainly for factual knowledge and skills, the shift to the conceptual level requires additional training and a new mindset.

Many teachers are confused about the difference between a *skill* and a *content objective*. Skills transfer, and they can be applied in different situations. "Analyze primary and secondary source documents to evaluate historical information" is a skill. If the transferable skill is applied to a specific topic, then it becomes a content objective or activity: "Analyze primary and secondary source documents to determine the perspectives of the North and South during the Civil War." Many teachers focus on the verb *analyze* and cite the entire statement as a skill. Marzano and Kendall (2008) clarify confusing terms for educators and help lay the groundwork for developing informed curricula that reflect critical factual knowledge, conceptual understanding, and skill.

Bransford, Brown, and Cocking have had a significant impact on curriculum and instruction with their book *How People Learn:*

*Brain, Mind, Experience, and School* (2000). This compilation of educational research and its implications for teaching and learning further supports the need for conceptually driven curricula and instruction. The authors remind us that experts organize knowledge around "key concepts and important ideas which suggests that curricula should also be designed to draw out conceptual understanding" (p. 42). They also make the case that having a deeper conceptual understanding of disciplines facilitates the efficient transfer of knowledge.

National and state academic standards provide a valuable service in framing critical content and skills for learning, but the design of curricula at the local level to meet academic demands is critical for the following reasons:

- The national and state standards are not a curriculum— they are a framework to be used in the design of local curricula.

- The national and state standards were developed independently and lack a coherent design across disciplines. Therefore, generally, the history standards are topic based, the science standards are concept based, and the mathematics standards are skill based. Yet all of these disciplines have an inherent conceptual structure. When local school districts design their curricula, they can bring coherence across the disciplines by contextualizing the state standards under a common design model that identifies what students must understand conceptually, know factually, and be able to do in processes and skills.

The design of concept-based curricula at the local level is difficult but necessary work. If national and state academic standards across the disciplines would articulate the important conceptual relationships for grade-level bands, it would facilitate local curriculum development work. The national science and economic standards address conceptual understandings, but there is still a great deal of conceptual work to do across the disciplines. In the next section, I reinforce reasons for moving to concept-based curriculum designs and identify contemporary initiatives that support this direction.

## Concept-Based Curriculum Designs

The transformation to a concept-based design for curriculum leaves most educators in the uncomfortable zone of cognitive dissonance—trying to integrate newer models and perspectives into the established and traditional pattern of design for curriculum and instruction. Technological advances, globalization, and growing complexity in living, learning, and working call for adaptation to our traditional designs if we are to significantly raise the achievement levels of students.

Conceptual designs for curriculum and instruction have been challenging traditional methods for decades. There are two main reasons:

1.  As the knowledge base of each discipline continues to expand, the futile nature of trying to "teach it all" becomes more apparent. There is so much information today that we need to move to a higher level of abstraction (the concepts and principles) to organize that knowledge and to help students see patterns and connections between factual knowledge and transferable understandings—an adherence to the refined principles of efficiency and utility, if you will.

2.  The complexity of the world we live in today, with its problems, promises, and interdependent relationships, requires that citizens use their minds well. Conceptual thinking, as well as creative, critical, and reflective thinking, cannot be assumed to be a byproduct of factual learning. When the requirement to think at higher levels is intentionally designed into curricular and instructional programs, it reinforces education as an intellectual process.

To counteract an anti-intellectual race to cover information, there has been a renewed interest in curriculum designs that engage higher levels of thinking. These designs value a solid foundation of factual knowledge, but they also ensure that teaching and learning go beyond the facts to the important concepts, principles, and transferable generalizations—the timeless constructs—of each discipline.

When I think about conceptually designed curriculum and instruction in relation to the New Taxonomy (Marzano & Kendall, 2008), I realize that my work has focused particularly on developing two aspects of the New Taxonomy: (1) the analysis level of cognition, especially the ability to derive conceptual understanding from content knowledge, and (2) the knowledge-utilization level, which requires the transfer of knowledge. My intense focus on these areas for more than twenty years has deepened my understanding of the absolutely integral role that thinking plays in the teaching and learning process. I now understand the following with great clarity:

- When the design of curriculum and instruction requires students to synergistically process the relationships between factual knowledge and related concepts, students develop conceptual structures in the brain for patterning and meaning making. Synergistic thinking is an interactive energy between the factual and conceptual levels of mental processing. Factual thinking by itself is not very powerful, and conceptual thinking by itself is impossible. The interplay of synergistic thinking, on the other hand, engages the personal intellect and develops the mind.

- Engaging the conceptual level of thinking motivates students for learning. Humans are uniquely intellectual animals, distinguished from other animals by their refined ability to think and find joy in thinking. Ask students to memorize facts about Martin Luther King, Jr., and they will comply with limited enthusiasm. Invite students to think, however, about Martin Luther King, Jr., through the lens of "leadership" or "beliefs and values" and they will feel intellectually engaged. They are thinking for themselves—a key motivator for learning.

A number of contemporary concept-based curriculum models exist. These include *Understanding by Design* (Wiggins & McTighe, 1999, 2005, 2007); *Concept-Based Curriculum and Instruction* (Erickson, 1995, 2002, 2007, 2008); *The Parallel Curriculum* (Tomlinson et al., 2009); *Essential Questions* (Jacobs, 1997, 2004); the Paideia Program (Roberts & Billings, 1999); and the International Baccalaureate Programme, which was started in 1968 in Geneva, Switzerland. These concept-based programs share certain characteristics:

- They are idea centered rather than coverage centered.

- They focus on the transfer of concepts and important ideas through time, across cultures, and across situations.

- They use factual knowledge as the foundational support for conceptual thinking and understanding.

- They create a synergy between the factual and conceptual levels of thinking to support greater retention of knowledge and deeper understanding.

- They clearly delineate three criteria for learning: understand (concepts), know (facts), and be able to do (processes and skills).

- They are concerned with building conceptual schemata in the brain so that new knowledge can be linked to prior knowledge, and so that knowledge can be patterned and sorted efficiently.

- They are designed to engage personal intellect so learners can construct meaning, determine relevance, and experience the joy of independent thinking.

The goal of concept-based curriculum designs is higher-order instruction for higher-order learning.

## Conceptual Curriculum Designs and Higher-Order Instruction

There are growing numbers of teachers, schools, and school districts throughout the world working diligently to design concept-based curricula across subjects and grade levels, prekindergarten to grade 12. Experienced educators realize that for the complex world we live in today, we need a higher-order curriculum model to support higher-order instruction. Concept-based curricula are supported by brain research and learning theory (Bransford et al., 2000; Caine, Caine, McClintic, & Klimek, 2005; Gardner, 2006a; Ritchhart, 2002; Sousa, 2006; Sylwester, 2005; Willis, 2006).

Judy Willis (2006), a neuroscience researcher who became a teacher, provides scientific explanations of how the brain makes conscious connections between stored memories and new information:

> Patterning is the process whereby the brain perceives and generates patterns by relating new with previously learned material or by chunking material into pattern systems it has used before. Whenever new material is presented in such a way that students see relationships, they generate greater brain cell activity (forming new neural connections) and achieve more successful long-term memory storage and retrieval. (pp. 15–16)

Concept-based curriculum creates structures in the brain to assist in patterning and relationship building, which leads to greater retention, retrieval, and understanding of information. By its very nature, concept-based instruction allows students to find personal meaning and relevance in new learning.

Concept-based curriculum and instruction are critical for all students regardless of whether they are in English as a second language, special education, advanced learning, or regular education classes. Focusing on developmentally appropriate concepts and generalizations supported by relevant facts helps all students build deeper disciplinary and interdisciplinary knowledge and understanding.

## Contemporary Forms of Conceptually Designed Curricula

A curriculum that promotes conceptual thinking needs a vehicle to engage the conceptual mind. Two methods are widely used today: (1) conceptual understandings and (2) essential questions. Both methods serve the purpose of creating an intellectual synergy between the factual and conceptual levels of thinking. The curriculum designers who work with conceptual understandings and essential questions realize that when students are encouraged to process factual knowledge using their conceptual mind, they develop deeper levels of understanding.

Adults often lament that they feel uncomfortable with mathematics. I believe this is because they learned how to perfunctorily carry out algorithms without understanding the conceptual language and relationships of mathematics. The language of mathematics communicates conceptual relationships that give meaning to the processes and skills of math. The language of mathematics is not a litany of isolated vocabulary terms and their definitions. Mathematics teachers find it difficult to state mathematical generalizations because they have been taught how to teach students to carry out skills devoid of the language of relationships. We need both the skill objectives and the statements of conceptual understanding to help guide mathematics instruction. To see the value in using both the objective and the understanding in curriculum and instruction, compare the following skill objective with the related statement of conceptual understanding:

*Skill:* Use angle measurements to classify angles as acute, obtuse, or right.

_____ 90 degrees _____ 180 degrees _____ 120 degrees

_____ 30 degrees _____ 60 degrees _____ 45 degrees

*Conceptual Understanding:* The arc of an angle, measured in degrees, indicates whether the angle is acute, obtuse, or right.

Peruse a set of mathematics standards written as skill objectives. How often do we ask students to carry out the skills and *assume* that they understand the related conceptual idea? In the previous example, students could memorize that right angles are always 90 degrees, or angles less than 90 degrees are acute. But if they do not state the idea we only assume they truly understand the conceptual relationship. As ideas become more complex, our assumptions of student understanding often fall short. Mathematics is a conceptual language, and helping students to converse in that language reinforces their learning.

When you ask a teacher in any discipline to state an important generalization based on factual study, he or she may struggle at first to articulate the thought. Teachers have no difficulty stating objectives related to factual content, but they need practice in stating conceptual understandings. Learning to articulate these important ideas is a skill that develops quickly with a shift in thinking and a little practice.

**Conceptual understandings.** Grant Wiggins, Jay McTighe, and I have worked on parallel paths over the years towards the same end goal: to help students develop deeper levels of thinking and conceptual understanding, to aid the transfer of knowledge, and to inform the pedagogy of classroom instruction (Erickson, 1995, 2007, 2008; Wiggins & McTighe, 1999, 2005, 2007). Every content subject area has a conceptual structure—the concepts, generalizations, and principles that portray the timeless nature of the discipline, as well as the processes and skills used by practitioners of the discipline. Yet teachers have not generally been taught to differentiate between the factual and conceptual levels of their disciplines. Nor have they been taught how to use the two levels to bring greater intellectual rigor to teaching and learning. They need this instruction. Every teacher who works within the conceptual structure of a discipline should be able to discuss the important conceptual relationships of that discipline for the grade level or course they teach.

Curriculum leaders often throw around terms like *facts, generalizations, principles*, and *theories*. The Structure of Knowledge in figure 1 helps teachers see the relationships between these terms (Erickson, 1995, 2007, 2008). This visual helps teachers understand the developing levels of abstraction as well as the relationships between the levels. Conceptually based instruction ultimately targets the generalization/principle level for deep understanding. The facts serve as support for these transferable ideas. Figure 2 shows an example from social studies.

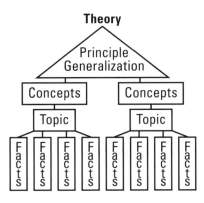

**Figure 1: The Structure of Knowledge showing relationships between the levels of learning (Erickson, 2007). Corwin Press Publishers, Thousand Oaks, CA. Reprinted with permission.**

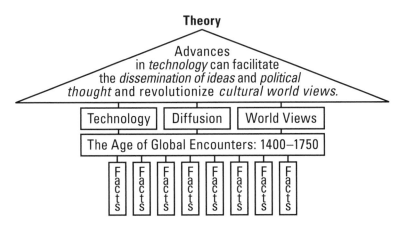

**Figure 2: An example of the Structure of Knowledge from Social Studies (Erickson, 2007). Corwin Press Publishers, Thousand Oaks, CA. Reprinted with permission.**

Concept-based instructors begin with the premise that deeper levels of thinking and understanding require students to use important facts not as an end point, but as a tool to think about and understand the related concepts and ideas that answer the critical questions, So what? What value or importance do these facts hold for lifelong learning? How can I transfer this understanding to use in other similar situations for thinking or problem solving?

For example, students may be studying the Palestinian/Israeli conflict in a high school history class. The teacher who is topic centered would be more concerned with presenting important facts for students to memorize. The concept-based teacher, on the other hand, would be teaching toward timeless ideas (generalizations) from the social studies curriculum. Two examples of these generalizations might be:

1.  Deeply held beliefs and values shape perspectives and make it difficult to overcome long-standing conflicts.

2.  Nations may intervene in the geopolitical conflicts of others when their political or economic self-interests are threatened.

The teacher may open the lesson by asking students to name a variety of conflicts from history, current events, the local community, or the school. The teacher records the specific examples on a chart and then asks the class to order the conflicts from most difficult to easiest to resolve. To guide students' thinking beyond the facts, the teacher then poses an essential question such as, "Why are long-standing conflicts more difficult to resolve?" and asks students to draw an inference from the examples and individually write an answer to the question. Students share their responses in collaborative groups to reach consensus on a generalization that reflects their most common inference. The generalization may convey the idea that "long-standing conflicts are the most difficult to resolve because they involve deeply held beliefs, values, and perspectives." The teacher writes a summary statement on the board to capture the main idea shared by the different groups. During the ensuing discussion of the Palestinian/Israeli conflict, the teacher uses guiding and essential questions to help students process the connections between the facts and the generalizations. The value of a universal generalization is that it stimulates synergistic thinking, which develops the intellect.

**Essential questions.** Essential questions are integral to conceptually based curriculum designs. Heidi Hayes Jacobs (1997) describes essential questions as "the essence of what you believe students should examine and know in the short time they have with you" (p. 26). Jacobs states the following:

> The [question] suggests investigation and inquiry. . . . The key is to create a question of genuine perplexity to the learner. The conceptual question is a conceptual commitment. . . . The teacher is saying, "I will put my teaching skills into helping my students examine the key concept implicit in the essential question." (p. 27)

Tomlinson et al. (2009), Tomlinson and McTighe (2006), Wiggins and McTighe (2007), and other conceptually based curriculum leaders today use essential questions to help students process the factual and conceptual levels of knowledge and understanding. Curriculum leaders may differ in the way they structure questions, but their end goal is the same: to ensure that students think beyond the facts to develop critical, creative, and conceptual thinking abilities.

Sometimes essential questions are open ended and have no apparent right or wrong answer: Is the twenty-first century man civilized? Does the image of a border fence between nations suggest a metaphor for relationships?

The presidential election of Barack Obama provided rich material for classroom instruction. It was a significant historical election in the sociopolitical evolution of the United States. A concept-based teacher would craft one or more conceptual understandings to draw out the significance. Questions of three basic types help students learn to link factual and conceptual levels of knowledge and understanding (Erickson, 2008). An essential debate question facilitates divergent, critical thinking. The feature box on page 185 shows examples of three kinds of questions, drawing on the presidential election, that relate to a universal generalization for history.

## Concept-Based Instruction

What does concept-based instruction look like? How is it different from traditional topic-based instruction? In a concept-based classroom there is a spirit of inquiry, and the teacher's focus is on how well students are processing the links between the factual and conceptual levels of understanding. The teacher artfully guides the students using questions and well-designed learning experiences to articulate one or more conceptual understandings.

For example, Mary Ellen Frick, of Round Rock, Texas, works with her fifth-grade students on the concept of transformations in mathematics. Since mathematics is a conceptual language, Mary Ellen designs the lesson using guiding questions and learning experiences that allow students to understand not only the attributes of individual concepts, but their relationships as well. After reviewing the definitions of the concepts of symmetry and line of symmetry, Mary Ellen asks students to determine the line of symmetry using their geomirrors. Once students recognize that reflections create symmetrical two-dimensional shapes, Mary Ellen uses a set of guiding questions to help her students understand and state the relationships between key concepts they have been learning related to transformations:

- Does symmetry require congruency?
- What is the relationship between symmetry, reflection, and congruency?
- Why are transformations and rotations of two-dimensional objects congruent?

## Three Kinds of Essential Questions

### Generalization

A significant historical event can illuminate the shifting sociopolitical landscape of a nation.

### Factual Questions

- Why was the election of Barack Obama a significant historical event in United States history?
- How did this election reflect social change in the United States? How did it reflect political change?
- What other major events in U.S. history have signaled changing social or political beliefs and attitudes?
- What personal qualities helped Barack Obama gain strong support across the nation (and across the world)?

### Conceptual Questions

- How can a single historical event often illuminate the shifting social character of a nation? How can it shift the political character?
- What role does leadership play in the evolution of a nation's identity?
- How do disruptive historical events, such as an international economic crisis, often serve as catalysts for change?

### Essential Debate Questions

- Is conflict inherent in the process of sociopolitical evolution? Why or why not?
- When is a leader considered transformational?
- What social, political, and economic factors coalesced to give Barack Obama the election?
- What events or issues could have interrupted this confluence of factors leading instead to the election of John McCain?

- Why are reflections, rotations, and translations called transformations when the concept is constancy of shapes?

After discussion, a student from one of the collaborative groups responds, "Reflections, rotations, and translations are all called *transformations* because the position or direction of the object may change, but the size or shape remains the same."

Mary Ellen uses collaborative groups to encourage use of the conceptual language as students carry out the learning experiences. As she asks the guiding questions, students discuss their answers. Her goal is to have students state the mathematical relationships using the conceptual terminology. She then asks them for specific examples to support their ideas.

Concept-based teachers do not assume students understand an idea. They ask students to articulate these understandings using the correct conceptual language. Concept-based teachers value and teach important factual content, but the focus is on developing students' thinking abilities and a deeper conceptual understanding of the topic under study. The concept-based teacher does the following:

- Plans the lesson to logically guide students to conceptual understanding
- Demonstrates a clear understanding of the relationship between facts, concepts, and transferable understandings
- Checks for prior knowledge of both concepts and factual knowledge, and listens for misconceptions
- Poses essential questions to engage students' intellect and interest
- Uses essential questions as a bridge between the factual content and the conceptual understandings
- Provides a clear focus and link between the content and concepts students are exploring
- Draws out required understandings, but celebrates when a student derives and can support new understandings

spontaneously; views autonomous conceptual thinking as the goal for all students

- Artfully employs disciplinary processes and skills to engage students with the content to develop knowledge and understanding

- Focuses learning on developing synergistic thinking and drawing out transferable conceptual understandings supported by factual knowledge

- Encourages students to use concepts and transferable understandings to see patterns and connections through time, across cultures, and across situations

- Views student performances and other assessments as reflections of the conceptual level of understanding as well as factual knowledge and skills

### The Conceptual Lens

The *conceptual lens* is an instructional tool that helps teachers create intellectual synergy and deeper levels of thinking and understanding (Erickson, 2002, 2007). It serves to focus each student's thinking when studying a particular topic. The lens integrates thinking at the conceptual level as students see patterns and connections between facts, concepts, and other applications. Consider the examples in the following feature box showing topics of study without, and then with, a conceptual lens.

| Sample Topics of Study and Conceptual Lenses | |
|---|---|
| **Topic** | **Possible Conceptual Lens** |
| The Holocaust | Humanity/Inhumanity |
| Global Warming | Responsibility/Sustainability |
| Linear Functions | Relationships |
| The Presidential Election | Ideologies/Conflict |

Once the student knows the attributes of the lens and has applied it to the particular topic, he or she can transfer the lens and apply it to other topics both within and across disciplines. The conceptual lens engages a student's personal thinking at the conceptual level. Material is not just "facts to memorize," but rather "ideas to understand" that are supported by facts. The use of a conceptual lens is another strategy to stimulate synergistic thinking.

### Paradigm Shifts for Teachers

Let there be no doubt that moving to a conceptually designed instructional model is a paradigm shift for the majority of teachers for the following reasons:

- **We tend to teach as we were taught**—Teachers teach with an emphasis on delivery of information rather than on thinking deeply with knowledge. There have been many innovations over the years that have tried to keep the focus on the child's development (such as constructivist learning [Brooks & Brooks, 1993], brain-based learning [Caine et al., 2005; Sousa, 2006; Willis, 2006], multiple intelligences [Gardner, 1993, 2006b], and differentiated instruction [Tomlinson et al., 2009]). But for every positive step on the road to child-centered learning, there have been powerful countervailing forces causing missteps (such as governmental legislation like NCLB and its heavy mandates, as well as institutionally ingrained tradition in educational practice).

- **Teachers are comfortable and familiar with teaching to objectives**—Shifting to a curriculum and instruction model that breaks objectives down into what students must understand conceptually, know factually, and be able to do in processes and skills requires the ability to view factual knowledge not as an end point, but as a tool to understand ideas that transfer through time, across cultures, and across situations. This is the paradigm shift required not only of teachers, but of their students as well.

- **Education, traditionally, has not required thinking deeply beyond the facts**—Concept-based teaching requires a shift from coverage-centered teaching to idea-centered teaching. Concept-based teachers have the ability to take critical facts and extrapolate the transferable ideas. If we as educators cannot articulate the deeper understandings, then how can we say we are teaching for understanding? The conceptual level of understanding provides the answer to the age-old question asked by so many students, Why do I have to learn this? The lessons of history are not the facts alone—they are the transferable understandings that humans can apply in addressing the social, economic, and political problems of today and tomorrow. Teachers find it challenging to articulate the conceptual understandings derived from the critical content they teach. But with practice, they can state the relevant ideas with clarity and power. There are specific strategies that can help teachers as they learn to craft these statements (Erickson, 2007, 2008).

- **Teachers generally have not been trained on the difference between factual and conceptual questions**—Conceptual designs that use essential questions train teachers on the difference between specific factual questions based on memorized knowledge and open-ended and/or essential questions that require thinking beyond the facts. Teachers learn to discern the differences in the way they word questions. They develop the ability to recognize the deeper meaning of factual knowledge in order to design questions that sharpen their students' mental processing skills of analysis, synthesis, and divergent thinking.

## An Art and a Science

Education in the twenty-first century is a complex endeavor. Educators working with curriculum and instruction models that value conceptual thinking and deeper understanding realize that they are but one cog in the overall system of schooling. Quality instruction requires a toolbox of knowledge and strategies—from collaborative learning, to differentiated instruction, to effective classroom management, to innovative techniques for reaching and motivating all students. Quality instruction is truly both an art and a science.

Educators who help design concept-based curriculum and instruction share a passion for this work because they see it as a critical need. What good is information if one cannot think with it, transfer it, understand it at a deeper level, or use it to solve problems? Information without intellect is useless. It is reassuring to see the growing recognition, once again, that education is as much about developing the mind as it is about gaining knowledge.

## References and Resources

Anderson, L., & Krathwohl, D. (Eds.). (2001). *A taxonomy for learning, teaching, and assessing: A revision of Bloom's taxonomy of educational objectives.* New York: Addison-Wesley Longman.

Bloom, B. S., Engelhart, M. D., Furst, E. J., Hill, W. H., & Krathwohl, D. R. (Eds.). (1956). *Taxonomy of educational objectives: The classification of educational goals: Handbook I. Cognitive domain.* New York: David McKay.

Brooks, J., & Brooks, M. (1993). *The case for constructivist classrooms.* Alexandria, VA: Association for Supervision and Curriculum Development.

Bransford, J., Brown, A., & Cocking, R. (Eds.). (2000). *How people learn: Brain, mind, experience, and school.* Washington, DC: National Academies Press.

Bruner, J. (1973). *Beyond the information given.* New York: W. W. Norton.

Caine, R., Caine, G., McClintic, C., & Klimek, K. (2005). *12 Brain/mind learning principles in action: The fieldbook for making connections, teaching, and the human brain.* Thousand Oaks, CA: Corwin Press.

Darling-Hammond, L. (2009). Teaching and the change wars: The professional hypothesis. In A. Hargreaves & M. Fullan (Eds.), *Change wars* (pp. 45–68). Bloomington, IN: Solution Tree Press.

Erickson, H. L. (1995). *Stirring the head, heart and soul: Redefining curriculum, instruction, and concept-based learning* (1st ed.). Thousand Oaks, CA: Corwin Press.

Erickson, H. L. (2002). *Concept-based curriculum and instruction: Teaching beyond the facts.* Thousand Oaks, CA: Corwin Press.

Erickson, H. L. (2007). *Concept-based curriculum and instruction for the thinking classroom.* Thousand Oaks, CA: Corwin Press.

Erickson, H. L. (2008). *Stirring the head, heart and soul: Redefining curriculum, instruction, and concept-based learning* (3rd ed.). Thousand Oaks, CA: Corwin Press.

Fullan, M., Hill, P., & Crevola, C. (2006). *Breakthrough.* Thousand Oaks, CA: Corwin Press and the National Staff Development Council and Ontario Principals' Council.

Gardner, H. (1993). *Multiple intelligences* (1st ed.). New York: Basic Books.

Gardner, H. (1999). *The disciplined mind.* New York: Simon & Schuster.

Gardner, H. (2006a). *The development and education of the mind: The selected works of Howard Gardner.* New York: Routledge.

Gardner, H. (2006b). *Multiple intelligences* (2nd ed.). New York: Basic Books.

Hargreaves, A., & Fullan, M. (Eds.). (2009). *Change wars.* Bloomington, IN: Solution Tree Press.

Hartman, H. (Ed.). (2002). *Metacognition in learning and instruction: Theory, research and practice.* Dordrecht, The Netherlands: Kluwer Academic Publishers.

Jacobs, H. H. (1997). *Mapping the big picture: Integrating curriculum and assessment K–12.* Alexandria, VA: Association for Supervision and Curriculum Development.

Jacobs, H. H. (2004). *Getting results with curriculum mapping.* Alexandria, VA: Association for Supervision and Curriculum Development.

Joyce, B., & Weil, M. (1986). *Models of teaching* (3rd ed.). Englewood Cliffs, NJ: Prentice Hall.

Marzano, R. (2007). *The art and science of teaching.* Alexandria, VA: Association for Supervision and Curriculum Development.

Marzano, R., & Kendall, J. (2007). *The new taxonomy of educational objectives* (2nd ed.). Thousand Oaks, CA: Corwin Press.

Marzano, R., & Kendall, J. (2008). *Designing and assessing educational objectives: Applying the new taxonomy.* Thousand Oaks, CA: Corwin Press with the American Association of School Administrators, National Association of Elementary School Principals, and the National Association of Secondary School Principals.

Ritchhart, R. (2002). *Intellectual character: What it is, why it matters, and how to get it.* San Francisco: Jossey-Bass.

Roberts, T., & Billings, L. (1999). *The Paideia classroom: Teaching for understanding.* Larchmont, NY: Eye on Education.

Sousa, D. (2006). *How the brain learns* (3rd ed.). Thousand Oaks, CA: Corwin Press.

Sylwester, R. (2005). *How to explain a brain: An educator's handbook of brain terms and cognitive processes.* Thousand Oaks, CA: Corwin Press.

Taba, H. (1966). *Teaching strategies and cognitive functioning in elementary school children.* Washington, DC: Office of Education, U.S. Department of Health, Education, and Welfare.

Tomlinson, C., & McTighe, J. (2006). *Integrating differentiated instruction and understanding by design.* Alexandria, VA: Association for Supervision and Curriculum Development.

Tomlinson, C., Kaplan, S., Renzulli, J., Purcell, J., Leppien, J., & Burns, D. (2009). *The parallel curriculum* (2nd ed.). Thousand Oaks, CA: Corwin Press and the National Association for Gifted Children.

Wiggins, G., & McTighe, J. (1999). *Understanding by design* (1st ed.). Alexandria, VA: Association for Supervision and Curriculum Development.

Wiggins, G., & McTighe, J. (2005). *Understanding by design* (2nd ed.). Alexandria, VA: Association for Supervision and Curriculum Development.

Wiggins, G., & McTighe, J. (2007). *Schooling by design.* Alexandria, VA: Association for Supervision and Curriculum Development.

Willis, J. (2006). *Research-based strategies to ignite student learning.* Alexandria, VA: Association for Supervision and Curriculum Development.

# Heidi Hayes Jacobs

Heidi Hayes Jacobs, Ed.D., has served as an education consultant to schools nationally and internationally on issues and practices pertaining to curriculum reform, instructional strategies to encourage critical thinking, and strategic planning. She is the author of numerous books and articles. She is president and founder of Curriculum Designers, Inc. and executive director of the Curriculum Mapping Institute. She has taught courses at Columbia University's Teachers College in New York since 1981.

In this chapter, Dr. Jacobs describes how curriculum mapping has directly impacted the role of the teacher and, ultimately, the role of the learner. She views this impact from various levels, from the classroom, to the professional learning community of the school, to the global learning community, and she describes the seven-phase Curriculum Mapping Review and Revision Model.

## Chapter 8

# Instructional Cartography: How Curriculum Mapping Has Changed the Role and Perspective of the Teacher

Heidi Hayes Jacobs

Mapmakers throughout history have influenced travelers by providing more accurate information about where they might go, where they have been, and where home is. In the same way, curriculum mapping has dramatically altered teachers' practice and the way they navigate the journey they make with their learners by giving a clear picture of students' educational experiences. *Curriculum mapping* is teaching and learning cartography. Communities of teachers collaborate to plot out future routes based on documentation of the pathways they have already traveled with their students. Mapping allows us to shape instruction with greater precision, and it provides a clear view—both vertically and across grade levels—that expands our perspective.

The power of mapping is reflected directly in student learning. Teachers make astute alterations in their plans in response to specific student needs in their specific settings. Mapping software has created a platform that expands educators' perspective while making collaborative communication natural and immediate. Both principals and teachers can see the actual curricular experiences of their students anchored in the reality of the school year and over the years.

In this chapter, I will describe how curriculum mapping has directly impacted the role of the teacher and, ultimately, the role of the learner. I will view this impact at various levels, from the classroom, to the professional learning community of the school, to the global learning community.

## A Twenty-First Century Strategy

It is important to understand that curriculum mapping is a replacement for old methods of decision making. The Curriculum Mapping Model (Jacobs, 1997) was designed to be a twenty-first century approach with its emphasis on immediate access via technology to the curriculum maps of others who share the same students within and between school settings. Schools that are actively mapping no longer use paper curricula in binders or on a wall in the faculty room; they are twenty-first century navigators for their twenty-first century learners. To provide a clear and thoughtful discussion of how the role of teachers and teaching has changed with this contemporary approach, I will focus on these key questions:

- What is mapping, and why is it powerful?
- What is the Curriculum Mapping Review and Revision Model?

To answer each of these questions, I explore a series of tenets and examples that demonstrate the shift from curriculum guidelines to curriculum planning through the mapping process. Throughout this discussion, I highlight specific ways that the roles of the teacher and the learner change through the mapping process.

## What Is Mapping, and Why Is It Powerful?

Calendar-based curriculum mapping is a twenty-first century procedure for collecting and maintaining a real-time database of the operational curriculum in a school and/or district. The Curriculum Mapping Review and Revision Model is a seven-stage process that provides educators with an opportunity to examine the mapping database vertically K–12, horizontally across grade levels, and in targeted groupings (Jacobs, 1997, 2004). From its inception, the model's goal was to make mapping an Internet-based program to provide ease in sharing and viewing curricula and assessments. Beyond the obvious use of mapping for classroom teachers, of interest is that administrators often map staff development, professors map courses, and now students are beginning to map their experiences via digital portfolio work. Curriculum mapping is active in every state in the United States and in countries throughout the world.

### Curriculum: A Path Run in Small Steps

The root of *curriculum* comes from the Latin *currere*, meaning "a path or course run in small steps." In formal education, the path begins for a child the day he or she starts school. A deeply held conviction in mapping is also a stark reality: learning is cumulative. Students develop and grow year to year as teachers create a pathway for and with the learner. Problems arise when teachers are unclear about the precise direction of the path the year before or when teachers make assumptions about the path that may not be accurate. This creates a series of gaps that forces students to jump from one stone in the pathway to another with minimal connectivity. Because of their transparency, curriculum mapping reviews provide honest information that impacts day-to-day decision making; educators have the ability to "go up periscope" to see the big picture. For example, a fourth-grade teacher is more likely to make better tactical choices in his or her lesson planning if he or she can find out with greater confidence what was actually covered and how a student fared in the third-grade math sequence.

Mapping reinforces and acts on the premise that teachers are interdependent in curriculum decision making. It also reinforces the critical nature of communication: professional learning communities within schools need to communicate about the actual experiences of students, otherwise what they are discussing is merely fiction. This underscores the importance of clarity about the operational curriculum versus the proposed curriculum. In my experience, there is sometimes confusion between the curriculum guidelines (the proposed curriculum) and the operational curriculum.

Curriculum guidelines provide direction and guidance to the teacher and school, but they do not reflect the actual and unfolding experience in real time. Guidelines are written generically and not adjusted for any specific group of learners. They do not take into account circumstances, resources, teacher aptitude, class size, and student ability. A good analogy is the difference between a proposed itinerary and the real trip. When a ship returns to port and the captain releases his sea log, it shows the actual experience with stormy seas, detours, and stops along the way. It is this actual experience that matters to everyone on board. The original itinerary would only surmise a likely scenario—it could not anticipate the realities. Simply put, in schools we need to talk about what learning students are actually experiencing and demonstrating in the course of the actual school year as opposed to what we hope happened. This disparity between targets and realities needs to be addressed, in what we often call *gap analysis*. When we see evidence of growth or regress in our assessment results, we need to initiate a corresponding change in the curriculum map. I have often said that there is no such thing as an eighth-grade math examination; rather, it is an "8, 7, 6, 5, 4, 3, 2, 1–K test." Educators must change and adjust the prescriptive curriculum cumulatively along *a path run in small steps.*

### Curriculum Mapping: A Coin With Two Sides

Curriculum mapping is like a coin with two sides. One side represents the actual maps themselves as documents or blueprints. The other side of the coin represents how the maps are actually used in the school setting. (I will address this second side in the next section on the seven-stage Curriculum Mapping Review and Revision Model on pages 202–207.) These sides are mutually dependent—simply having maps will not help our learners; using them and revising them will. Let us examine each side with more detail and begin with the maps themselves as documents.

**Curriculum maps as blueprints.** Curriculum maps are a kind of planning blueprint to help teachers lay out their units of study, courses, lessons, and students' classroom experiences using a clear template. In architecture, there are basic elements to consider in construction, such as the style of the building, the materials, and the proportion, and the blueprint aligns them internally to make a cohesive and attractive design. Architects also realize the need for external alignment as blueprint plans must meet local building standards and codes. Similarly, there are basic elements of curriculum planning that are integral to the curriculum layout that need to align internally as well as externally to local standards. In a mapping template (the blueprint), these elements include the targeted standard, essential questions, key concepts (big ideas), specific content and knowledge points, skills and strategies, matching assessments (both formative and summative), and resources. Each of these elements in the map is mutually dependent on the others. In short, just "putting something" in the map arbitrarily does not mean the design will hold up anymore than a building would had an architect simply chosen a design feature without considering the materials involved. Mapping requires four types of alignment making for effective designs that have a natural counterpoint to architectural planning: internal alignment, external alignment, alignment to client need, and alignment to context:

1. **Internal alignment**—In architecture, this is the style and proportion of the building, and the choice of complimentary materials. In curriculum mapping, this is alignment of the essential question, the concept/big idea, the targeted skills and strategies, and the assessment, which must match and support one another.

2. **External alignment**—In architecture, this is when the blueprint meets the standards and specifications established by the local community. In curriculum mapping, this is achieved when the map meets the standards and/or mission statement of the local, school, and/or provincial community of professional educators.

3. **Alignment to client needs**—In architecture, professionals attempt to devise a blueprint that matches the needs and characteristics of the actual users of the building in order to provide them with an environment that compliments the building's function. In curriculum mapping, educators make choices that specifically match the number, age, stage of development, learning characteristics, aspirations, and needs of the actual students whom they serve in a specific school setting.

4. **Alignment connected to context**—In architecture, good plans take into account the context of the building: the neighborhood, the surrounding structures, and most simply, the connections between floors. Curriculum maps are deliberately and diligently planned to connect learners and learning vertically K–12 and across grade levels.

The amount of detail included in a map depends on the type of map. To clarify this point, I will use a MapQuest analogy that has proven helpful for educators.

**Mapping the critical details.** Most of us are familiar with using MapQuest to obtain information about a geographical location or for driving directions. Based on the scope of the information needed, an individual determines the level of detail requisite on the MapQuest zoom-in and zoom-out feature. For example, if I am trying to find the location of a country such as Guatemala and its proximity to the United States, I need a wide-angle map of the northern hemisphere. If I am looking for the location of Ohio in the United States, I can zoom in on a map of the continental United States. From there, I can zoom in to find the city of Columbus if I need driving directions from the Center of Science and Industry in Columbus on 333 West Broad Street to the Cincinnati Art Museum at 953 Eden Park Drive. This last choice will be highly detailed with specific places to enter the highway, make exits, and the precise distances between each step.

With the help of curriculum mapping software, every educator who logs onto their mapping site has a similar opportunity to obtain the degree of specificity needed to navigate and plan for his or her learners. With this software, users can have the following:

- Immediate access to national and international standards and guidelines
- Immediate access to state or provincial standards, benchmark maps, or guidelines
- Immediate access to the maps of any teacher in any building to obtain an immediate and timely view of what is operational in that classroom in real time
- Individual teachers' detailed lesson plans
- Direct access to student maps (linked to teacher maps) with digital portfolios containing both formative and summative data, products, and performances

The role of the teacher has changed fundamentally with this immediate access to all grades and levels in real time; teachers now have the critical details needed for more informed decision making. Classroom life is no longer "covert activity" with limited knowledge of what is transpiring from one class to the next. Thus, the first side of the mapping coin—the maps themselves—provides a source of information with many levels of detail. It is now natural to consider the other side of the coin: the review process.

## What Is the Curriculum Mapping Review and Revision Model

Mapping is an active approach to solving teaching and learning problems. To provide impetus for this work, I have suggested that schools establish a reason for it that is tied to specific and discrete site-based learning issues that need tackling. Mapping teams try to solve some of the most common practical problems by doing the following:

- Gaining information about the operational curriculum in any class

- Analyzing gaps in student achievement and the gaps in corresponding maps

- Editing for needless redundancies and repetitions

- Validating standards

- Integrating content, skills, and assessments for natural connections

- Updating maps for timeliness to remove old curriculum and replace it with contemporary curriculum

The Latin for revision is *re visere*, which means "to view again." Mapping is an active process where we view our work again and again and again, then revise it to keep it alive and functioning. Genuine viability is at the heart of the mapping review and revision process. The goal is to make alterations cumulatively, classroom to classroom, so that students can have continuity. The seven-phase Curriculum Mapping Review and Revision Model (Jacobs, 1997) allows for strategic groups of teachers to analyze and make key decisions about sets and sequences of maps openly, efficiently, and effectively. The power of the model is its employment of technology as a key communication device. Through the use of a district website, an individual classroom teacher can log into an Internet-based site that houses ongoing information about what is being taught at any point in the school calendar year. Teachers can click into the assessment entries for their units and courses and store student work and records about the performance of individual learners.

The accessibility of mapping nationally and internationally has grown proportionately with the increase in educators' comfort with computer technologies. The leading commercial software groups and nonprofit educational organizations have created programs that are easy to use to make this level of communication not only possible but now mainstream (Jacobs, 2006); mapping is no longer the passive activity of putting a static paper curriculum on a shelf to collect dust.

Now let us turn to a strategic summary of the seven-phase Curriculum Mapping Review and Revision Model and examine each phase with a strategic eye on how the roles of the teacher and administrator become more dynamic and refined with each step.

### Phase One: Mapping Data Collection

In phase one, teachers, staff members, and administrators gather data (key curricular elements) to enter electronically on the map: essential questions, big ideas and concepts, content, skills, assessments, and resources that are linked to standards. There are two types of maps: project maps and diary maps. A *project map* is a planning map in which teachers enter what they expect they will do, and then they alter the maps as they go. In navigation terms, it is akin to the planned itinerary of a voyage and then the actual trip. Sometimes there are obstacles, sometimes we linger on a journey, and sometimes we find a better way. What is new is that teachers can now easily make alterations in their documentation electronically. A *diary map* is made up of an individual teacher's entries for his or her own classroom; the information is entered in real time for ongoing units of study and classroom experiences. The quality of both types of maps is contingent on solid preparation.

### Phase Two: First Read Through

In this phase, individual teachers read targeted sets of maps to address specific tasks and problems, such as gap analysis or standards validation. *Targeted sets of maps* are a precise group of classroom maps that must be examined to solve a specific problem. For example, if there is a precipitous drop in math scores in a seventh-grade state math examination, teachers might target math maps in grades 7, 6, 5, 4, and 3 for examination. This is because learning is cumulative, and if a school wishes to treat causes and not just symptoms of math problems, then educators must review and revise the entire sequence of math instruction and assessment practices. This phase represents one of the most dramatic changes from past protocol: all members of the professional community can access a teacher's map. There are two implications here: first, the teacher can make informed entries because of his or her access to data from other grades and classes; second, the teacher can see how his or her work connects or does not connect with the child's overall journey. Individual teachers read these maps, gather their observations, and move on to the next phase: small-group reviews.

### Phase Three: Mixed Small-Group Reviews

With these new views immediately accessible, it is possible to set up mixed groups of teachers who break from traditional like groups to share totally new perspectives. We call this a *strategic read through*. For example, instead of a grade-level team meeting, we can have vertical perspectives, because a fifth-grade teacher might see something that the first-grade teacher misses and vice versa. Instead of the isolated "silo" department meeting, there can be cross-grade-level views. In short, sometimes professionals outside of the usual group (the subject department, for example) can see things that other colleagues miss. A broad generic reading of maps is not particularly helpful; rather, this is a structured phase so that a group of teachers might read math maps from grades 2 through 7 to analyze gaps in computational skills that lead to dividing fractions. Students take a path through their schooling that needs to be nurtured and monitored, and if teachers in certain grade levels spend insufficient time or do not thoughtfully assess student skills, such as computation, there will likely be gaps in student performance. English and science teachers, who in the past would not look at the math curriculum, will examine maps to see if there are potential reading problems that might lead to poor student performance in math. Science teachers might be able to assist in designing assessments showing math applications in physics.

### Phase Four: Large-Group Reviews

Phase four involves the entire faculty or larger groupings of the faculty. The principal, headmaster, teacher leader, or staff developer leading the mapping efforts leads the group to review the findings of the smaller mixed-group reviews. These sessions are often organized around role-alike groups such as departments and grade levels. The goal is to share findings openly, which will eventually lead into sorting and setting priorities in the next two phases: identifying places in the sets of maps where revisions can be handled with relative ease and then moving on to identifying those problems that will require long-term study and development of systemic solutions.

### Phase Five: Determining Points for Immediate Revision

With observations available from earlier targeted reviews, a faculty can now begin to sift through and sort their findings to identify those areas in need of immediate revisions. For example, examination in small groups might have revealed that two teachers were teaching the same book two years in a row in back-to-back grade levels. Or examination could reveal the need to resequence shared science materials across a grade level so that material might be better shared. The examination may have revealed "curriculum habits," such as when a teacher views her curricula as personal real estate that she then carries with her from one grade level to another. For example, a fourth-grade teacher loves to teach a unit on weather in which she creates anemometers with her students. She is moved to fifth grade and takes her anemometers with her, even though they are not part of fifth-grade science. Not every curriculum revision is for a big problem, and, in fact, many can be handled easily between teachers. Making these minor changes to the curriculum adds up to create a better path flow for the learner.

### Phase Six: Determining Areas Needing Long-Term Research and Development

In contrast to phase five's immediate fixes, phase six deals with areas needing extensive research and investigation prior to developing alternatives. Many times these larger concerns are what drive schools to mapping in the first place. Some examples might be when a school has adopted a new approach to mathematics that will need to be instituted K–8 or when test scores reflect a huge gap in literacy, necessitating literacy integration across the disciplines (Jacobs, 2006). Or a state education department might adopt new and improved standards, and schools will need to respond coherently K–12 with long-term planning. In this phase, traditional curriculum committees can be replaced with energized task forces that do the scouting work for research and begin to develop alternatives for the larger faculty to ultimately consider, critique, and adopt for schoolwide reform. These task forces disband once they have completed their research and development and made the appropriate recommendations for reform.

### Phase Seven: Continued Planning for the Next Review Cycle

Curriculum reviews should be cyclical, active, and integrated into the fabric of school life. It has long been my view that most curriculum committees should be eliminated because they meet out of habit as opposed to being targeted on a task. The one group that our curriculum mapping work does support is an ongoing school curriculum council that monitors mapping reviews. Professionals in a building should meet for solution finding to address specific problems only, and not purely out of habit. Hence, the task force model proves to be a more efficient approach. The council can set up review cycles to monitor certain subject areas and set up task forces for research and development as per phase six. Councils are made up of both teacher and administrator representatives with the number of members based on the size of the school. Many schools have existing site-based councils that are natural leadership groups and could handle this responsibility. A significant change with this model is that each professional in a building knows that there is a place to go to consider curriculum concerns from a full range of mapping levels—from the classroom, school, and district levels.

## Using Assessment Data to Diagnose and Curriculum to Prescribe

With the seven-phase model in place, it is possible to engage in what many consider its most important and significant benefit: integrating assessment data formally into curriculum planning K–12. Ultimately, this is the most critical focus for mapping reviews, and it certainly is where we see a direct impact on instruction. Teachers make informed, shared, examined, and expanded decisions on how to lay out instruction based on collaborative analysis of the learners in their care. Instructional decisions are seen as part of the child's larger K–12 experience.

To reinforce this key tenet in the curriculum-mapping process, a medical analogy is helpful. The notion of diagnosis and prescription is at the heart of the doctor/patient relationship. Patients go to health professionals because they cannot improve their performance within the limitations of what they know. For example, a symptom presents itself to John. He wakes up in the morning with some dizziness and irritation in his eyes. He tries all that he knows, from aspirin to over-the-counter eye drops, and nothing improves, so he goes to his doctor for some assistance. His physician, Dr. Roberts, runs highly specific tests to find out the cause behind the symptoms, and on the basis of those tests, she makes a diagnosis. She analyzes this information and then gives John a prescription. Dr. Roberts is giving John something to do differently; she is revising John's routine with a new eye drop that should make a difference. What is important here is that *all* of John's doctors in the practice in which he is a patient will have immediate computerized access to John's records so that they do not inadvertently give him a medicine that might contradict Dr. Robert's judgment. They work as a team.

Curriculum mapping produces a similar outcome. School professionals can diagnose student learning with shared assessment data available to all professionals responsible for a child. Let us say there is a sixth-grade student named Maria. Through gap analysis, Maria's teaching professionals can make the determination that she is missing certain skill competencies in her math performance. Maria struggles with dividing and multiplying fractions. Teachers note that a number of children in the class share Maria's problem. They decide that students in grades 3 to 6 need to be working on a more consistent basis on the requisite skills to divide and multiply fractions. Thus, they decide that a change is needed in Maria's pathway through sixth grade into seventh. This prescription is entered into the curriculum maps; this is the instruction teachers will give Maria, her classmates, and those who follow in subsequent years.

Maps should be responsive to what the assessment data suggest is needed. Just as a connected band of doctors and nurses communicates clearly about what procedures and medicines are necessary for any given patient, with mapping, a connected group of teachers works both vertically and across a grade level to help Maria with her progress. Mapping reviews, as detailed in the seven-phase model, are often totally focused on this critical need to analyze gaps in student performance and achievement, to seek the holes in the curriculum, fill those with thoughtful and sequenced strategies, and integrate monitoring mechanisms through cornerstone or benchmark assessments.

If curriculum is not responsive, it is robotic. Imagine if your doctor said, "I always give the same medicine every September. So be sure, when you enter the hospital, that your illness matches what I am prepared to give."

## A Guaranteed and Viable Curriculum: Consensus and Diary Maps

With the use of real-time information available at a full range of detail, curriculum mapping can provide the vehicle for achieving what Marzano (2003) has found to be central for successful student achievement: a guaranteed and viable curriculum. The guaranteed focus of mapping is obvious when schools or education organizations develop what we call *consensus maps*. This level of mapping replaces the curriculum guideline. Through consensus mapping, educators make strategic choices about where consistency is critical for student learning as well as where flexibility is equally as important. One of the most sophisticated levels of consensus mapping is when educators unpack assessment data on a specific student population to locate skill gaps in performance. With this information, school faculty and administration create a series of benchmark or cornerstone assessments and lay them out developmentally on consensus maps to monitor over the course of a year or several years. Rather than feeling "ambushed" by state education testing, the educators in a school can take active measures to provide the proper response to student needs (Jacobs, 2004, p. 114). Once mapping is in place, the members of a faculty and administration can meet to make cumulative changes and share their new entries that address learner needs. The process uses imagination and rigor on the part of professionals in order to help students try to achieve curricular goals and targets.

The word *viable* comes from the Latin meaning *able to live*. With mapping reviews, teachers identify ways to engage specific learners with what they actually need at a given time and place in their lives. Unlike in the past process when curriculum was drafted and placed on a shelf, there is vibrancy to the mapping process. Teachers can make changes that respond to the world of each individual child.

The notion of viability is particularly intriguing and can be actualized through mapping with diary maps. Diary maps are more detailed than consensus maps. As discussed earlier, they are made up of the individual teacher's entries for his or her own classroom. Teachers add entries to their map to reflect actual classroom experiences in real time; thus, diary maps show the operationalized curriculum. These maps are a tool for an accountable professional teacher since they show how he or she composes the classroom experience over the course of an academic year. Diary maps are based on the reality that no two groups of students are identical, that no two teachers are identical, and that no two curricula are delivered identically. The lesson plans and individualized nature of a class are seen on the more detailed diary map level.

### Linking the World With Vibrant Connections

Curriculum mapping equips teachers and school leaders with the tools needed to help them become responsive professionals working in concert with others in their school location and beyond. The mapping model and software tools allow for not only vibrant connections between colleagues, but also build links across states, nations, and countries. A fourth-grade teacher in Pierre, South Dakota, can search her state's mapping database to import a map from Sioux Falls about a physics unit on magnetism. That same fourth-grade teacher could put in a national search to see how others present key concepts and skills to their learners. She can also become part of Global Mapping Learning Communities and access a map from Australia and interact with a teacher in Brisbane about teaching magnetism in the southern hemisphere. All of these levels of access occur when teachers use a common blueprint to assist the learners in their care. They become twenty-first century cartographers charting dynamic and responsive instruction.

What is more, administrators and staff developers create professional development maps for their buildings based on what is specifically needed at a site. This allows for differentiated staff development and even differentiated building or site development (Jacobs & Johnson, in press). There are now programs that allow students to map and link their work directly to teacher maps (Niguidula, 2005). The future bodes well for exciting instructional possibilities, but at the core, mapping has changed teachers and their teaching.

## References

Jacobs, H. H. (1997). *Mapping the big picture: Integrating curriculum and assessment K–12*. Alexandria, VA: Association for Supervision and Curriculum Development.

Jacobs, H. H. (2004). *Getting results with curriculum mapping*. Alexandria, VA: Association for Supervision and Curriculum Development.

Jacobs, H. H. (2006). *Active literacy across the curriculum: Strategies for reading, writing, speaking, listening*. Larchmont, NY: Eye on Education.

Jacobs, H. H., & Johnson, A. W. (in press). *The Curriculum Mapping Planner: Templates, tools, and resources for effective professional development*. Alexandria, VA: Association for Supervision and Curriculum Development.

Marzano, R. (2003). *What works in schools: Translating research into action*. Alexandria, VA: Association for Supervision and Curriculum Development.

Niguidula, D. (2005). Documenting learning with digital portfolios. *Educational Leadership, 63*(3), 26–29.

# Robert J. Marzano

Robert J. Marzano, Ph.D., is CEO of Marzano Research Laboratory. Dr. Marzano focuses on translating research and theory into practical programs and tools K–12 teachers and administrators can put to use in their classrooms for immediate gains. During his forty years in education, Dr. Marzano has worked with educators in every state and a host of countries in Europe and Asia. He has authored more than 30 books, 150 articles and chapters, and 100 sets of curriculum materials. His work focuses on reading and writing, instruction, thinking skills, school effectiveness, restructuring, assessment, cognition, and standards implementation.

In this chapter, Dr. Marzano addresses the need for systematic development of expert teachers through a well-articulated knowledge base and deliberate practice. He argues that the knowledge base on teaching must be organized to make it a viable tool for developing teacher expertise. He describes organizing strategies through lesson segments using a nine-segment framework. The nine segments are organized into three categories: segments involving routine events, segments involving academic content, and segments involving issues that must be addressed as they occur.

# Chapter 9

# Developing Expert Teachers

### Robert J. Marzano

Today it is considered common knowledge that a classroom teacher is probably the single most powerful influence on student achievement that is within the control of the educational system. We know that effective teachers enhance student achievement. Impressive findings from a wide variety of researchers attest to this fact. For example, when reporting on their findings of achievement scores across five subject areas (mathematics, reading, language arts, social studies, and science) for sixty thousand students across grades 3 and 5, Wright, Horn, and Sanders (1997) note:

> The immediate and clear implication of this finding is that seemingly more can be done to improve education by improving the effectiveness of teachers than by any other single factor. *Effective teachers appear to be effective with students of all achievement levels regardless of the levels of heterogeneity in their classes* [emphasis in original]. (p. 63)

More recently, Nye, Konstantopoulos, and Hedges (2004) have quantified the relationship between teacher effectiveness in a randomized controlled study involving seventy-nine schools in forty-two school districts. Using their findings, one could make the inferences in table 1 regarding the relationship between teacher competence and student achievement.

**Table 1: The Relationship Between Teacher Competence and Student Achievement**

| Teacher Skill Percentile Rank | Expected Percentile Gain in Achievement for a Student Starting at the 50th Percentile | Predicted Percentile Rank for a Student Starting at the 50th Percentile |
|---|---|---|
| 50th | 0 | 50th |
| 70th | 8 | 58th |
| 90th | 18 | 68th |
| 98th | 27 | 77th |

Table 1 depicts the expected percentile gain in achievement for a student starting at the 50th percentile if that student is taught by teachers of varying degrees of competence. The first row depicts a teacher at the 50th percentile in terms of his pedagogical competence. With this teacher, the student would not gain in her relative standing regarding other students. She would remain at the 50th percentile. She would, of course, increase in her knowledge, but it would be at the same rate as her cohort group. Next, consider the second row. Here the teacher is at the 70th percentile in terms of his pedagogical competence. Now the student is expected to gain 8 percentile points, raising her to the 58th percentile. In the classroom of a teacher at the 90th percentile, a student starting at the 50th percentile would be expected to increase her achievement to the 68th percentile. The inference from table 1 is clear: if the skill of teachers in a building or district could be raised dramatically, student achievement would be expected to increase dramatically.

But just how does a school or district go about achieving such a feat? How does a school or district ensure that highly skilled teachers are in their classrooms? Certainly one step toward this goal is to recruit and retain effective teachers. Marzano and Waters (2009) underscore the importance of this approach. As a result of their review of research on district leadership, they recommend that districts and schools provide the necessary incentives to recruit and retain high-quality teachers. This, of course, is in keeping with the U.S. Department of Education (2002) mandate that all schools provide highly qualified teachers as part of the No Child Left Behind Act (NCLB). It is also consistent with many of the recommendations made by Darling-Hammond (2009) based on her extensive reviews of the research on district and school effectiveness. Finally, it is consistent with the mandate for the new role of federal policy in education spelled out in the report *Democracy at Risk: The Need for a New Federal Policy in Education* (The Forum for Education and Democracy, 2008).

While recruiting and retaining high-quality teachers is certainly a strategy every district and school should employ, there is another equally (if not more) important strategy for ensuring high-quality teachers in classrooms: actively developing expert teachers. That is, in addition to recruiting and retaining expert teachers, districts and schools should provide direct experiences that develop expertise. Fortunately, there is research providing guidance to this end. (For reviews, see Ericsson & Charness, 1994; and Ericsson, Krampe, & Tesch-Romer, 1993).

Some type of metric, of course, is required to operationally define expertise. Ericsson and Charness (1994) explain that *expertise* is traditionally defined as performance that is two standard deviations above the mean in a specific domain. Performance that is two standard deviations above the mean would put a teacher at the 98th percentile in terms of pedagogical skill. As we see in table 1, this is associated with an increase of 27 percentile points for students at the 50th percentile. Simply stated, students in the classrooms of expert teachers learn well beyond expected rates.

Relatively speaking, it was not that long ago that expertise was considered something that could not be developed. To illustrate, as a result of his historical analysis of perceptions of expertise, Murray (1989) concluded that it was generally believed that talent was considered "a gift from the gods." About this notion, Ericsson and Charness (1994) note:

> One important reason for this bias in attribution . . . is linked to immediate legitimization of various activities associated with the gifts. If the gods have bestowed a child with a special gift in a given art form, who would dare to oppose its development, and who would not facilitate its expression so everyone could enjoy its wonderful creations. This argument may appear strange today, but before the French Revolution the privileged status of kings and nobility and birthright of their children were primarily based on such claims. (p. 726)

Talent bestowed by the gods, then, was considered the prime determiner of expertise. Over time, the fallacies in this perspective emerged. Ericsson and Charness explain that "it is curious how little empirical evidence supports the talent view of expert and exceptional performance" (p. 730). They note that over the centuries, the talent hypothesis was inevitably challenged once it became evident that individuals could "dramatically increase their performance through education and training if they had the necessary drive and motivation" (p. 727).

Akin to the talent hypothesis is the intelligence hypothesis: highly intelligent people have the capacity to learn more, quicker. Over time, this trajectory leads to expertise. Again, Ericsson et al. (1993) note that this hypothesis has little backing: "The relationship of IQ to exceptional performance is rather weak in many domains" (p. 364).

If expertise is not a function of talent or intelligence, then what are its determiners? The research points to two critical factors: a well-articulated knowledge base and deliberate practice.

## A Well-Articulated Knowledge Base

A well-articulated knowledge base is a prerequisite for developing expertise in any systematic way within any domain. Ericsson et al. (1993) note that the knowledge base has increased and is continuing to increase in a variety of domains. This has resulted in an increased ability to develop experts in many fields:

> As the level of performance in the domain increased in skill and complexity, methods to explicitly instruct and train individuals were developed. In all major domains there has been a steady accumulation of knowledge about the best methods to attain a high level of performance and the associated practice activities leading to this performance. (p. 368)

As is the case with most fields of study, education has experienced exponential growth in its knowledge base, particularly regarding effective pedagogy. There have been many attempts to codify this knowledge base (see Hattie, 1992; Hattie, Biggs, & Purdie, 1996; and Wang, Haertel, & Walberg, 1993). While these efforts have succeeded in listing the various strategies and activities that occur in effectively run classrooms, they have not attempted to articulate the context in which specific strategies should be used. Ericsson and Smith (1991) identify this as a necessary characteristic of expert performance—not only knowing the "moves" to be made in a given domain, but also knowing the "right move" for a specific situation. One challenge, then, in organizing the knowledge base on teaching to make it a viable tool for developing expertise is to classify it in a way that identifies the context or situations in which to employ specific strategies.

Drawing on a considerable amount of design theory (see Berliner, 1986; Doyle, 1986; Good, Grouws, & Ebmeier, 1983; Leinhardt & Greeno, 1986; and Stodolsky, 1983), Leinhardt (1990) proposes the *lesson segment* as a way of classifying the myriad strategies and behaviors (moves) employed by expert teachers:

> This research-based information points to the fact that lessons are constructed with multiple parts, or lesson segments, each of which has important characteristics. Each segment contains different roles for teachers and students. Each segment has multiple goals, which can be more or less successfully met by a variety of actions. Further, these segments are supported by fluid, well-rehearsed routines. (pp. 21–22)

Following Leinhardt's lead, this chapter organizes what is known about instructional strategies into lesson segments using the framework described in *The Art and Science of Teaching* (Marzano, 2007). That framework identifies nine types of segments that might occur in classrooms:

1. Communicating learning goals, tracking student progress, and celebrating success
2. Establishing or maintaining rules and procedures
3. Introducing new content (critical input lessons)
4. Knowledge practicing and deepening lessons
5. Hypothesis generating and testing lessons (knowledge-application lessons)
6. Increasing student engagement
7. Recognizing and acknowledging adherence and lack of adherence to classroom rules and procedures
8. Establishing and maintaining effective relationships with students
9. Communicating high expectations for every student

These nine segments are organized into three categories: segments involving routine events, segments involving academic content, and segments involving issues that must be addressed as they occur. The relationships between these categories are depicted in figure 1.

In figure 1, the first two of the nine lesson segments are organized into the "routine events" category. The next three segments all involve academic content. The last four segments involve issues that must be addressed as they occur. The following sections present the research supporting each segment along with a brief description of how the behaviors associated with the segment might manifest in the classroom along with a list of specific behaviors for each segment.

### Segments Involving Routine Events

Every day in every classroom, teachers and students will exhibit certain routine behaviors regardless of the content being taught or the age of the students. As shown in figure 1,

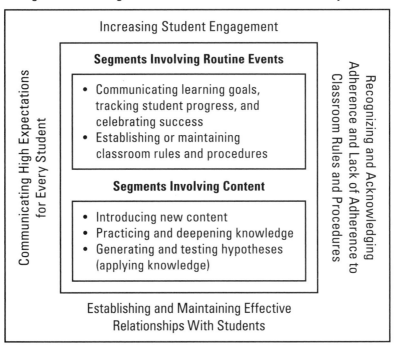

**Figure 1: Categories of lesson segments.**

two segments are classified as routine events: (1) communicating learning goals, tracking student progress, and celebrating success; and (2) establishing or maintaining classroom rules and procedures.

**Communicating learning goals, tracking student progress, and celebrating success.** Each of the nine segments identified in *The Art and Science of Teaching* (Marzano, 2007) are themselves an amalgamation of a number of instructional strategies and behaviors. The segment involving communicating learning goals, tracking student progress, and celebrating success is supported by research on the effects of goal setting (Lipsey & Wilson, 1993; Walberg, 1999; Wise & Okey, 1983), feedback (Bangert-Drowns, Kulik, Kulik, & Morgan, 1991; Haas, 2005; Hattie & Timperley, 2007; Kumar, 1991), reinforcing effort (Hattie et al., 1996; Kumar, 1991; Schunk & Cox, 1986), use of praise (Bloom, 1976; Wilkinson, 1981), and use of rewards (Deci, Ryan, & Koestner, 2001).

Specific behaviors associated with this segment include the following (Marzano, 2008):

- The teacher reminds students about learning goals or introduces new learning goals.

- The teacher provides formative feedback to students (through quizzes, tests, informal forms of assessment) relative to their individual progress on learning goals.

- The teacher provides students with some form of recognition for their progress on learning goals.

To illustrate how these behaviors might interact, consider a middle school science teacher who daily reminds students of the learning goals for the unit. In addition, using formative assessments, the teacher helps students track their progress regarding the learning goals for the unit. This is done routinely if not daily. Finally, as a matter of course, the teacher provides opportunities for students to celebrate their knowledge gain as well as their achievement status at any given moment.

**Establishing or maintaining classroom rules and procedures.**
Another segment that is classified as a type of routine behavior
involves establishing or maintaining classroom rules and procedures. This segment draws from the research on establishing rules
and procedures early on in the school year and addressing those
rules and procedures in a logical and systematic fashion throughout
the school year (Anderson, Evertson, & Emmer, 1980; Brophy &
Evertson, 1976; Eisenhart, 1977; Emmer, Evertson, & Anderson,
1980; Good & Brophy, 2003; Moskowitz & Hayman, 1976).

Specific behaviors associated with this segment include the
following (Marzano, 2008):

- The teacher has clear routines and procedures that
  contribute to the effective functioning of the class.
- The teacher has organized the classroom for effective
  learning with appropriate traffic patterns and bulletin
  boards that display student work.

To illustrate the interplay of these behaviors in the classroom,
consider an elementary language arts teacher who takes time
at the beginning of the school year to establish clear rules and
procedures regarding appropriate behavior in the classroom.
Additionally, as a matter of routine, the teacher systematically
reviews these rules and procedures, making changes as necessary. Finally, the teacher helps establish routine and order by
organizing classroom materials, displays, and traffic patterns
in a manner that facilitates learning.

### Segments Involving Content

There are three types of content segments: (1) segments
that involve the introduction of new content, (2) segments that
involve reviewing content or practicing content, and (3) segments
that involve applying content. Each of these typically manifest
as a distinct lesson, although more than one type of content
segment may be addressed in a single class period—especially
when classes are extended due to block scheduling.

**Introducing new content.** Some lessons are devoted to the introduction of new content. Marzano (2007) refers to these lessons as critical input lessons—students are being introduced to new content that is critical to their ability to attain learning goals. The behaviors important to these types of lessons draw from the research on presentation formats that enhance retention of new knowledge (Nuthall, 1999), previewing new content (Ausubel, 1968; Mayer, 1989, 2003; West & Fensham, 1976), organizing new knowledge for efficient processing (Linden et al., 2003; Rosenshine, 2002), summarizing new information (Anderson & Hidi, 1988/1989; Hidi & Anderson, 1987), representing new knowledge in multiple ways (Alvermann & Boothby, 1986; Aubusson, Foswill, Barr, & Perkovic, 1997; Druyan, 1997; Newton, 1995; Sadoski & Paivio, 2001; Welch, 1997), teacher questioning (Pressley et al., 1992; Reder, 1980; Redfield & Rousseau, 1981), and student self-reflection (Cross, 1998).

Specific behaviors associated with introducing new content include the following (Marzano, 2008):

- The teacher engages students in activities that help them preview the new content (such as overt linkages, preview questions, brief teacher summary, skimming, teacher-prepared notes, and asking, "What do you think you know?").

- When appropriate, the teacher presents new content in ways that involve a variety of mediums (such as lecture, demonstration, and video).

- When appropriate, the teacher augments new content with narratives and anecdotes.

- The teacher presents new content in small, digestible "chunks."

- After each chunk, students are asked to process the new content by generating brief summaries and making predictions, or the teacher uses some formal type of group-interaction technique (such as reciprocal teaching, jigsaw, or concept attainment).

- After presenting new content, teachers ask students to elaborate on the content by addressing inferential questions and defending their answers.

- After presenting new content, teachers ask students to record and represent their understanding of the new content (such as by summarizing their understanding, creating graphic representations of the new content, generating notes on the new content, or drawing pictures representing the new content).

- When appropriate, the teacher engages students in the use of dramatic enactments or mnemonic devices to help them remember and better understand the new content.

- At the end of the lesson (or segment), the teacher asks students to reflect on their understanding and their learning process (for example, "What are you clear about?" "What are you unclear about?").

- The teacher uses grouping effectively to help students process the new content (for example, students are organized in small groups as they process new content).

To illustrate the interaction of these behaviors, consider a high school mathematics teacher who designs a lesson to introduce new information about the concept of function. The teacher begins by briefly previewing the concept. She asks students what they think they know about functions. As students volunteer answers, she records their responses on the whiteboard. Next, she shows a video that describes and illustrates defining characteristics of various types of functions. Prior to showing the video, the teacher has organized students into groups of three to facilitate interaction about the information in the video. She plays about two minutes and then stops. She then asks one student in each group of three to summarize what they have seen so far. The other two students in each group pose questions that are either answered in the triad or posed to the teacher. Next, the teacher plays another two minutes of the video and repeats the same process by having one student in each triad summarize the content. When the video is completed, the teacher asks some inferential questions of the entire class to provide a different perspective on the content. Next, each triad is asked to develop a summary of the content in the video along with a graphic or pictographic representation of the content. The lesson ends with students reflecting on their understanding of the content as presented in the lesson. They do so by answering the following question in their academic notebooks: What am I still confused about?

**Practicing and deepening knowledge.** Once the teacher has introduced the knowledge, one or more lessons are typically devoted to helping students practice a new skill or deepen their understanding of information. The behaviors important to these types of lessons draw from the research on practice (Kumar, 1991; Ross, 1988), revising and analyzing errors (Halpern, 1984; Hillocks, 1986; Rovee-Collier, 1995), examining similarities and differences (Halpern, Hansen, & Reifer, 1990; McDaniel & Donnelly, 1996), and homework (Cooper, Robinson, & Patall, 2006). When considering lessons that involve practicing and deepening knowledge, it is important to keep in mind the distinction between declarative and procedural knowledge. *Procedural knowledge* includes skills, strategies, and processes. *Declarative knowledge* includes details, sequences of information, generalizations, and principles.

Specific behaviors associated with segments devoted to practicing and deepening knowledge include the following (Marzano, 2008):

- The teacher engages students in a brief review of the content.

- The teacher asks students to review and revise notes they have taken on the new content.

- Teachers use grouping in ways that help students deepen their understanding (for declarative knowledge) or move toward fluency (for procedural knowledge).

- When appropriate, the teacher assigns homework that helps students deepen their understanding (for declarative knowledge) or move toward fluency (for procedural knowledge).

*If the content is information based (declarative):*

- The teacher engages students in activities that require them to examine similarities and differences regarding content (such as comparison activities, classification activities, metaphor activities, and analogy activities).

- The teacher engages students in activities that require students to examine their own logic regarding the new content or the logic underlying the presentation of the new content.

*If the content is skill or process based (procedural):*

- The teacher involves the students in practice activities that are appropriate to their level of development toward fluency.

To illustrate these behaviors, consider two teachers. The first is a primary language arts teacher who has previously presented a strategy for editing a composition to make sure there is a clear beginning, middle, and end (procedural knowledge). This strategy would have been presented earlier in a lesson specifically designed for introducing new knowledge (a critical input lesson). The second teacher is a middle school history teacher who has previously presented students with information about republics as a form of government (declarative knowledge). Both would begin their knowledge practice and deepening lesson with a brief review of the content presented in the earlier introductory lesson. Both might also organize students into small groups to facilitate the processing of information. Because the language arts teacher is dealing with procedural knowledge, she would engage students in some type of practice activity. For the initial practice activity, she might provide students with a set of sample compositions, none of which have clear beginnings, middles, and ends. Individually or in small groups, students would use these contrived examples to practice the revising strategy by rewriting the compositions to include an effective beginning, middle, and end. Because the middle school teacher is dealing with declarative knowledge, she might have students engage in a comparison activity designed to help students contrast republics with other forms of government. For example, the teacher might ask students to contrast republics with democracies and monarchies. Finally, both teachers would determine if the activities begun in class would be extended as homework.

**Generating and testing hypotheses (applying knowledge).** Ultimately, knowledge must be applied in some meaningful situation. In the classroom, these situations typically manifest as projects. Marzano (2007) provides evidence that to maximize the instructional effect of these projects, students must generate and test hypotheses. Strategies for these types of lessons that focus on applying knowledge draw on the research from problem-based learning (Gijbels, Dochy, Van den Bossche, & Segers, 2005) and hypothesis generation and testing (Hattie et al., 1996; Ross, 1988).

Specific strategies associated with lessons devoted to applying knowledge include the following (Marzano, 2008):

- The teacher engages students in a brief review of the content.

- The teacher asks students to work individually or in groups on their hypothesis generation and testing tasks.

- The teacher assumes the role of resource provider and facilitator.

To illustrate the interaction of these strategies, consider a physical education teacher who has previously introduced and had students practice a variety of stretching techniques, each with its own unique purpose. To apply this procedural knowledge in tasks, students might carry out three very different types of physical activities—one involving lifting weights, another involving running slowly for an extended distance, and the third involving sprinting short distances. Students would be asked to construct warm-up and cool-down stretching protocols for each of the three types of activities using the techniques they had previously learned. Prior to executing their protocols, students would generate hypotheses regarding the specific effects of their protocols and then examine their findings in light of these hypotheses.

### Segments Involving Issues That Must Be Addressed as They Occur

A number of teacher behaviors must be used as specific situations occur. They involve instructional elements that might not be a part of every lesson. However, when they are called for, a teacher must attend to them immediately or the learning environment will quickly erode. As depicted in figure 1 on page 219, there are four segments that fit into this category: (1) increasing student engagement, (2) recognizing and acknowledging adherence and lack of adherence to classroom rules and procedures, (3) establishing and maintaining effective relationships with students, and (4) communicating high expectations for every student.

**Increasing student engagement.** Segments devoted to increasing student engagement might be called for at any point in time during a lesson. If students are not engaged in the classroom activities, then they have little if any chance of taking advantage of the instruction that is occurring. Consequently, effective teachers continuously scan their classrooms to determine if students are engaged and then act deliberately to reengage students if they are not. This type of lesson segment draws from the research on the nature of engagement and ways that engagement can be elicited (Connell, Spencer, & Aber, 1994; Connell & Wellborn, 1991; Reeve, 2006).

Specific behaviors associated with segments devoted to increasing student engagement include the following (Marzano, 2008):

- When appropriate, the teacher involves students in academic games that include inconsequential competition.

- When appropriate, the teacher manages response rates through use of wait time, response cards, choral response, or response chaining.

- When appropriate, the teacher engages students in activities that require physical movement.

- The teacher maintains a lively and appropriate pace throughout the lesson.

- When appropriate, the teacher demonstrates intensity and enthusiasm for the content.

- When appropriate, the teacher engages students in friendly controversy.

- When appropriate, the teacher provides opportunities for students to talk about themselves.

- When appropriate, the teacher provides students with unusual information regarding the content.

To illustrate how these behaviors might be used, consider a technology teacher who notices that her students are simply not paying attention to her presentation on ways to determine the accuracy of information on websites. Noting this lack of engagement, the teacher selects from a list of prepared activities designed to reenergize and reengage students. For example, the teacher might ask questions that require students to answer using response cards, thus ensuring that all students are engaged in responding to each question. Alternatively, the teacher might engage students in a brief physical activity that helps increase their short-term energy, thus increasing engagement.

**Recognizing and acknowledging adherence and lack of adherence to classroom rules and procedures.** Segments devoted to acknowledging students' adherence to rules and procedures and acknowledging lack of adherence to rules and procedures may be required throughout the course of a lesson or a day. This type of segment draws from the general research on classroom management (Wang, Haertel, & Walberg, 1993) and discipline (Marzano, Marzano, & Pickering, 2003).

Specific behaviors associated with this segment include the following (Marzano, 2008):

- When appropriate, the teacher provides positive consequences for student adherence to rules and procedures (such as simple verbal and nonverbal acknowledgments, tangible recognition, and involving the home).

- When appropriate, the teacher provides negative consequences for lack of adherence to classroom rules and procedures (such as being proactive about possible classroom disruptions, occupying the entire room, noticing potential problems, using a series of graduated actions when rules and procedures have been broken, using direct consequences, using overcorrection, and using home contingency or group contingency).

To illustrate the use of these behaviors, consider a primary teacher who notices that students are not following the procedure for putting away materials after a science lesson. The teacher points this out to students and takes some time to briefly review the procedure. On another occasion, the teacher notices that students have done a particularly good job at following the rule for raising their hands to ask a question. Again, the teacher points this out to students noting how smoothly the class went and thanking students for their efforts.

**Establishing and maintaining effective relationships with students.** Perhaps a necessary but not sufficient condition for effective instruction is effective teacher/student relationships. If sound relationships exist between teacher and students, classroom activities progress more smoothly than if sound relationships are not in place. Lesson segments that address teacher/student relationships draw on the research regarding the need for a balance between student perceptions that the teacher is in control of the classroom and student perceptions that the teacher is their advocate (Brekelmans, Wubbels, & Creton, 1990; Wubbels, Brekelmans, den Brok, & van Tartwijk, 2006).

Specific behaviors associated with segments devoted to enhancing teacher/student relationships include the following (Marzano, 2008):

- When appropriate, the teacher demonstrates knowledge of students' interests and backgrounds.

- When appropriate, the teacher engages in verbal behaviors that indicate affection for students (for example, compliments, humor, and informal conversations).

- When appropriate, the teacher engages in physical behaviors that indicate affection for students (for example, smiles, appropriate physical proximity, and contact).

- When appropriate, the teacher brings students' interest into the content.

- When appropriate, the teacher demonstrates a demeanor of emotional objectivity and a cool exterior.

To illustrate the use of these behaviors, consider a middle school teacher who notices that while he has behavioral issues well under control, there is little levity in his classroom. Additionally, students seem reluctant to approach him regarding problems they are having with the content. In response, the teacher decides that he must enhance the perception that he is there to help students, not just to keep them under control. He, therefore, decides to lighten up the classroom atmosphere using humor and good-natured banter with students.

**Communicating high expectations for every student.** The final type of lesson segment involves communicating high expectations for all students. Directly or indirectly, students pick up messages that they are expected to do well or poorly academically and then behave in accordance with these expectations (Rosenthal & Jacobson, 1968). Behaviors for this type of lesson segment draw from the research on establishing an appropriate affective tone with all students and providing equal opportunities for complex academic interactions (Weinstein, 2002).

Specific behaviors associated with segments devoted to communicating high expectations include the following (Marzano, 2008):

- The teacher provides low-expectancy students with verbal and nonverbal indications that they are valued and respected (for example, makes eye contact, smiles, makes appropriate physical contact, maintains appropriate proximity, and engages in playful dialogue).

- The teacher asks questions of low-expectancy students.

- When low-expectancy students do not answer a question correctly or completely, the teacher stays with them.

To illustrate how these behaviors might manifest, consider a high school AP calculus teacher who realizes that she asks questions almost exclusively of students who readily participate in class and seem to be doing quite well with the content. In contrast, she leaves other students alone not wishing to embarrass them or force them to respond to questions with which they are not comfortable. Realizing that her behavior is communicating high expectations for some students and low expectations for others, she institutes a policy of asking difficult questions of every student in class. At first, this is challenging for some students since it represents a dramatic shift in her previous behavior.

However, over time, students accept the fact that all students are expected to address complex content, and their thinking will be respected even if it has some flaws in it.

## Using the Knowledge Base to Identify Areas of Greatest Pedagogical Need

The nine segments organized into three categories depicted in figure 1 (page 219) provide an organizational scheme that allows teachers seeking improvement in their pedagogical expertise to pinpoint their areas of strength and their areas of weakness. For example, upon introspection and feedback from instructional coaches and superiors, a teacher might determine that her area of greatest need pedagogically is routines. Another teacher might identify critical input lessons as an area on which to work. Still a third teacher might identify student engagement as a focus of personal improvement.

### Providing Deliberate Practice

In addition to a well-articulated knowledge base, the second factor important to developing expert teachers is providing opportunities for deliberate practice. Where a comprehensive knowledge of pedagogy is important to developing expertise, deliberate practice is the vehicle that transforms knowledge into behavior. It is the *sine qua non* of expertise (Ericsson & Charness, 1994). Deliberate practice has at least three defining characteristics: (1) clear and focused tasks, (2) clear criteria for success, and (3) the motivation to engage in deliberate practice. Due to the resources necessary to implement these three characteristics, the development of expert teachers most probably should be a districtwide initiative. Necessary resources include an identified cadre of expert teachers, time for expert teachers and aspiring teachers to interact about effective teaching, and time for expert teachers and aspiring teachers to observe each other teaching. These resources are more readily available at the district level than at the school level.

## Clear and Focused Tasks

One characteristic of deliberate practice is that it involves tasks for the aspiring expert that are consistent with his or her current skill and knowledge levels. Ericcson et al. (1993) explain: "The design of the task should take into account the preexisting knowledge of the learner so that the task can be correctly understood after a brief period of instruction" (p. 367). This implies that specific areas of strength and weakness have been identified for aspiring experts. To this end, Marzano (2008) recommends the use of rubrics like that in figure 2 (pages 234–235).

The rubric in figure 2 provides a scale for evaluating teacher performance in content lessons that involve introducing new knowledge. Rubrics like this one have been designed for each of the segments described in the previous section. The combination of teacher self-ratings, ratings by expert supervisors, and ratings by instructional coaches can be used to establish a baseline profile of a teacher's greatest area of pedagogical need.

After identification of a high-need segment, an aspiring teacher would receive targeted instruction from a recognized expert in the district. To illustrate, an aspiring teacher might be mentored by an expert in the area of routines. Using the knowledge base described previously, the mentor would review the information regarding effective use of routines. This initial interaction would constitute what Ericcson et al. (1993) refer to as "a brief period of instruction." Next, the aspiring teacher would observe the master teacher using specific strategies regarding effective use of routines. The purpose of this is to allow aspiring teachers to observe what Ambady and Rosenthal (1992, 1993) refer to as "thin slices" of behavior that typically characterize expertise. Ambady and Rosenthal explain that expert behavior is often determined by and recognizable within relatively short episodes. Another way of saying this is that expertise occurs in the moment-to-moment adaptations a teacher makes regarding the use of a specific strategy. Consequently, describing teaching

**Score 4.0:** In addition to Score 3.0 behaviors, uses adaptations that enhance students' learning.

**Score 3.5:** In addition to Score 3.0 behaviors, has partial success with adaptations that enhance students' learning.

**Score 3.0:** While engaged in classroom activities that involve students interacting with new knowledge, the teacher makes no major errors or omissions regarding the following behaviors:

- Identifies critical input experiences
- Employs previewing activities that make linkages between new knowledge and what has been previously addressed
- Organizes students into small groups to facilitate the processing of new knowledge
- Breaks input experiences into small chunks appropriate to the students
- When pausing after a small chunk of new knowledge, teacher engages students in description, discussion, and prediction activities that enhance their understanding of the new knowledge
- Engages students in activities that require them to elaborate on the new knowledge
- After the input experience, teacher engages students in activities that require them to write out and represent their conclusions
- Engages students in concluding activities that require them to reflect on their own learning

**Score 2.5:** No major errors or omissions regarding the simpler behaviors (Score 2.0 performance) and partial success at the more complex behaviors (Score 3.0 performance).

**Score 2.0:** No major errors or omissions regarding the following simpler behaviors:

- Identifies experiences that provide students with new information, but does not distinguish between critical and noncritical experiences
- Employs previewing activities, but does not highlight linkages between new knowledge and what has been previously addressed
- Organizes students into small groups, but those groups do not enhance the processing of new knowledge
- Breaks input experiences into small chunks, but those chunks are not appropriate to the students' level of readiness
- When pausing after a small chunk of new knowledge, teacher engages students in activities, but those activities do not necessarily enhance students' understanding of new knowledge

**Figure 2: Rubric for lessons involving introduction of new knowledge.**

- Engages students in activities that are inferential but not focused on elaborating on the content of the input experience
- After the input experience, engages students in review activities, but those activities do not require students to write out and represent their conclusions
- Engages students in concluding activities, but those activities do not require students to reflect on their own learning

The teacher exhibits major errors or omissions regarding the more complex behaviors (Score 3.0 performance).

**Score 1.5:** Partial success at the simpler behaviors (Score 2.0 performance) but major errors or omissions regarding the more complex behaviors (Score 3.0 performance).

**Score 1.0:** With help, partial success at some of the simpler behaviors (Score 2.0 performance) and some of the more complex behaviors (Score 3.0 performance).

**Score 0.5:** With help, partial success at some of the simpler behaviors (Score 2.0 performance) but not the more complex behaviors (Score 3.0 performance).

**Score 0.0:** Even with help, no success with the Score 2.0 or 3.0 behaviors.

**Figure 2: Rubric for lessons involving introduction of new knowledge.**

expertise in terms of use or nonuse of specific instructional strategies makes little sense. It is not the case that experts use routines and nonexperts do not. Rather, it is how the expert adapts the use of routines to specific classes and environments that distinguish her from the nonexperts. Only observation of an expert teacher in action can help the aspiring expert discern the thin slices of behavior that characterize expertise.

After an aspiring teacher has a working knowledge of how specific strategies are used by expert teachers, he would practice the identified strategy in his own class. Extrapolating from the research summarized by Ericsson and his colleagues (Ericsson & Charness, 1994; Ericcson et al. 1993), it can be estimated that about two to four hours of practice per day over an extended period of time is required to master the skills associated with a specific lesson segment. This requirement would fit well into the lives of aspiring teachers who spend more time than this with students each day.

It is important to note that during practice sessions, it is not sufficient for aspiring teachers to simply repeat a strategy they have seen employed by an expert. Rather, feedback from the expert is needed. As Ericcson et al. (1993) explain: "In the absence of feedback, efficient learning is impossible and improvement only minimal even for highly motivated subjects. Hence, mere repetition of an activity will not automatically lead to improvement" (p. 367). This is quite consistent with the findings reported by Hattie and Timperley (2007) from their analysis of twelve meta-analyses incorporating 196 studies and 6,972 effect sizes. The average effect size for providing feedback was .79, which they note is approximately twice the average effect size (.40) associated with most educational innovations.

To provide effective feedback, expert teachers would have to observe aspiring teachers. This might be done in person with expert teachers visiting the classrooms of aspiring teachers. This, of course, would require a great deal of time. A more efficient technique would be for expert teachers to review videos of aspiring teachers practicing a specific strategy. Again, the work on thin slices of behaviors by Ambady and Rosenthal (1992, 1993) is relevant in that expert teachers would not have to observe the video of an entire lesson to provide effective feedback on the use of specific instructional strategies for a specific lesson segment.

### Clear Criteria for Success

Deliberate practice must be accompanied by a clear criterion for success. This means that expertise cannot be assumed of an individual simply because he or she exhibits the behaviors associated with expertise. Indeed, an individual can work in a domain for years and have a great deal of knowledge regarding the domain, but not exhibit superior performance (Camerer & Johnson, 1991). About this, Ericsson and Charness (1994) explain that expertise should be judged by superior performance, not by knowledge of the domain. A logical question is, What should be the criterion for superior performance regarding classroom pedagogy? In answer to this question, it is easy to embrace the position that appropriate use of specific instructional strategies should be the measure of superior performance. This is a tempting but faulty position to take. While the reasoned use of specific instructional strategies is certainly a necessary ingredient of expertise, the ultimate criterion for expert performance in the classroom is student achievement. Anything else misses the point. As an analogy, consider the domain of chess. A chess player might demonstrate knowledge of a wide variety of moves and even knowledge of when those moves are most appropriate; however, if the chess player cannot actually use that knowledge to win chess matches, she cannot be considered an expert. The same logic applies to the classroom teacher. The ultimate criterion for successful teaching must be student learning. Indeed, in their review of teacher evaluation programs, Tucker and Stronge (2005) demonstrated the power of using student knowledge gain as the ultimate criterion for successful teaching.

Marzano (2008) has provided specific recommendations about how teachers might collect data on student knowledge gain. He recommends two types of data: (1) knowledge gain based on a pretest and posttest from students, and (2) perceived level of learning as reported by students. To obtain the first type of data, teachers would select a unit of instruction and administer a pretest and a posttest over the context of the unit. The differences between posttest and pretest scores would constitute a measure of knowledge gain for each student. This is quite similar to the achievement data used in the Oregon Teacher Work Sample Methodology reviewed by Tucker and Stronge (2005). In addition to knowledge gain as measured by pre-post gains, student self-report perceptions of learning can be collected at the end of each unit by asking students to complete one or more Likert-type items that represent how much they thought they had learned.

Aspiring experts would use knowledge-gain data to determine the effectiveness of their efforts to master the use of instructional strategies within a particular segment selected for improvement. Specifically, the extent to which student knowledge gain increases as indicated by one or both measures would be used as an indicator of the effectiveness of the teacher's performance.

### The Motivation to Engage in Deliberate Practice

The final characteristic of deliberate practice is that it is engaged in continuously and wholeheartedly by aspiring teachers. As mentioned previously, two to four hours of focused practice are required per day. Additionally, this level of practice must continue for about a decade—a fact that has been referred to as the "ten-year rule" (Simon & Chase, 1973). Ericcson et al. (1993) demonstrate the ubiquity of the ten-year rule. Regardless of the domain, about ten years of deliberate practice is required to reach expert performance.

Given the importance of the ten-year rule, it is easy to conclude that acquiring expert status in teaching requires a high level of motivation on the part of aspirants. As Ericcson et al. (1993) explain:

> On the basis of several thousand years of education, along with more recent laboratory research on learning and skill acquisition, a number of conditions for optimal learning and improvement of performance have been uncovered. . . . The most cited condition concerns subjects' motivation to attend to the task and exert effort to improve their performance. (p. 367)

It is probably unreasonable to expect all teachers, even the majority of teachers, to seek the lofty status of expert. Indeed, the natural human condition appears to be to stop development once an acceptable level of performance has been reached. Ericsson and Charness (1994) explain: "Most amateurs and employees spend a very small amount of time on deliberate practice efforts to improve their performance once it has reached an acceptable level" (p. 730).

What, then, would be a reasonable expectation for teachers in a school or district? One reasonable expectation would be that all teachers in a school or district should improve from year to year. Even small increments in teacher expertise over time could translate into substantial gains. To illustrate, assume that teachers in a district were expected to gain 2 percentile points each year in their effectiveness. For those teachers who begin their improvement at the 50th percentile in terms of pedagogical skill, one would expect their students' achievement to increase by 8 percentile points over a ten-year period of time.

Another reasonable expectation is that teachers who aspire to achieve expert status and are willing to put in the necessary work for the requisite period of time (ten years), should receive the support to do so. As outlined earlier, such support would include tutorial and consultative sessions with teachers who have already attained expert status, opportunities to observe expert teachers, and feedback on their use of specific instructional strategies related to specific types of lesson segments.

## Support to Become Experts

This chapter addresses the systematic development of expert teachers. Such an initiative is not easy to implement. It requires a redistribution of resources to free up the time for expert teachers to interact with aspiring teachers. It requires willingness on the part of the district to recognize expertise, and it requires willingness on the part of expert teachers to stand and be counted as leaders. While this idea is challenging, it is not new. Using different terminology and different specific recommendations,

Darling-Hammond (2009) cites examples in the United States and other countries of many of the practices outlined in this chapter. Although Darling-Hammond lays out a very comprehensive reform agenda that goes well beyond the scope of this chapter, one of her basic tenets is that school systems should ensure "that all practitioners have the support to become expert" (p. 64). This chapter has attempted to articulate specific steps districts can take to this end.

## References and Resources

Alvermann, D. E., & Boothby, P. R. (1986). Children's transfer of graphic organizer instruction. *Reading Psychology, 7*(2), 87–100.

Ambady, N., & Rosenthal, R. (1992). Thin slices of expressive behavior as predictors of interpersonal consequences: A meta-analysis. *Psychological Bulletin, 111*(2), 256–274.

Ambady, N., & Rosenthal, R. (1993). Half a minute: Predicting teacher evaluations from thin slices of nonverbal behavior and physical attractiveness. *Journal of Personality and Social Psychology, 64*(3), 431–441.

Anderson, L., Evertson, C., & Emmer, E. (1980). Dimensions in classroom management derived from recent research. *Journal of Curriculum Studies, 12,* 343–356.

Anderson, V., & Hidi, S. (1988/1989). Teaching students to summarize. *Educational Leadership, 46,* 26–28.

Aubusson, P., Foswill, S., Barr, R., & Perkovic, L. (1997). What happens when students do simulation-role-play in science. *Research in Science Education, 27*(4), 565–579.

Ausubel, D. P. (1968). *Educational psychology: A cognitive view.* New York: Holt, Rinehart & Winston.

Bangert-Drowns, R. L., Kulik, C. C., Kulik, J. A., & Morgan, M. (1991). The instructional effects of feedback in test-like events. *Review of Educational Research, 61*(2), 213–238.

Berliner, D. C. (1986). In pursuit of the expert pedagogue. *Educational Researcher, 15*(7), 5–13.

Bloom, B. S. (1976). *Human characteristics and school learning.* New York: McGraw-Hill.

Bloom, B. S. (1985). Generalizations about talent development. In B. S. Bloom (Ed.), *Developing talent in young people* (pp. 507–549). New York: Ballantine Books.

Brekelmans, M., Wubbels, T., & Creton, H. A. (1990). A study of student perceptions of physics teacher behavior. *Journal of Research in Science Teaching, 24,* 335–350.

Brophy, J. E., & Evertson, C. M. (1976). *Learning from teaching: A developmental perspective.* Boston: Allyn & Bacon.

Camerer, C. F., & Johnson, E. J. (1991). The process-performance paradox in expert judgment: How can the experts show so much and predict so badly? In K. A. Ericsson & J. Smith (Eds.), *Toward a general theory of expertise: Prospects and limits* (pp. 195–217). Cambridge, England: Cambridge University Press.

Connell, J. P., Spencer, M. B., & Aber, J. L. (1994). Educational risk and resilience in African-American youth: Context, self, action, and outcomes in school. *Child Development, 65,* 493–506.

Connell, J. P., & Wellborn, J. G. (1991). Competence, autonomy, and relatedness: A motivational analysis of self-system processes. In M. Gunnar & L. A. Sroufe (Eds.), *Minnesota Symposium on Child Psychology* (Vol. 23, pp. 21–56). Chicago: University of Chicago Press.

Cooper, H., Robinson, J. C., & Patall, E. A. (2006). Does homework improve academic achievement? A synthesis of research, 1987–2003. *Review of Educational Research, 76*(1), 1–62.

Cross, K. P. (1998). Classroom research: Implementing the scholarship of teaching. In T. Angelo (Ed.), *Classroom assessment and research: An update on uses, approaches, and research findings* (pp. 5–12). San Francisco: Jossey-Bass.

Darling-Hammond, L. (2009). Teaching and the change wars: The professional hypothesis. In A. Hargreaves & M. Fullan (Eds.), *Change wars* (pp. 45–70). Bloomington, IN: Solution Tree Press.

Deci, E. L., Ryan, R. M., & Koestner, R. (2001). The pervasive effects of rewards on intrinsic motivation: Response to Cameron (2001). *Review of Educational Research, 71*(1), 43–51.

Doyle, W. (1986). Classroom organization and management. In M. C. Wittrock (Ed.), *Handbook of research on teaching* (3rd ed., pp. 392–431). New York: Macmillan.

Druyan, S. (1997). Effects of the kinesthetic conflict on promoting scientific reasoning. *Journal of Research in Science Teaching, 34*(10), 1083–1099.

Eisenhart, M. (1977, May). *Maintaining control: Teacher competence in the classroom.* Paper presented at the American Anthropological Association, Houston, TX.

Emmer, E. T., Evertson, C., & Anderson, L. (1980). Effective classroom management at the beginning of the school year. *Elementary School Journal, 80*(5), 219–231.

Ericsson, K. A., & Charness, N. (1994). Expert performance: Its structure and acquisition. *American Psychologist, 49*(8), 725–747.

Ericsson, K. A., Krampe, R. T., & Tesch-Romer, C. (1993). The role of deliberate practice in the acquisition of expert performance. *Psychological Review, 100*(3), 363–406.

Ericsson, K. A., & Smith, J. (1991). Prospects and limits of the empirical study of expertise: An introduction. In K. A. Ericsson & J. Smith (Eds.), *Toward a general theory of expertise: Prospects and limits* (pp. 1–39). Cambridge, England: Cambridge University Press.

The Forum for Education and Democracy. (2008). *Democracy at risk: The need for a new federal policy in education.* Washington, DC: Author.

Gijbels, D., Dochy, F., Van den Bossche, P., & Segers, M. (2005). Effects of problem-based learning: A meta-analysis from the angle of assessment. *Review of Educational Research, 75*(1), 27–61.

Good, T. L., & Brophy, J. E. (2003). *Looking in classrooms* (9th ed.). Boston: Allyn & Bacon.

Good, T. L., Grouws, D. A., & Ebmeier, H. (1983). *Active mathematics teaching* (Research on Teaching monograph series). New York: Longman.

Haas, M. (2005). Teaching methods for secondary algebra: A meta-analysis of findings. *NASSP Bulletin, 89*(642), 24–46.

Halpern, D. F. (1984). *Thought and knowledge: An introduction to critical thinking.* Hillsdale, NJ: Lawrence Erlbaum.

Halpern, D. F., Hansen, C., & Reifer, D. (1990). Analogies as an aid to understanding and memory. *Journal of Educational Psychology, 82*(2), 298–305.

Hattie, J. A. (1992). Measuring the effects of schooling. *Australian Journal of Education, 36*(1), 5–13.

Hattie, J., Biggs, J., & Purdie, N. (1996). Effects of learning skills interventions on student learning: A meta-analysis. *Review of Educational Research, 66*(2), 99–136.

Hattie, J., & Timperley, H. (2007). The power of feedback. *Review of Educational Research, 77*(1), 81–112.

Hidi, S., & Anderson, V. (1987). Providing written summaries: Task demands, cognitive operations, and implications for instruction. *Reviewing Educational Research, 56*, 473–493.

Hillocks, G. (1986). *Research on written composition.* Urbana, IL: ERIC Clearinghouse on Reading and Communication Skills and National Conference on Research in English.

Kumar, D. D. (1991). A meta-analysis of the relationship between science instruction and student engagement. *Educational Review, 43*(1), 49–66.

Leinhardt, G. (1990). Capturing craft knowledge in teaching. *Educational Researcher, 19*(2), 18–25.

Leinhardt, G., & Greeno, J. (1986). The cognitive skill of teaching. *Journal of Educational Psychology, 78*(2), 75–95.

Linden, D. E., Bittner, R. A., Muckli, L., Waltz, J. A., Kriegekorte, N., Goebel, R., et al. (2003). Cortical capacity constraints for visual working memory: Dissociation of FMRI load effects in a fronto-parietal network. *Neuroimage, 20*(3), 1518–1530.

Lipsey, M. W., & Wilson, D. B. (1993). The efficacy of psychological, educational, and behavioral treatment. *American Psychologist, 48*(12), 1181–1209.

Marzano & Associates. (2006). *Observational protocol for teacher feedback.* Centennial, CO: Author.

Marzano, R. J. (2007). *The art and science of teaching: A comprehensive framework for effective instruction.* Alexandria, VA: Association for Supervision and Curriculum Development.

Marzano, R. J. (2008). *Getting serious about school reform.* Bloomington, IN: Marzano Research Laboratory.

Marzano, R. J., & Waters, T. (2009). *District leadership that works: Striking the right balance.* Bloomington, IN: Solution Tree Press.

Marzano, R. J. (with Marzano, J. S., & Pickering, D. J.). (2003). *Classroom management that works: Research-based strategies for every teacher.* Alexandria, VA: Association for Supervision and Curriculum Development.

Mayer, R. E. (1989). Models of understanding. *Review of Educational Research, 59*, 43–64.

Mayer, R. E. (2003). *Learning and instruction.* Upper Saddle River, NJ: Merrill, Prentice Hall.

McDaniel, M. A., & Donnelly, C. M. (1996). Learning with analogy and elaborative interrogation. *Journal of Educational Psychology, 88*(3), 508–519.

Moskowitz, G., & Hayman, J. L. (1976). Success strategies of inner-city teachers: A year-long study. *Journal of Educational Research, 69*, 283–289.

Murray, P. (1989). Poetic genius and its classic origins. In P. Murray (Ed.), *Genius: The history of the idea* (pp. 9–31). Oxford, England: Basil Blackwell.

Newton, D. P. (1995). Pictorial support for discourse comprehension. *British Journal of Educational Psychology, 64*(2), 221–229.

Nuthall, G. (1999). The way students learn: Acquiring knowledge from an integrated science and social studies unit. *Elementary School Journal, 99*(4), 303–341.

Nuthall, G., & Alton-Lee, A. (1995). Assessing classroom learning: How students use their knowledge and experience to answer classroom achievement test questions in science and social studies. *American Educational Research Journal, 32*(1), 185–223.

Nye, B., Konstantopoulos, S., & Hedges, L. V. (2004). How large are teacher effects? *Educational Evaluation and Policy Analysis, 26*(3), 237–257.

Pressley, M., Wood, E., Woloshyn, V., Martin, V., King, A., & Menke, D. (1992). Encouraging mindful use of prior knowledge: Attempting to construct explanatory answers facilitates learning. *Educational Psychologist, 27*, 91–109.

Reder, L. M. (1980). The role of elaboration in the comprehension and retention of prose: A critical review. *Review of Educational Research, 50*(1), 5–53.

Redfield, D. L., & Rousseau, E. W. (1981). A meta-analysis of experimental research on teacher questioning behavior. *Review of Educational Research, 51*(2), 237–245.

Reeve, J. (2006). Extrinsic rewards and inner motivation. In C. Evertson, C. M. Weinstein, & C. S. Weinstein (Eds.), *Handbook of classroom management: Research, practice, and contemporary issues* (pp. 645–664). Mahwah, NJ: Lawrence Erlbaum.

Rosenshine, B. (2002). Converging findings on classroom instruction. In A. Molnar (Ed.), *School reform proposals: The research evidence.* Tempe, AZ: Arizona State University Research Policy Unit. Accessed at http://epsl.asu .edu/epru/documents/EPRU%202002-101/Chapter%2009-Rosenshine-Final .rtf on June 1, 2006.

Rosenthal, R., & Jacobson, L. (1968). *Pygmalion in the classroom.* New York: Holt, Rinehart & Winston.

Ross, J. A. (1988). Controlling variables: A meta-analysis of training studies. *Review of Educational Research, 58*(4), 405–437.

Rovee-Collier, C. (1995). Time windows in cognitive development. *Developmental Psychology, 31*(2), 147–169.

Sadoski, M., & Paivio, A. (2001). *Imagery and text: A dual coding theory of reading and writing.* Mahwah, NJ: Lawrence Erlbaum.

Schunk, D. H., & Cox, P. D. (1986). Strategy training and attributional feedback with learning disabled students. *Journal of Educational Psychology, 73*(3), 201–209.

Simon, H. A., & Chase, W.G. (1973). Skill in chess. *American Scientist, 61*, 394–403.

Stodolsky, S. (1983). *Classroom activity structures in the fifth grade.* (Final report, NIE contract No. 400-77-0094). Chicago: University of Chicago. (ERIC Document Reproduction Service No. ED242412).

Tucker, P. D., & Stronge, J. H. (2005). *Linking teacher evaluation and student learning.* Alexandria, VA: Association for Supervision and Curriculum Development.

U.S. Department of Education. (2002). *Meeting the highly qualified teachers challenge: The secretary's annual report on teacher quality.* Washington, DC: U.S. Department of Education, Office of Postsecondary Education.

Walberg, H. J. (1999). Productive teaching. In H. C. Waxman & H. J. Walberg (Eds.), *New directions for teaching practice research* (pp. 75–104). Berkeley, CA: McCutchan.

Wang, M. C., Haertel, G. D., & Walberg, H. J. (1993). Toward a knowledge base for school learning. *Review of Educational Research, 63*(3), 249–294.

Weinstein, R. S. (2002). *Reaching higher: The power of expectations in schooling.* Cambridge, MA: Harvard University Press.

Welch, M. (1997, April). *Students' use of three-dimensional modeling while designing and making a solution to a technical problem.* Paper presented at the annual meeting of the American Educational Research Association, Chicago.

West, L. H. T., & Fensham, P. J. (1976). Prior knowledge or advance organizers as affective variables in chemical learning. *Journal of Research in Science Teaching, 13,* 297–306.

Wilkinson, S. S. (1981). The relationship between teacher praise and student achievement: A meta-analysis of selected research. *Dissertation Abstracts International, 41,* 3998A.

Wise, K. C., & Okey, J. R. (1983). A meta-analysis of the effects of various science teaching strategies on achievement. *Journal of Research in Science Teaching, 20*(5), 415–425.

Wright, S. P., Horn, S. P., & Sanders, W. L. (1997). Teacher and classroom context effects on student achievement: Implications for teacher evaluation. *Journal of Personnel Evaluation in Education, 11,* 57–67.

Wubbels, T., Brekelmans, M., den Brok, P., & van Tartwijk, J. (2006). An interpersonal perspective on classroom management in secondary classrooms in the Netherlands. In C. Evertson & C. S. Weinstein (Eds.), *Handbook of classroom management: Research, practice, and contemporary issues* (pp. 1161–1191). Mahwah, NJ: Lawrence Erlbaum.

# Carol Ann Tomlinson

Carol Ann Tomlinson, Ed.D., spent twenty-one years as a public school teacher, including twelve years as a program administrator of special services for struggling and advanced learners. She is a faculty member at the University of Virginia's Curry School of Education, where she is currently William Clay Parrish, Jr. Professor in Education and chair of Educational Leadership, Foundations and Policy. She is also codirector of the university's Institutes on Academic Diversity. Dr. Tomlinson was named Outstanding Professor at Curry School of Education in 2004 and received an All University Teaching Award in 2008. Special interests throughout her career have included curriculum and instruction for struggling learners and advanced learners, effective instruction in heterogeneous settings, and encouraging creative and critical thinking in the classroom.

In this chapter, Dr. Tomlinson advocates for quality differentiation in the classroom. She explores the context for effective differentiation, which is marked by five indicators of quality and three core elements.

# Chapter 10

# Differentiating Instruction in Response to Academically Diverse Student Populations

Carol Ann Tomlinson

In *Understood Betsy* (Fisher, 1999), a children's novel set near the turn of the twentieth century, third-grader Betsy transfers midyear from a consolidated school to a one-room schoolhouse. Her teacher welcomes her, and as a matter of course, immediately begins assigning her tasks to determine her level of knowledge and skill in the various content areas. Ultimately, she asks Betsy to join the level-seven readers during reading time. Betsy, a very precocious reader, is excited at the prospect of reading a "real" book. In her previous school, round robin reading of simple texts was standard fare. Nonetheless, Betsy tells her new teacher that it would not be wise for her to read with the level-seven students because she is not nearly good enough in math to handle level-seven work in that subject. The teacher replies that one has little to do with the other.

By the end of the day, the teacher has determined Betsy's points of entry in each subject and assigned her work that matches her readiness to learn in each area. Betsy, however, is confused and says to her teacher, "Why—why, I don't know what I am at all. If I'm second grade math and third grade spelling, and seventh grade reading, what grade *am* I?" (p. 83).

Her teacher laughs and replies, "*You* aren't any grade at all, no matter where you are in school. You're just yourself, aren't you? What difference does it matter what grade you're in, and what's the point of reading little baby things that are too easy for you just because you don't know your multiplication tables?" (pp. 83–84).

Betsy was a student in a time of transition. One-room schoolhouses—once a staple of the American educational landscape—were losing popularity to consolidated schools deemed more efficient. Surely it made better sense to put eight-year-olds in a room together so they could be taught alike, rather than having them mixed in with six- to eighteen-year-olds. Betsy, however, was not a standard-issue third grader, and a classroom where a teacher was prepared to match instruction to students' particular needs served her better than her original classroom where the assumption was that students should fit the curriculum rather than the curriculum fitting the student.

The argument can be made that schools are again in a time of transition—a period in which it again seems evident that one-size-fits-all approaches to curriculum and instruction are a misfit for too many students, a period in which teachers are once more trying to understand what it means to calibrate instruction based on the varying needs of an increasingly diverse student population.

### Guess Who's Coming to School

Fisher's portrayal of Betsy, whose academic development is uneven and whose learning is influenced by conditions at home that are out of her control, is a more accurate representation of reality than the convenient notion that as long as a teacher covers a prescribed curriculum in a prescribed timeframe, it will work for all students of a given age. In most contemporary classrooms, the premise that students are essentially alike is a delusion. School populations are increasingly diverse in terms of student experience, culture, language, race, economics, gender, handicapping conditions, home support, and a myriad of other factors that undeniably shape how students learn. Thus, diversity in each of those areas results in academic diversity as well.

Changes in language and culture in the classroom have been swift and dramatic. In 1970, 12 percent of the United States' population was nonwhite. By 2000, 30 percent of the population was of non-Anglo, non-European ancestry. In the period between 1980 and 2000, the white, non-Hispanic population grew by 7.9 percent. The population that identifies itself as nonwhite or Hispanic grew by 88 percent (Lynch & Hanson, 2004).

More immigrants arrived in the United States in the 1980s than in any other decade on record. Students in the United States now speak more than 450 languages. In 2004, approximately 12 percent of students were considered English language learners—a number expected to grow to about 50 percent by 2030 (Flynn & Hill, 2005; Gray & Fleischman, 2004).

Students with identified disabilities are also growing in number and their presence in "regular" classrooms is a reality. Approximately 96 percent of teachers have students with disabilities in their classrooms—resulting in about three to four students with individualized education plans (IEPs) in each classroom. Further, three-quarters of students with disabilities spend about 40 percent of their time in regular classrooms (U.S. Department of Education, 2001). In the majority of these classrooms, there is scant evidence of consistent instructional adaptation to attend to the particular learning needs of students with learning difficulties (Graham et al., 2008).

Approximately 6 percent of students are identified as gifted, with services for these students being uneven across sites (National Association for Gifted Children, 2008). As is the case with students identified for special education, many of these students spend a substantial portion of their time in regular or general classrooms in which there is little evidence of instructional adaptation in response to their learning status (Archambault et al., 1993).

Economic disparities among students also impact learning. The United States has the highest child poverty rate of the seventeen wealthiest nations in the world (Mishel, Bernstein, & Allegretto, 2008). Children of poverty are approximately 1.4 times as likely as their nonpoor peers to have learning disabilities or developmental delays, twice as likely to repeat grades and to be suspended from school, and 2.2 times as likely to drop out of school (Brooks-Gunn & Duncan, 1997).

Despite progress in race relations in the United States, a long history of racial inequity and discrimination continues to cast a shadow in contemporary classrooms. Many students of color still struggle with what it means to be both true to their race and academic achievers—the latter still associated with a white and more affluent culture—and to fit in in schools and classes that often still operate from a Caucasian perspective (Delpit, 1995; Perry, Steele, & Hilliard, 2003; Tatum, 1997).

In addition, experts argue that classrooms are often ineffective for students who have behavioral and emotional difficulties (Greene, 2008) and for those who have experienced trauma such as abuse or violence (Craig, 2008), because many teachers do not understand or attend to the challenges and needs of these students. There is even the hypothesis and some evidence that the generic nature of classroom instruction inappropriately serves both girls and boys by failing to consider gender-specific learning needs and patterns (Flood & Shaffer, 2000; Gurian, 2001; Pipher, 1994; Pollack, 1998; Sadker & Sadker, 1994; Salomone, 2003; Sax, 2005).

Thus, in a time when academic diversity is a given, when most students need to be educated at a level once reserved for elite learners (Marx, 2000), and when single-size instruction is the prevailing instructional approach, many educators are again seeking instructional paradigms that are not totally alien to the one-room schoolhouse to proactively support student variability in the classroom.

## A Need in Search of a Different Approach

The advent of the grade-level classroom did not eliminate student variability, of course. It simply offered an illusion that all six-year-olds or all eleventh graders were essentially alike and could be taught as a single entity rather than more individually. The idea is understandably appealing to teachers who are inevitably stretched for time, resources, and energy.

It is perhaps not surprising, then, that the two dominant approaches to academic variance in the classroom accept the efficacy of standardized teaching and learning. One approach has been to retain heterogeneity but largely *not* address student learning differences. The second, historically preferred by teachers (National Educational Association, 1968), is homogeneous grouping of students based on perceptions of student ability. Both approaches have consistently proven problematic in terms of student achievement and attainment of equity of access to excellence in school, a fundamental goal of education in a democratic society (Burris & Garrity, 2008; Gamoran, 2002; Glass, 2002).

A third option, less common but persistent over time in various forms, suggests that educators acknowledge that human diversity is both normal and enriching, and that they adopt instructional approaches that address inevitable student variance in the context of heterogeneity. Among iterations of this approach are multiage classrooms (Stone, 1996), various forms of collaborative or cooperative learning (for example, Cohen et al., 1999; Johnson & Johnson, 1999; and Slavin, 1999), and inclusive classrooms including universal design (Rose, Meyer, & Hitchcock, 2005) and response to intervention (Mellard & Johnson, 2008).

Each of these student-centered approaches to developing classrooms that are effectively responsive to student learning differences presupposes implementation of what we now call *differentiated instruction* (for example, Tomlinson, 1999, 2001, and 2003). This approach to instruction is rooted in theory suggesting that student readiness, interest, and learning preferences impact learning and that cognitive, affective, behavioral, and social outcomes for a wide range of students will improve when teachers plan and teach with those elements in mind (Tomlinson et al., 2003). While research indicates that the majority of teachers persist in teaching as though student variance was of minimal importance (Johnsen, Haensly, Ryser, & Ford, 2002; Scruggs & Mastropieri, 2004; Morocco, Riley, Gordon, & Howard, 1996; Schumm & Vaughn, 1995), research also indicates improved student engagement, behavior, and achievement when instruction addresses student readiness, interest, and learning preferences separately and in a unified model of classroom instruction (Tomlinson et al., 2003; Tomlinson, Brimijoin, & Narvaez, 2008; Tomlinson & McTighe, 2006).

## The Context for Effective Differentiation

As is the case with other robust instructional approaches, effective differentiation will reflect general high-quality educational practice. That is, defensible differentiation is a part of, not apart from, good teaching. There are at least five contextual indicators of quality differentiation. It is not the case that the five must be firmly in place for differentiation to begin, but rather that they evolve as teacher skill and will in attending to student variance evolve. They are a root system that at once grows through and nourishes growth toward responsive teaching. Each of the five elements plays a role in strengthening teaching and learning in any classroom, and each is necessary in a particular way to support differentiation.

### 1. A Positive or Growth Mindset About Student Potential

Schools and the educators in them are often representative of what Carol Dweck (2006) calls a *fixed mindset*. That is, they reflect a belief that ability is a matter of heredity and home environment. Some people come to school smart, others do not. A manifestation of a fixed mindset is the almost unquestioned assumption that educators can figure out who is smart and who is not, and that they can then sort students into groups that can and groups that cannot achieve at high levels. The alternative to a fixed mindset is what Dweck calls a *growth* or *fluid mindset*. This perspective holds that success and achievement are not artifacts of birth, but rather of effort.

Educators with a fluid mindset believe that most students can learn most things as long as both the student and teacher are willing to work hard to ensure that outcome. The role of the teacher is to hold high expectations and provide the necessary support system so that students achieve those goals. Teachers with a fixed mindset are likely to struggle with the concept of differentiation and to differentiate for some students by "watering down" the curriculum. By contrast, teachers with a fluid mindset see differentiation as a given—as a part of what it takes to maximize student potential. Teachers with a fluid or growth mindset find it logical to "teach up"—extend the reach of students and provide support for the stretch—and to differentiate as a means of ensuring student access to high-level goals. Dweck is clear that individuals can change their mindset. At the very least, differentiation calls on teachers to reflect on their current mindsets and to ensure development or strengthening of a growth mindset.

### 2. Teacher-Student Connections to Support Learning

Learning involves risk. Substantive learning inevitably involves failures. For many students, taking the risk of learning comes only after a teacher has earned their trust. Teachers who build bridges of trust with students make learning seem both desirable and possible. As Powell (1996) reports, "Positive relationships with their instructors can motivate students when other incentives fail. Personalization should not be confused with social work; it is directly linked to the promotion of academic learning" (p. 197). In an effectively differentiated classroom, a teacher asks each student to work consistently at a point a bit beyond the student's reach. A student at any point on an achievement continuum must therefore continually have confidence that there will be scaffolding for support as they navigate the unknown. Further, evolving connections with each student both inform and fuel the teacher's determination to invest in student success. It is much more difficult to give up on a person you know and understand than on one who remains relatively generic and anonymous. Further, unless teachers are willing to reflect on students as individuals, the temptation to teach them as a "pack" remains strong.

### 3. Developing Community

In classrooms that invite student learning, the teacher's respect for and connections with individuals progressively lead to student respect and connection and ultimately result in a sense of classroom community. Michael Fullan (2001) notes:

> The new common ground for both cognitive scientists and sociologists concerns motivation and relationships. That is, it is only when schooling operates in a way that connects students relationally in a relevant, engaging, and worthwhile experience that substantial learning will occur. That only a small proportion of any students are so engaged is a measure of the seriousness of the problem. (p. 152)

In a differentiated classroom, a sense of community or team not only energizes learning, but also enables students to trust one another, support one another's growth, and celebrate one another's successes.

### 4. High-Quality Curriculum as the Target for Virtually All Students

Helene Hodges (1991) describes what she calls a *pedagogy of plenty,* which is typically found in classes designed for a school's "best" students. In such settings, there is emphasis on meaning making, complex thought, use of authentic resources, student-created products for meaningful audiences, substantive discussion, and working in a variety of groupings. By contrast, Martin Haberman (1991) details the traits of what he labels a *pedagogy of poverty*. Such classes are heavily populated by students from low-income and minority backgrounds and are typified by right-answer questions, low-level tasks, lots of review, correcting work, settling disputes, and dispensing punishments. An effectively differentiated classroom—one predicated on a growth mindset and intent on creating trust, respect, and community—will necessarily opt for a pedagogy of plenty as the starting point for all students, with the possible exception of those who have IEPs indicating an alternate set of curricular goals (National Research Council, 1999; Tomlinson & McTighe, 2006). Ample evidence (Tomlinson & McTighe, 2006) and common sense dictate that students achieve more when they are expected to understand, apply, and transfer the big ideas or fundamental principles of the disciplines they study than when they are asked only to feed back rote information and practice decontextualized skills. In an effectively differentiated classroom, trust and community also erode when students observe (and they clearly do) that some among them are prisoners of drill and practice while others are earmarked as thinkers and creators of knowledge. A teacher who differentiates instruction must differentiate *something*. The quality of that something is predictive of the success of individual students and to the quality of the classroom environment. Differentiation guides teachers to develop "respectful tasks" designed to ensure that all students (1) find their work appealing and engaging, (2) work with the core principles or big ideas of the discipline, and (3) are cast as critical and creative thinkers who use what they learn in meaningful and challenging contexts. It also asks teachers to "teach up" by extending the reach of students and providing support for the stretch.

## 5. Assessment to Inform Instruction

A number of contemporary educators (for example, Earl, 2003; and Stiggins, Arter, Chappius, & Chappius, 2007) distinguish between assessment *of* learning, assessment *for* learning, and assessment *as* learning. Differentiation is predicated upon a teacher's increasing consistency and effectiveness in implementing assessment *for* learning. That is, plans for differentiation stem from a teacher's ongoing collection of information that details each student's proximity to specified and essential knowledge, understanding, and skill that form curricular frameworks. A teacher who sees the central goals of teaching as ensuring that each student understands, applies, and transfers key content uses preassessment and formative assessment as a sort of daily GPS to know how to steer instruction for individual students, small groups of students, and the class as a whole to achieve that goal (Tomlinson, 2007/2008). Formative assessment thus becomes a primary vehicle to guide teacher reflection on individual learners and to move them away from thinking only about "the class" as the unit of instruction. Ultimately, teachers in effectively differentiated classrooms come to understand and emphasize assessment *as* learning. That is, they help students use assessment as a window into their own growth and identity as learners so they develop the power and agency necessary to take charge of their learning (Tomlinson, 2008).

### Key Elements of Differentiation

There are three core elements in the practice of differentiated instruction: (1) categories of variance in student learning, (2) classroom elements that teachers can modify or differentiate in response to the categories of student learning variance, and (3) flexible management of classroom resources to enable students to work in ways and with tasks that maximize their learning.

### Categories of Variance in Student Learning

Research indicates that students inevitably vary in at least three aspects: readiness to learn particular content at a particular time, personal interests, and mode of learning or learning profile (Tomlinson, 2003; Tomlinson et al., 2003). Readiness is not synonymous for the more fixed constructs of aptitude or intelligence, but rather refers to a student's current knowledge, understanding, and skill as they relate to specified content goals. In differentiating based on student readiness, the intent of the teacher is to provide materials and tasks that are just ahead of the student's current comfort zone, as well as the support necessary to help the student achieve proficiency at the new level of challenge. Readiness is determined largely by current classroom assessments and will change often for each student.

Interest refers to a student's affinity for particular content or topics. Students' motivation to learn increases when they perceive a topic or task to be interesting and relevant. Teachers who differentiate instruction based on student interests attempt to (1) identify student interests, (2) help students see themselves and their interests in required content, (3) provide opportunities for students to use their particular talents in exploring and expressing content, and (4) develop new interests and abilities that will enhance their success as learners.

*Learning profile* refers to ways in which students learn most efficiently and can be shaped by culture, gender, learning style, intelligence preference, and interactions among those four factors. Teachers who differentiate instruction based on student learning profile preferences attempt to provide options for exploring and expressing learning so that students have ample opportunity to develop essential knowledge, understanding, and skill, and to adequately demonstrate what they have learned.

A goal of differentiation is to respond to student readiness, interest, and mode of learning often enough and in enough ways to support each student's engagement with and understanding of essential content goals.

### Classroom Elements That Allow Differentiation

There are at least three classroom elements that teachers can modify in response to student readiness, interest, and learning profile needs. Those are (1) content, (2) process, and (3) product. Again, purposeful modifications of these elements, informed by ongoing assessment information, enhance the likelihood of each student's academic success.

**Content.** *Content* can refer either to what students should know, understand, and be able to do as the result of a sequence of learning or to how students gain access to that knowledge, understanding, and skill. Most of the time, teachers differentiate how students gain access to key content rather than differentiating the content itself. Examples of varying student access to content might include using a variety of peer reading structures, presenting information in multiple modes or formats, and making available reading and web-based materials at a range of reading levels or in varied languages. Teachers can appropriately differentiate the actual content (versus ways in which students access the content) when formative assessment demonstrates that a student lacks prerequisite knowledge or skills or that a student has mastery of knowledge or skills in an upcoming unit of study. It is also appropriate to differentiate content for students with IEPs indicating a set of learning outcomes different from the general outcomes for a grade or subject (Tomlinson & McTighe, 2006).

**Process.** *Process* refers to activities designed to ensure that students master, internalize, or make sense of essential knowledge, understanding, and skill. Whereas content occurs when students are introduced to ideas or skills, process begins when students move from hearing about, reading about, or watching demonstrations of content to trying out and putting the content to use. Process can be a synonym for what educators call *learning activities*.

**Product.** *Product* refers to ways in which students demonstrate what they know, understand, and can do and tends to focus more on summative rather than formative tasks. While more conventional measures such as multiple-choice or fill-in-the-blank tests can be useful in determining student mastery of essential content, more authentic tasks such as applications, demonstrations, and proposing solutions to real-world problems are not only more likely to demonstrate genuine understanding but also "make room" for a greater variety of learners who will inevitably approach and express learning in a variety of ways. While products can be differentiated in response to student readiness, interest, and/or learning profile, the learning goals that products are designed to measure should remain constant (Tomlinson & McTighe, 2006). Table 1 (pages 260–261) provides a few examples of ways in which teachers can modify content, process, and product in response to student readiness, interest, and learning profile needs.

### Flexible Classroom Management

Early on, novice teachers tend to strive for a sort of "flock control" in the classroom as a survival tool. Their expectation is that everyone will do the same work, using the same materials, starting and ending the work at the same moment, and doing the work with a bare minimum of movement and conversation. Mastering this approach to classroom management may be the quintessential badge of becoming a teacher who is "in charge" of his or her classroom. Perhaps the greatest challenge to teachers in differentiation, then, is learning to establish a classroom in which, some of the time, individuals and groups of students can work effectively and efficiently on different tasks, for different lengths of time, using different materials and different working parameters. As is the case with most other aspects of differentiation, this sort of flexible management reflects an evolving set of teacher competencies. It also calls on teachers to help students understand and contribute to a classroom in which both teamwork and individual focus are important components of success.

**Table 1: Examples of Differentiating Content, Process, and Product in Response to Student Readiness, Interest, and Learning Profile**

| | Readiness | Interest | Learning Profile |
|---|---|---|---|
| **Content** | • Using materials at varied reading levels<br>• Providing vocabulary lists in English and students' first language<br>• Referencing word walls during explanations<br>• Using small-group instruction<br>• Providing miniworkshops<br>• Preteaching vocabulary to students who lack key academic vocabulary<br>• Teaching reading and writing skills in all subjects for students weak in those areas | • Using a range of materials showing application of important ideas/skills to varied fields<br>• Providing illustrations of ideas at work in varied areas and drawing from varied cultures<br>• Using enrichment reading to learn about contributors to varied domains | • Teaching in varied modes (for example, visual, kinesthetic, and verbal)<br>• Using creative, analytical, and practical examples<br>• Using video and audio to accompany text<br>• Providing options to read text before or after lectures, depending on student learning needs<br>• Using whole-to-part phonics and part-to-whole phonics explanations |

| | Readiness | Interest | Learning Profile |
|---|---|---|---|
| **Process** | • Using tiered activities<br>• Using learning centers with tasks tailored to student skill needs<br>• Providing tape-recorded task directions<br>• Specifying a skilled reader to read directions for small groups<br>• Assigning "experts of the day" to provide task-specific help | • Forming expert groups<br>• Using jigsaw groups<br>• Allowing choice of applications to varied hobby areas/vocations<br>• Providing interest centers<br>• Encouraging independent investigations<br>• Encouraging web quests and web inquiries | • Using complex instruction<br>• Providing tasks that allow exploration and expression via varied intelligence preferences<br>• Providing work-alone and work-with-a-peer options<br>• Using review groups that capsule key ideas in multiple modes<br>• Using culture- and gender-relevant modes of expression |
| **Product** | • Using tiered products<br>• Setting personal goals for products<br>• Using varied resource options<br>• Requiring varied check-in requirements for product work | • Creating student-generated product options<br>• Using problem-based products that require varied student interests<br>• Using product applications relevant to varied cultures | • Providing varied expression options<br>• Using group products designed to tap the learning preferences of each student in the group |

Establishing and guiding a flexible classroom includes flexible use of classroom tools such as time, materials, space, student groupings, and support mechanisms or scaffolding. It also includes using those tools in ways that support the various affective needs of learners, including those who can work at advanced levels of independence and those who need a great deal of informed teacher support in order to survive and thrive in a world that seems confusing or alienating (Craig, 2008; Greene, 2008). Table 2 (pages 263–264) illustrates some ways in which teachers can use classroom elements flexibly to support and maximize individual academic development.

## The Common Sense of Differentiation

The wealth of diversity in today's schools could well be the catalyst for creating schools and classrooms in which the goal of educating *each* learner replaces the goal of educating *all* learners, and where it is no longer acceptable to sort students by perceived learning capacity by assigning robust expectations to only a small proportion, but instead where access to the best curriculum is the right of each student. Differentiated instruction is a research-based model aimed at maximizing the capacity of each learner in the context of rich and complex curriculum. While materials related to the model provide considerable guidance to teachers and educational leaders about how to implement the model and evaluate fidelity to it, the model is best represented as a set of guiding principles, not a recipe book. It calls on teachers to be persistently reflective about both their content and their students, and to seek an instructional match between students and content. Few who have tried teaching have found it easy, and it is certainly demanding to teach with the intent to ensure maximum growth for each learner in an academically diverse classroom. Nonetheless, there is a great deal of common sense in the concept of differentiation.

**Table 2: Examples of Flexible Use of Key Classroom Elements to Address Student Readiness, Interest, and Learning Profile**

| | Teaching | Time | Materials/Tasks | Groups | Space |
|---|---|---|---|---|---|
| **Readiness** | • Providing notes or note frames for students who struggle with note taking<br>• Stopping often for student summaries and questions<br>• Using student work as models<br>• Using cues to prompt recall and thinking | • Allowing students to move ahead in texts/work as ready<br>• Providing second chances for demonstrating mastery<br>• Providing option to turn in drafts early for critique<br>• Providing time for lesson closure and focus | • Using web and text materials at varied reading levels<br>• Using contacts, tiering, stations, and centers with multiple tasks based on student need<br>• Using computer programs for review and extension | • Using small-group instruction to reteach and extend<br>• Varying homogeneous and heterogeneous groupings of students for practice, application, and review | • Providing space for peer collaboration<br>• Using cue boards, word walls, and help walls<br>• Providing space for learning centers<br>• Providing space for student access to varied learning materials |
| **Interest** | • Relating key ideas to student interests<br>• Allowing students to coteach in areas of interest | • Dedicating time to high-relevance tasks<br>• Allowing time for student-generated inquiry | • Using biography and autobiography as tools to connect content with real life | • Creating interest-alike groups for in-depth application tasks | • Assigning space for student inquiry<br>• Allowing space for student collaboration<br>• Using interest centers or boards |

continued on next page →

**Table 2: Examples of Flexible Use of Key Classroom Elements to Address Student Readiness, Interest, and Learning Profile**

| | Teaching | Time | Materials/Tasks | Groups | Space |
|---|---|---|---|---|---|
| **Interest** | • Sharing your own interests in content areas | • Concluding lessons with "so what?" time<br>• Using interest-based anchor activities | • Using interest-based RAFTs, journal prompts, and performance tasks<br>• Providing interest-based materials for research, reading, and enrichment<br>• Using contemporary technologies (such as blogs, vlogs, video, and digital portfolios) as an option for student exploration and expression | • Creating multi-interest groups for addressing complex issues<br>• Creating student-expert groups | • Displaying student work related to hobbies and interests |
| **Learning Profile** | • Giving presentations in multiple modes<br>• Modeling and sharing your own learning preferences<br>• Answering in multiple modes | • Allowing for variance in student pace<br>• Honoring varied cultural perspectives on time | • Guiding students in using visual, auditory, or kinesthetic preferences when studying<br>• Providing options for collaboration and competition | • Using complex instruction groups<br>• Using similar and mixed learning profile groups | • Providing areas where students can work alone<br>• Providing areas with little visual distraction<br>• Providing areas (and ear plugs) for quiet time |

The journey toward creating an academically responsive classroom may seem more attainable when it is seen as a teacher's daily response to four key questions:

1. What should students know, understand, and be able to do as a result of this segment of learning?

2. How will I know where each student is relative to essential knowledge, understanding, and skill throughout a unit of study?

3. What will I do when I find that students are not all in the same place relative to essential knowledge understanding and skill?

4. How can I create classroom systems and procedures that allow me to attend to varied learners when there is a need to do so?

Teachers who keep these four questions in the foreground of their thinking and planning will readily adopt the skills and mindsets of differentiation, and their students will be the beneficiaries.

## References

Archambault, F., Westberg, K., Brown, S., Hallmark, B., Emmons, C., & Zhang, W. (1993). *Regular classroom practices with gifted students: Results of a national survey.* Research Monograph 93102. Storrs, CT: National Research Center on the Gifted and Talented.

Brooks-Gunn, J., & Duncan, G. (1997). The effects of poverty on children. *The Future of Children: Children and Poverty, 7*(2), 55–71.

Burris, C., & Garrity, D. (2008). *Detracking for excellence and equity.* Alexandria, VA: Association for Supervision and Curriculum Development.

Cohen, E., Lotan, R., Whitcomb, J., Balderrama, M, Cossey, R., & Swanson, P. (1999). Complex instruction: Higher order thinking in heterogeneous classrooms. In S. Sharan (Ed.), *Handbook of cooperative learning methods* (pp. 82–95). Westport, CT: Praeger.

Craig, S. (2008). *Reaching and teaching children who hurt: Strategies for your classroom.* Baltimore: Brookes.

Delpit, L. (1995). *Other people's children: Cultural conflict in the classroom.* New York: The New Press.

Dweck, C. (2006). *Mindset: The new psychology of success.* New York: Random House.

Earl, L. (2003). *Assessment as learning: Using classroom assessment to maximize student learning.* Thousand Oaks, CA: Corwin Press.

Fisher, D. (1999). *Understood Betsy.* New York: Henry Holt.

Flood, C., & Shaffer, S. (2000, November). Safe boys, safe schools. *WEEA Digest,* 3–8. Accessed at www2.edc.org/WomensEquity/pdffiles/males.pdf on March 2, 2009.

Flynn, K., & Hill, J. (2005). English language learners: A growing population. *McREL Policy Brief.* Accessed at http://www.mcrel.org/PDF/PolicyBriefs/5052PI_PBEnglishLanguageLearners.pdf on April 30, 2009.

Fullan, M. (2001). *The new meaning of educational change* (3rd ed.). New York: Teachers College Press.

Gamoran, A. (2002). The production of achievement inequality in high school English. *American Educational Research Journal, 39,* 801–807.

Glass, G. (2002). Grouping students for instruction. In A. Molnar (Ed.), *School reform proposals: The research evidence* (pp. 95–112). Greenwich, CT: Information Age.

Graham, S., Morphy, P., Harris, S., Fink-Chorzempa, Saddler, B., Moran, S., et al. (2008). Teaching spelling in the primary grades: A national survey of instructional practices and adaptations. *American Educational Research Journal, 45,* 796–825.

Gray, T., & Fleischman, S. (2004). Successful strategies for English language learners. *Educational Leadership, 62*(4), 84–85.

Greene, R. (2008). *Lost at school: Why our kids with behavioral problems are falling through the cracks, and how we can help them.* New York: Scribner.

Gurian, M. (2001). *Boys and girls learn differently: A guide for teachers and parents.* San Francisco: Jossey-Bass.

Haberman, M. (1991). The pedagogy of poverty vs. good teaching, *Phi Delta Kappan, 73,* 290–294.

Hodges, H. (1991). Overcoming a pedagogy of poverty. In R. Cole (Ed.), *More strategies for educating everybody's children* (pp. 1–9). Alexandria, VA: Association for Supervision and Curriculum Development.

Johnsen, S., Haensly, P., Ryser, G., & Ford, R. (2002). Changing general education classroom practices to adapt for gifted students. *Gifted Child Quarterly, 46,* 45–63.

Johnson, D., & Johnson, R. (1999). Learning together. In S. Sharan, (Ed.), *Handbook of cooperative learning methods* (pp. 51–65). Westport, CT: Praeger.

Lynch, E., & Hanson, M. (2004). *Developing cross-cultural competence* (3rd ed.). Baltimore: Paul H. Brookes.

Marx, G. (2000). *Ten trends: Preparing children for a profoundly different future.* Arlington, VA: Educational Research Service.

Mellard, D., & Johnson, E. (2008). *RTI: A practitioner's guide to implementing response to intervention.* Thousand Oaks, CA: Corwin Press.

Mishel, L., Bernstein, J., & Allegretto, S. (2008). *The state of working America, 2006–2007.* Washington, DC: Economic Policy Institute.

Morocco, C., Riley, M., Gordon, S., & Howard, C. (1996). The elusive individual in teachers' planning. In G. Brannigan (Ed.), *The enlightened educator* (pp. 154–176). New York: McGraw-Hill.

National Association for Gifted Children (2008). NAGC at a glance. Accessed at www.nagc.org/index.aspx?id=31 on December 30, 2008.

National Education Association. (1968). *Ability grouping research summary, 1968–53.* Washington, DC: Author.

National Research Council. (1999). *How people learn: Brain, mind, experience, and school.* Washington, DC: National Academies Press.

Perry, T., Steele, C., & Hilliard, A. (2003). *Young, gifted, and black: Promoting high achievement among African-American students.* Boston: Beacon.

Pipher, M. (1994). *Reviving Ophelia: Saving the selves of adolescent girls.* New York: Putnam.

Pollack, W. (1998). *Real boys: Rescuing our boys from the myth of boyhood.* New York: Holt.

Powell, A. (1996). *Lessons from privilege: The American prep school tradition.* Cambridge, MA: Harvard University Press.

Rose, D., Meyer, A., & Hitchcock, C. (2005). *The universally designed classroom: Accessible curriculum and digital technologies.* Cambridge, MA: Harvard Education Press.

Sadker, M., & Sadker, D. (1994). *Failing at fairness: How America's schools cheat girls.* New York: Scribner.

Salomone, R. (2003). *Same, different, equal: Re-thinking single-sex schooling.* New Haven, CT: Yale University Press.

Sax, L. (2005). *Why gender matters: What parents and teachers need to know about the emerging science of sex differences.* New York: Broadway Books.

Schumm, J., & Vaughn, S. (1995). Getting ready for inclusion: Is the stage set? *Learning Disabilities Research & Practice, 10,* 169–179.

Scruggs, T., & Mastropieri, T. (Eds.). (2004). *Research in secondary schools: Advances in learning and behavioral disabilities* (Vol. 17). Oxford, UK: Elsevier Science.

Slavin, R. (1999). Student teams-achievement divisions. In S. Sharan (Ed.), *Handbook of Cooperative Learning Methods* (pp. 3–19). Westport, CT: Praeger.

Stiggins, R., Arter, J., Chappius, J., & Chappius, S. (2007). *Classroom assessment for student learning: Doing it right—using it well.* Portland, OR: ETS Assessment Training Institute.

Stone, S. (1996). *Creating the multiage classroom*. Tucson, AZ: Goodyear.

Tatum, B. (1997). *"Why are all the black kids sitting together in the cafeteria?" and other conversations about race*. New York: Basic Books.

Tomlinson, C. (1999). *The differentiated classroom: Responding to the needs of all learners*. Alexandria, VA: Association for Supervision and Curriculum Development.

Tomlinson, C. (2001). *How to differentiate instruction in mixed-ability classrooms* (2nd ed.). Alexandria, VA: Association for Supervision and Curriculum Development.

Tomlinson, C. (2003). *Fulfilling the promise of the differentiated classroom: Strategies and tools for responsive teaching*. Alexandria, VA: Association for Supervision and Curriculum Development.

Tomlinson, C. (2007/2008). Learning to love assessment. *Educational Leadership, 65*(4), 8–13.

Tomlinson, C. (2008). The goals of differentiation. *Educational Leadership, 66*(3), 26–30.

Tomlinson, C., Brighton, C., Hertberg, H., Callahan, C., Moon, T., Brimijoin, K., et al. (2003). Differentiating instruction in response to student readiness, interest, and learning profile in academically diverse classrooms: A review of literature. *Journal for the Education of the Gifted, 27*(2,3), 119–45.

Tomlinson, C., Brimijoin, K., & Narvaez, L. (2008). *The differentiated school: Making revolutionary changes in teaching and learning*. Alexandria, VA: Association for Supervision and Curriculum Development.

Tomlinson, C., & McTighe, J. (2006). *Integrating differentiated instruction and understanding by design: Connecting content and kids*. Alexandria, VA: Association for Supervision and Curriculum Development.

U.S. Department of Education (2001). *23rd annual report to Congress on the implementation of the Individuals with Disabilities Act (IDEA)*. Washington, DC: U.S. Government Printing Office.

# Jay McTighe

Jay McTighe is an educational consultant with an extensive background in professional development. He is a regular speaker at international, national, state, and district conferences and workshops.

McTighe served as director of the Maryland Assessment Consortium and was involved with school improvement projects at the Maryland State Department of Education. He is well known for his work with thinking skills, having coordinated statewide efforts to develop instructional strategies, curriculum models, and assessment procedures for improving the quality of student thinking. In addition to his work at the state level, he has experience as a classroom teacher, resource specialist, and program coordinator. He also served as director of a state residential enrichment program for gifted and talented students.

McTighe is an accomplished author who has coauthored numerous books and more than thirty articles and book chapters.

In this chapter, the author explores the Understanding by Design (UbD) framework and its implications for instructional planning and teaching. More specifically, he examines seven teaching practices suggested by UbD and considers a set of concomitant indicators of their application in classrooms.

Chapter 11

# Understanding by Design and Instruction

## Jay McTighe

As its title suggests, the Understanding by Design (UbD) model (Wiggins & McTighe, 2005) reflects the confluence of two independent ideas: (1) research on learning and cognition that highlights the centrality of teaching and assessing for understanding, and (2) a time-honored process for curriculum design. This chapter explores the UbD framework and its implications for instructional planning and teaching. More specifically, it examines seven teaching practices suggested by UbD and considers a set of concomitant indicators of their application in classrooms.

### Understanding as an Instructional Aim

The heading of this section may strike readers as unnecessary. Doesn't every teacher want her students to understand what she teaches? Perhaps, but the proof is in the pudding. Indeed, an examination of many classrooms in North America today reveals that instruction is often focused on covering lots of content specified in national, state, or provincial standards or contained in bulging textbooks. The frequently cited problem of "mile wide, inch deep" curriculum encourages superficial coverage at the expense of teaching for greater depth. Moreover, the high-stakes pressures associated with accountability testing have elevated "test prep" to an increasingly prominent position on the instructional landscape. As a result, teaching becomes skewed toward what is tested, minimizing instruction on those subjects, topics, or skills that are not tested. Furthermore, instruction on tested content may simply mimic the format of the test, resulting in multiple-choice teaching and drilling of formulaic responses (for example, the five-paragraph essay).

Ironically, such test-prep methods are not likely to yield long-term achievement gains on accountability tests for two reasons:

- Most students will not find a steady diet of test-prep drills and worksheets to be particularly meaningful, and accordingly, they will not put forth optimal learning effort. Also, many teachers resent the pressures they feel to prepare for tests in ways that do not reflect their best teaching toward the most important outcomes. Principals may demand a full commitment to test prep, but teachers' actions are likely to be halfhearted.

- Analyses of international (TIMSS, PISA), national (NAEP), and state assessments reveal that the most widely missed items are those requiring higher-order thinking and the ability to transfer learning to a new context, not those testing basic knowledge and skills (of the sort that are typically "practiced" in a decontextualized fashion).

The contention we express throughout *Understanding by Design* (Wiggins & McTighe, 2005) is straightforward: long-term achievement gains are more likely when teachers teach for understanding of transferable concepts and processes while giving learners multiple opportunities to apply their learning in meaningful (authentic) contexts. Students learn the requisite knowledge and skills through the process of actively constructing meaning (coming to an understanding) and in transferring learning to new situations. An instructional fixation on the format of the test confuses measures and goals. This is akin to practicing for your physical exam as a means of becoming healthier.

Further support for an understanding-based approach to instruction and classroom assessment comes from research in cognitive psychology. A readable synthesis of this research may be found in *How People Learn: Brain, Mind, Experience, and School* (Bransford, Brown, & Cocking, 2000). Following are summaries of several key findings that provide a conceptual base for specific instruction and assessment approaches in UbD (cited in McTighe, Seif, & Wiggins, 2004):

- Views on effective learning have shifted from a focus on the benefits of diligent drill and practice to a focus on students' understanding and application of knowledge.

- Learning must be guided by generalized principles in order to be widely applicable. Knowledge learned at the level of rote memory rarely transfers; transfer most likely occurs when the learner knows and understands underlying concepts and principles that can be applied to problems in new contexts. Learning with understanding is more likely to promote transfer than simply memorizing information from a text or a lecture.

- Experts first seek to develop an understanding of problems, and this often involves thinking in terms of core concepts or big ideas. Novices' knowledge is much less likely to be organized around big ideas; novices are more likely to approach problems by searching for correct formulas and pat answers that fit their everyday intuitions.

- Research on expertise suggests that superficial coverage of many topics may be a poor way to help students develop the competencies that will prepare them for future learning and work. Curricula that emphasize breadth of knowledge may prevent effective organization of knowledge because there is not enough time to learn anything in depth. Curricula that are mile wide and inch deep run the risk of developing disconnected rather than connected knowledge.

- Many assessments measure only propositional (factual) knowledge and never ask whether students know when, where, and why to use that knowledge. Given the goal of learning with understanding, assessments and feedback must focus on understanding, and not simply on memory for procedures or facts.

- The teaching of metacognitive skills should be integrated into the curriculum in a variety of subject areas. Because metacognition often takes the form of an internal dialogue, many students may be unaware of its importance unless teachers explicitly emphasize these processes.

Research findings such as these provide a conceptual underpinning for the UbD framework and should guide instructional practice.

## Planning Precedes Teaching

Teaching is a means to an end. The most successful teaching begins with clarity about important learning outcomes *and* about the evidence that will show that learning has occurred. The UbD model reflects this view. Grant Wiggins and I (2005) recommend that teachers use a three-stage "backward design" process to plan curriculum units that include desired understandings and performance tasks that require transfer. Teachers then develop specific lesson plans in the context of a more comprehensive unit design.

The concept of planning curriculum backward from desired results is certainly not new. In 1948, Ralph Tyler advocated this approach as an effective process for focusing instruction, and more recently, William Spady (1994) endorsed the idea of "designing down" from exit outcomes. Although not a new idea, we have found that the intentional use of backward design results in more clearly defined goals, more appropriate assessments, and more purposeful teaching.

The following is a summary of the UbD three-stage design process for planning units, courses, and programs of study.

### Stage One: Identify Desired Results

What should students know, understand, and be able to do? What are the "big ideas" worthy of understanding? What enduring understandings do we desire from students? What essential questions will we explore?

In Stage One, we consider our long-term goals and examine established content standards and related curriculum expectations such as twenty-first century skills. It is often necessary to "unpack" the standards to identify the big ideas of the content and to frame companion essential questions. Finally, we identify more particular knowledge and skill objectives. This first stage in the design process calls for clarity about instructional priorities.

### Stage Two: Determine Acceptable Evidence

How will we know if students have achieved the desired results? What will we accept as evidence of student understanding and proficiency?

Backward design encourages teachers to "think like an assessor" *before* planning lesson activities, which comes in Stage Three. This approach requires us to consider in advance the assessment evidence needed to validate that the learning outcomes targeted in Stage One have been achieved. Doing so sharpens and focuses teaching.

Educators obtain evidence of understanding through performance tasks that ask students to *apply* their learning to new situations (transfer) and *explain* (support their answer and show their reasoning). We recommend that the performance assessments be set in a meaningful and authentic context whenever possible. Other assessments (such as a quiz on facts or a skills check) provide evidence of knowledge acquisition and skill proficiency.

## Stage Three: Plan Learning Experiences and Instruction

What instruction will students need in order to achieve the desired results and perform effectively? How should we teach to help learners make meaning of the big ideas and equip them to transfer their learning?

With clearly identified results and appropriate assessment evidence in mind, we now plan the most appropriate instructional activities for helping learners acquire targeted knowledge and skills, come to understand important ideas, and apply their learning in meaningful ways.

We have found that when teachers follow this three-stage planning process, they are more likely to avoid two familiar "twin sins" of planning and teaching. The first sin, "activity-oriented teaching," occurs more widely at the elementary and middle school levels. The activities teachers conduct may be engaging, hands on, and kid friendly. These are fine qualities as long as the activities are purposefully focused on clear and important goals *and* if they yield appropriate evidence of learning. However, we have all seen examples of classroom activities that fail these tests. Such activities are like cotton candy—pleasant enough in the moment, but lacking long-term substance.

The second sin, more prevalent at the secondary and collegiate levels, goes by the name of "coverage." In this case, planning simply requires a review of the teacher's edition while teaching consists of marching chronologically through the textbook. We have all known teachers who act as if they believe that their job is to cover the book and seem to resent any suggestions to the contrary.

The challenge of content overload is familiar to all teachers, regardless of subject and grade level. Since there is typically more material to be learned than can reasonably be addressed within the available time, we are constantly challenged by the tension between coverage and meaningful learning. Of course, if covering more content is our aim, we can always talk faster in class! But meaningful and lasting learning requires that the learner *make sense* of the content and see its usefulness in the long term. Thus, a teacher's job is to teach to the big ideas in the standards in ways that enable students to apply their learning to relevant situations (see Wiggins, page 7 of this volume). The textbook may very well provide an important resource in this regard, but it should *not* constitute the syllabus.

Thinking in a backward design way not only asks teachers to carefully align their goals, assessments, and learning activities; it also asks us to consider what a learner should eventually be able to *do* with the targeted content. This way of planning may prove uncomfortable to those teachers who are used to following the pages of a text or presenting a string of activities. Indeed, many teachers have reported that while the backward design process makes sense, it sometimes feels awkward, since it requires a break from familiar planning habits. The good news is that with some practice, backward design becomes more natural and a way of thinking. Once instilled, we have found that teachers become much clearer about curriculum priorities, the longer-term performance outcomes they seek, and the instruction needed to attain those aims.

## The Instructional Implications of Understanding by Design

Let us now turn attention to the practical implications of a UbD approach to teaching and explore seven suggested instructional practices. I will begin with two overarching ideas in teaching for understanding, followed by a set of more specific methods. As you read these, think about your own teaching and that of your colleagues. Which of these instructional approaches do you and your colleagues currently use? Which of these that you are not currently using will you try?

### 1. Frame Content Instruction Around Big Ideas and Essential Questions

In *Understanding by Design* (Wiggins & McTighe, 2005), we propose that content standards need to be unpacked in order to identify the big ideas and core processes that we want students to come to understand. These ideas are then framed by essential questions to focus teaching and learning. This approach is consistent with the recommendations of other curriculum experts, such as Lynn Erickson (1998), who calls for developing concept-based curriculum, and Douglas Reeves (2002), who advocates targeting "power" standards as a means of prioritizing content. Following are three examples of unpacking standards in this manner.

**English/language arts content standard.** Students will read world literature and examine the cultural context in which it was written to determine the similarities of the human condition.

- *Big idea understanding*: Great literature from various cultures explores enduring themes and reveals recurrent characteristics of the human condition.

- *Essential question*: How can stories from other places and times be about us?

**Mathematics content standard.** Students will determine the line of best fit for data to interpret patterns and make predictions.

- *Big idea understanding*: Statistical analysis and display often reveal patterns in data, enabling us to make predictions with degrees of confidence.

- *Essential questions*: Can you predict the future? What will happen next? How sure are you?

**Visual arts content standard.** Students will recognize how technical, organizational, and aesthetic elements contribute to the ideas, emotions, and overall impact communicated by works of art.

- *Big idea understanding*: An artist's culture and personal experiences inspire the ideas and emotions they express. Available tools and technologies influence the ways in which artists express their ideas.

- *Essential questions*: Where do artists get their ideas? In what ways do culture and experience inspire artistic expression? In what ways do artists stimulate thinking and evoke feeling in viewers? How does the medium influence the message?

Notice that in these examples, the transferable big ideas and essential questions provide a conceptual lens through which the specific content in the standards may be taught. They help bring the standards to life; they provide specificity without being reductionist. As a teacher friend of mine noted, the big ideas and essential questions serve as "conceptual Velcro" to help learners connect discrete facts and skills to larger ideas and questions that transfer across topics.

This focus on big ideas helps to prioritize teaching (an antidote to mile-wide, inch-deep curricula), while the use of essential questions fosters an inquiry approach whereby students are actively engaged in making meaning. The aforementioned research on learning endorses this practice.

As a practical matter, I suggest posting the essential questions in a prominent place in the classroom at the start of a new unit of study. These visible questions provide an advance organizer for the unit's central ideas, while stimulating thinking and signaling ongoing inquiry.

### 2. Frame Learning Around Authentic Assessment Tasks Requiring Transfer Application

Sixth-grade students are given the following assessment task at the beginning of a unit on nutrition:

Since we have been learning about nutrition, the camp director at the Outdoor Education Center has asked us to propose a nutritionally balanced menu for our three-day trip to the center later this year. Using the USDA Food Pyramid guidelines and the nutrition facts on food labels, design a plan for three days, including the three main meals and three snacks (morning, evening, and campfire). Your goal is a healthy and tasty menu. In addition to your menu, prepare a letter to the director explaining how your menu meets the USDA nutritional guidelines. Include a chart showing a breakdown of fat, protein, carbohydrates, vitamins, minerals, and calories for designated portion sizes. Finally, explain how you have tried to make your menu tasty enough for your fellow students to want to eat.

A secondary mathematics teacher surprises his classes with the following announcement at the beginning of a new unit on statistics:

I will allow you to select the measure of central tendency (in other words, mean, median, or mode) by which your quarterly grade will be calculated. As the quarter comes to an end, you will have the opportunity to review your grades for quizzes, tests, a math project, and homework. Then determine which measure of central tendency will be best for your situation. You will write me a note explaining which method you selected and show why it will give you the best mark. If I agree, you will receive that grade.

What did you notice in these two examples? Presumably, you observed that both tasks ask students to apply their learning, and that they require reasoning and not mere recall. Also, you saw that the tasks are contextualized in real-world situations having relevance for the students.

The characteristics of these tasks reflect a fundamental recommendation of UbD (Wiggins & McTighe, 2005)—that teachers set up realistic, authentic contexts for assessment, for it is when students are able to transfer their learning thoughtfully and flexibly that they demonstrate true understanding. An old educational adage applies here: "what we measure signals what we value." When we call for authentic application, we signal to students that we want them to understand the content and be able to transfer their learning thoughtfully and flexibly in realistic situations.

Framing teaching and learning around authentic tasks has at least two benefits. First, the culminating assessments clarify the desired learning results for teachers and students. In other words, the assessments define the evidence that will determine whether or not students have learned the targeted content. By knowing what the culminating assessments will be, students are better able to focus on what teachers expect them to know (for example, what constitutes a balanced diet for healthy eating) and on what they will be expected to do with that knowledge (such as develop a nutritious meal plan).

Please note I am using the term *authentic* here in two senses: (1) authentic to the way in which people outside of school use knowledge and skills (realistic), and (2) authentic to the experiences and interests of the learners (relevant). The most authentic tasks address both connotations of the term, and the two earlier examples are illustrative of this. A second benefit is that presenting an authentic task at the start of a unit provides a meaningful learning goal for students. Such tasks inherently answer those familiar student questions, Why do we have to learn this? and Who ever uses this stuff?

It is worth noting again that students learn the necessary factual knowledge (for example, knowing the food groups and the USDA Food Pyramid recommendations) and skills (such as interpreting nutritional information found on food labels) in the context of accomplishing something genuine, *not* for their own sake.

Consider a sports analogy: coaches of team sports regularly run practice drills intended to develop and refine basic skills. The players, parents, and coaches all realize that these practices are intended to improve individual and team performance in the (authentic) game. While this orientation is the norm in athletics, the arts, and other extracurricular activities, it is not always acted upon in classrooms. Indeed, there is a tendency in academic instruction and assessment for teachers to overemphasize decontextualized practice drills on facts and skills, while offering few if any opportunities for students to actually "play the game" with their knowledge. We regularly ask our students to read the chapter and answer the questions, complete the worksheets, do the odd-numbered problems, learn a formulaic response to open-ended test items, and so on. Yet in the absence of a clear and meaningful performance goal, it should not be a surprise that some students lack motivation or seem satisfied with doing the bare minimum. How many track or cross-country runners would endure endless laps and grueling intervals if they were not trying to lower their times in forthcoming meets? How many nonprofessional basketball players would run repeat 3-on-3 fast breaks or shoot a hundred free throws at practice if they were not interested in improving their scoring in the game?

In other words, this quest for authenticity is not just about coming up with cool tasks. It addresses the fundamental issue of student motivation by presenting meaningful real-world performance goals achieved through purposeful learning.

In addition to the previous two overarching considerations, Wiggins and I suggest that teachers include five elements contained in the acronym WHERE to guide their instruction (Wiggins & McTighe, 2005). These five elements reflect best practices of pedagogy. Let us examine the ideas behind each letter, beginning with an illustrative classroom vignette for each element.

### 3. Let Students Know Where We Are Going, Why This Is Worth Learning, and What Is Expected

*On the first day of a new unit on research skills and research report writing, a middle school language arts teacher describes the expectations and tells students that they can pick a topic of interest (with her approval). She then distributes several examples of student research papers collected from previous years (with student names removed), and asks students to discuss which are the strongest and the reasons why. She then presents the district's rubric for judging research papers, and the students can see that the rubric is consistent with their own analysis of the samples. Throughout the unit, the teacher uses the student examples and the criteria in the rubric to help students better understand the nature of high-quality research and report writing.*

*At the start of a fitness unit, an elementary physical education teacher shows a video of previous years' students demonstrating both skill and enjoyment while jumping rope. She finds that her youngsters are more motivated to try to learn the skill and to practice because they want to be able to jump rope like the students they watched.*

Research and experience underscore a truism in our profession: learners of all ages are more likely to focus their efforts when they can see a clear and worthwhile learning goal. Conversely, when the goal is unclear or irrelevant to the students, it is less likely that they will try their best. At its essence, the "W" in WHERE simply asks teachers to identify *what* is most important to learn (and what is not), *why* it is worth learning (relevance), and *what* is expected (assessment evidence—how successful learning will be determined). Of course, this is common practice in the performance-based teaching areas, such as the arts and career/technical education; however, in academic classrooms it is not uncommon for students not to know the expected performance for a unit (especially when the assessments are kept secure), or even why the targeted knowledge and skills are worth learning.

There are a number of practical actions that teachers can take *at the start* of a new learning segment (such as a unit) to counter this lack of clarity (McTighe & Wiggins, 2004). These include the following:

- Presenting the desired learning results *and* major assessment tasks at the beginning of a unit

- Presenting the rationale for the unit goals, including the long-term benefits of acquiring this knowledge and skill

- Identifying people and places beyond the classroom where this knowledge and these skills are applied

- Asking students to identify personal learning goals related to the unit topic

- Presenting the culminating performance task requirements

- Reviewing the accompanying scoring rubric(s)

- Showing models/exemplars of expected products/performances so learners see what quality looks like

- Involving students in identifying preliminary evaluation criteria

- Posting and discussing essential question(s) as an advance organizer at the start of the unit

- Inviting students to generate questions about the unit topic (such as the "W" in K-W-L)

When students have clarity about the purpose of the targeted learning, the expected assessment evidence, and what quality work looks like, they are better able to see the relevance of learning and are more likely to put forth effort.

### 4. Plan to "Hook and Hold" the Learner's Interest

*As an opener to a new unit on the five senses, a primary grade teacher asks her students to only use their senses of hearing and touch to try to determine what objects she has placed in brown paper bags. The kids listen intently with eyes closed as she shakes each bag. Then they take turns reaching in with one hand to feel the object and excitedly venture guesses about what each object is. Correct guesses are accompanied by loud squeals. This purposeful hook relates directly to one of the unit's essential questions: How can our senses help us understand our world?*

*At the start of a new unit on the Vietnam War, a U.S. history teacher presents his classes with excerpts from a Canadian and a Chinese textbook describing this historical period from different perspectives. The varied accounts immediately raise student questions and link to one of his essential questions for the course: Whose "story" is this?*

Another education adage applies here: "before you can teach them, you have to get their attention." Think back to your own school experiences and recall your most memorable *and* effective teachers. No doubt, the ones you identify were noteworthy in part because they opened a new learning experience in an interesting, thought-provoking, surprising, or unorthodox manner. In all likelihood, their approach was unforgettable because it kindled your interest in a topic, sparked your thinking, or otherwise hooked you.

Thankfully, one need not be a superstar or unconventional teacher to meaningfully engage learners. There are time-honored and proven ways of provoking thought, awakening and sustaining interest, and making learning exciting. Here are some approaches for *hooking* and *holding* students (the "H" in WHERE), especially in the beginning of a new unit or course.

- Present an odd fact, anomaly, or counterintuitive example (for example, note that butterflies taste with their feet or dolphins sleep with one eye open to introduce the big idea of "form and function in nature").

- Present a question related to student interests (for example, ask "Can what you eat help prevent zits?" at the start of a ninth-grade health unit on nutrition).

- Present a challenge (for example, ask, "Which group can create the tallest straw structure with given materials?" and then ask students to generalize about the most supportive structures and the geometric shapes that they contained).

- Present a problem or contemporary issue (for example, ask, "Should our country require compulsory military or social service from citizens eighteen to twenty-four years of age?" as an opener to exploring the big ideas of rights and responsibilities in a democracy).

- Present a simple experiment or demonstration and ask students to predict the outcome (for example, show students various objects and ask which ones will sink and which will float as an introduction to scientific reasoning in the elementary grades).

- Present a mystery (for example, ask students to use logical reasoning to solve a "whodunit" involving various characters, as in the game of Clue).

- Present a role play or simulation (for example, set up an imaginary class government in which a few select students have absolute power and the rest of the class must obey their directives to introduce the concepts of absolute power and checks and balances).

- Present personal experiences (for example, ask, "Have you ever had a friend who let you down? How do you know who your *true* friends are?" at the start of a literature unit exploring the theme of friendship).

- Present students with choices for assignments or projects (for example, allow students to select a book on any topic or theme that they wish, with teacher approval).

- Use emotional connection (for example, show the opening of Ken Burns' documentary on the United States Civil War to introduce the personal toll and horrors of war).

- Use humor (for example, show cartoons and humorous objects depicting exaggerated proportion at the beginning of a unit on ratio and proportion).

Effective teachers are mindful of the importance of trying to engage student interest, especially for topics that may not be inherently motivating to young people. Hooks such as those listed can and should be a part of instructional planning. Of course, we must always keep the end in mind and make sure that our hooks are purposefully linked to the unit goals, and not just engaging activities for their own sake.

### 5. Equip Learners to Come to an Understanding and Successfully Transfer Their Learning

*A high school English teacher facilitates a Socratic seminar to engage her students in a thoughtful interpretation of* The Glass Menagerie. *Initially, the students are passive, waiting for the teacher to confirm their responses. Instead, she continually probes (What in the text led you to that conclusion?) and calls on other students to give their thoughts. Gradually, over the course of the unit, the students become more and more active. On the last day, the teacher removes herself from the literature circle and watches as the students discuss and debate the meaning of the novel on their own.*

*A mathematics teacher has students work in interest groups to develop their own original problems in which recently learned mathematical concepts and skills are applied to various real-life situations. For example, a group of algebra students developed equations to use in calculating costs for different cell phone and text message plans. In geometry, a group of surfing enthusiasts used geometric concepts to plot the optimal starting place on shore based on the distance to the surf break and the prevailing current.*

The first "E" in WHERE reminds us to think about a key instructional question: In what ways will I help students come to understand the big ideas and *equip* them to transfer their learning? If we perceive our job as simply covering content in a textbook, then this question will seem irrelevant. However, if we are teaching for understanding and transfer as the UbD model recommends, the question gets to the heart of the matter.

In order for students to come to an understanding of important ideas, they must be intellectually engaged in constructing meaning, and this requires a much different approach than simply presenting content for rote learning. A number of general approaches have proven effective at actively involving students in meaning making. These include problem-based learning, Socratic seminar, inquiry-oriented mathematics and science programs, primary source (document based) investigations in history, and process writing. In addition to such general methods for developing understanding, Robert Marzano and his colleagues (Marzano, Pickering, & Pollock, 2004) have identified a specific set of research-based active learning techniques, applicable across the curriculum. These include comparing and contrasting, summarizing, creating graphic (nonlinguistic) representations, and cooperative learning.

The logical extension of helping learners acquire knowledge and skills and come to an understanding of important ideas is *transfer*. We want learners to be able to apply their learning on their own to new situations (for example, make sense of a new text, solve an unfamiliar problem, think through a contemporary issue, and express themselves clearly to a target audience). When transfer is the goal, teachers of academic subjects can learn a great deal from the performance-based areas of coaches and teachers in the visual and performing arts. Consider what they *do* to develop and improve autonomous performance. Grant Wiggins and I have identified ten characteristics that we have observed in teaching for transfer (2007):

1. Establish explicit performance targets clearly related to long-term transfer goals.

2. Show models and exemplars for all goals.

3. Design practice and assess progress backward from the ultimate transfer performances.

4. Assess from the start to see where learners are.

5. Devote most of the time together to having learners perform so the coach is freed up to coach.

6. Personalize coaching by being mindful of individual profiles (ability and personality).

7. Provide ongoing feedback and immediate opportunities to use it.

8. Provide just-in-time teaching in small focused doses.

9. Adjust plans in light of unexpected or inappropriate results.

10. Strive to make learners autonomous, thus making self-assessment and self-adjustment a key goal.

Such practices are not restricted to athletics, the arts, and extracurricular activities; they are applicable in any teaching situation in which transfer is the goal.

Thus far, I have discussed facilitative teaching to help students actively make meaning (in other words, come to understand meaning) and coaching for transfer. You might be asking, where then is the place for direct instruction? Of course, there is a role for explicit teaching, especially to help students acquire needed knowledge, skills, and strategies. But direct instruction need not be the starting point, as Bransford et al. (2000) note in *How People Learn*:

> A common misconception regarding "constructivist" theories of knowing is that teachers should never tell students anything directly but instead should always allow them to construct knowledge for themselves. This perspective confuses a theory of pedagogy (teaching) with a theory of knowing. There are times, usually after people have first grappled with issues on their own, that "teaching by telling" can work extremely well. (p. 11)

We can summarize the instructional implications of teaching for understanding and transfer as follows: when the learning goal is to ensure that ideas are understood and misconceptions overcome, *facilitate* active processing of information and student inquiry so that learners *make meaning* for themselves. When the aim is for the learner to *transfer* knowledge and skills to new specific situations, then *coach* for the desired performances. When students need to *acquire* specific knowledge, skill, and strategies (especially in the context of meaningful performance), *direct* instruction is in order (Wiggins & McTighe, 2008).

### 6. Provide Opportunities for Students to Rethink, Revise, and Retry Based on Feedback

*Sixth-grade students are learning watercolor painting techniques. The art teacher models proper technique for mixing and applying the colors, and the students begin working. As they paint, the teacher provides feedback both to individual students and to the class as a whole. She targets common mistakes, such as using too much paint and not enough water, a practice that reduces the desired transparency effect. Benefiting from continual feedback from the teacher, students experiment with the medium on sheets of paper. The next class provides additional opportunities to apply various watercolor techniques to achieve such effects as color blending and soft edges.*

*As a culminating performance task for a high school government course, the teacher has students work in teams to investigate a current issue in the community or state, and then write a letter to a policymaker (such as a city council member or state delegate) advocating a particular position on the issue. He provides students with exemplary letters from previous classes to illustrate the qualities of an effective position paper. Students discuss and debate the issues as a means of helping them clarify their thinking before drafting their letters. The drafts are then circulated among the teams for peer review. The teacher also gives specific feedback on the drafts and provides time for revision before the letters are mailed.*

The "R" in WHERE acknowledges the fact that a learner will rarely achieve in-depth understanding of an abstract idea on the first encounter; rather, the learner will need to *rethink*, *revise*, and *retry*. The phrase *come to an understanding* suggests that comprehension is a process, occurring over time. Similarly, few people can produce a perfect product or flawless performance on the first try. We need feedback and opportunities to retry in order to develop proficiency and achieve quality in our work. Legendary football coach Vince Lombardi once quipped that "feedback is the breakfast of champions." Indeed, in every field of endeavor, feedback is the fuel for continuous improvement.

To serve learning, feedback must meet three criteria: it must be timely, specific, and understandable to the receiver (Wiggins, 1998). Feedback on strengths and weaknesses needs to be "just in time" in order to inform needed adjustments. Waiting two weeks to find out how you did on a test is not likely to help you improve on the tested area, especially if the class has already moved on to a new topic. Students also need specificity to help them understand the areas in which they need to improve. By themselves, grades (such as C+) and scores (such as 92%) fail the specificity test, and are no more helpful than generic comments such as "Good work!" or "Did you try your best?" Although positive remarks and top grades may make a student feel good, they do not advance learning in and of themselves.

Specific feedback sounds different, as in this example from a swimming coach:

> Your arms are relaxing well during the recovery; however, your underwater pull is stopping short so that you are not getting all of the power out of your arm stroke. Make sure that you pull all the way through until you feel your thumb graze your thigh before beginning your recovery.

Accompanied by a brief demonstration, the swimmer now has highly specific information to help his speed in the water.

Of course, it is important to be careful with our language, especially when giving feedback and guidance to younger learners. For instance, instead of saying, "Document your reasoning process," a teacher might say, "Show your work in a step-by-step manner so that a reader can see what you were thinking and follow what you did."

Here is a straightforward test for a feedback system: can a learner tell *specifically* from the given feedback what he or she has done well and what he or she needs to do to improve? If not, then the feedback is not yet specific or understandable enough to help the learner. In addition to timely, specific, and understandable feedback, learners must have the opportunity *and* the expectation to act on it (for example, to revise their explanation, to fine tune their argument, to practice and retry their performance, to rethink their approach to the problem). Providing feedback without a chance to use it is like eating without digesting. It does not make sense to spend time on formative assessments and giving feedback if we do not allow learners time to rethink and revise their work or performance. We need to include time for this—by design. A high school teacher told me that he always builds a "speed bump" into his unit plans to allow for the needed adjustments (such as reteaching, more practice, revision opportunities, and so on) that feedback reveals. He went on to say that he learned this from his experience as an athletic coach. This is not surprising since the essence of coaching involves ongoing assessment and feedback.

We tend to see the best feedback given in the performance-based subjects, such as career/technical education and the arts, and in extracurricular activities, such as drama, chorus, and athletics. Shouldn't feedback be a centerpiece of *every* classroom?

### 7. Encourage Self-Evaluation and Reflection

*Before turning in their science lab reports, students review their work against a list of explicit criteria. On the basis of their self-assessments, a number of students make revisions to improve their reports before handing them in. Their teacher observes that the overall quality of the lab reports has improved since he started requiring students to evaluate their work before submitting it.*

*A middle school mathematics teacher periodically distributes "exit cards" in which he asks students to identify what is working for them in his class and what isn't working. Students complete the cards, which he collects as they leave at the end of the period. He has found that this simple practice has dual benefits: (1) it gives the students an opportunity to reflect on their learning, and (2) it provides him with feedback to use in reflecting on his teaching. In fact, he has made several improvements to his instructional methods as a direct result of these student reflections.*

Research findings in cognitive psychology, reading, and problem solving underscore the importance of metacognition in learning. Metacognition refers to processes by which learners think about their thinking, actively monitor their comprehension (Am I getting the author's meaning here?), employ and evaluate strategies (Is this approach working?), and reflect on their learning and set goals (How can I do better next time?). The second "E" in WHERE reminds us of the importance of regularly *engaging* our students in self-evaluation and reflection.

Metacognition has been characterized as a habit of mind involving an internal dialog or "self-talk" (Costa & Kallick, 2000). While this may occur spontaneously for some students, there is a recognized need to make the "invisible visible" for all learners. Here are ways in which teachers can explicitly cultivate the metacognitive capabilities of their students:

- At the beginning of the year, ask students to develop a personal profile of their strengths and weaknesses as learners (perhaps using a formal learning styles instrument). The students should consider how they learn best, what strategies work well for them, what type of learning is most difficult, and what they wish to improve upon (such as with goal setting). Then, include periodic opportunities for journaling when students can monitor their efforts, think further about their profile, and reflect on their struggles and successes.

- Use "think alouds" to model your own thinking process for your students. It is especially valuable to show them what you do when you are stuck (such as when you do not understand a portion of text or get stuck during problem solving). Let them hear your struggles, your shift of strategy, your evaluation of progress, and so on. As learners become more comfortable with the process, you can ask them to think aloud and share their own thinking.

- Teach students to evaluate the same way that teachers are trained to be judges in Advanced Placement or statewide writing assessment. Ask them to score sample papers so that they will come to understand the meaning of the evaluative criteria and become more accurate as self-assessors.

- Ask students to include a self-assessment for every important product or performance that they produce. This can be easily accomplished when using a rubric or criteria sheet by adding a checkbox for the students to evaluate their work according to the listed elements. (See McTighe & O'Connor, 2005, pp. 15–16.) With practice, students become increasingly capable of honest criterion-based self-assessment.

- Periodically, have students respond to self-reflection questions, such as the following:

  + What do you really understand about _____?

  + What questions/uncertainties do you still have about _____?

  + What was most effective in _____?

  + How could you improve _____?

  + What would you do differently next time?

  + What are you most proud of?

  + What are you most disappointed in?

+ How difficult was _____ for you?

+ What grade/score do you deserve? Why?

+ How has what you've learned changed your thinking?

+ How does what you've learned relate to the present and future?

Noted educator John Dewey once quipped, "We don't learn from experience, we learn by *reflecting* on it." Indeed, the most effective learners self-assess and reflect on their work, set personal learning goals, and employ proven strategies. Teachers help cultivate metacognition through modeling and by expecting students to apply these metacognitive habits regularly.

## Classroom Indicators

This chapter has explored the general instructional implications of the UbD framework and suggested seven associated teaching practices. Let us conclude by considering what we would see in classrooms where these practices are in use.

Over the years, classroom observations have tended to focus on the teacher, often in the form of checklists or descriptors of teacher behaviors. Today, we see a growing emphasis on learner-focused observations in which attention is directed to what the students are doing—that is, the *effects* of the teacher's actions on learners and the learning process. Accordingly, I offer a set of observable indicators (see table 1 on pages 296–298) related to the seven instructional practices for both teachers and learners.

These indicators can be used for self-assessments by teachers, during classroom walk-throughs by school leaders, and as part of an induction/mentoring/coaching program. Of course, the entire list could be overwhelming, especially for a novice teacher or first-time observer. Thus, it makes sense to begin by focusing on a few selected indicators targeted to school priority areas or a teacher's professional growth plan.

**Table 1: Observable Indicators of Suggested Instructional Practices**

| Instructional Practice | The Teacher | The Learners |
|---|---|---|
| 1. Frame content instruction around big ideas and essential questions (EQs). | a. Posts EQs in the classroom<br>b. Actively uses the EQs to frame instruction and learning activities<br>c. Connects specific facts and skills to the big ideas and invites students to make such connections | • Can describe how the EQs relate to the content being studied<br>• Can relate specific facts and skills to the big ideas |
| 2. Frame learning around authentic assessment tasks requiring transfer application. | d. Frames the key learning goals in terms of authentic assessment tasks requiring learners to transfer their learning | • Can explain how the transfer tasks reflect the key learning goals (for example, "By doing _____, I will show that I have learned _____.")<br>• Are engaged by the tasks because of their relevance |
| 3. Help students know where the learning is going, why it is important, and how it will be assessed and evaluated. | e. Presents the learning goals at the start of a new unit or course<br>f. Explains the purpose and relevance of the targeted learning<br>g. Describes the major assessments that will show the extent of student learning<br>h. Presents the evaluative criteria (for example, scoring rubrics) | Can answer the following questions:<br>• What is the main learning goal in this unit?<br>• How will this learning be assessed? Or, How will I show this learning?<br>• How will my work be evaluated or my grade determined?<br>• What are the qualities I am striving for in my work? |

| Instructional Practice | The Teacher | The Learners |
|---|---|---|
| | i. Shows exemplars of quality work along with examples of poor quality so that students can see the differences, and links the examples to the rubric | • How does today's work relate to the unit goal? How does it relate to what we have already learned? |
| 4. Hook and hold student interest. | j. Begins a new instructional segment with a hook to engage student thinking, wonder, interest, emotion<br>k. Uses hooks that directly link to important learning goals (not simply engaging activities) | • Are genuinely hooked and display interest, curiosity, excitement, puzzlement, laughter related to the targeted learning topic<br>• Raise genuine and relevant questions about the topic as a result of the hook |
| 5. Equip learners to come to an understanding and successfully transfer their learning. | l. Facilitates active meaning making on the part of the student<br>m. Shows models of excellent work and expected performance (contrasted with poor examples or weak performances)<br>n. Explicitly teaches needed skills and strategies related to the transfer performances | • Are actively engaged in comparing, summarizing, and generating graphic representations of key ideas<br>• Work in cooperative teams on meaningful tasks<br>• Have opportunities to transfer their learning to relevant situations |
| 6. Provide opportunities for students to Rethink, Revise, and Retry based on feedback. | o. Provides specific and timely feedback in kid-friendly language<br>p. Offers opportunities for students to revise their work, practice and retry a performance, or rethink an initial conception | • Can explain in their own words specifically what they have done well and what needs improvement based on feedback<br>• Take the opportunities to revise, retry, and rethink to improve their performance based on feedback and results |

continued on next page →

**Table 1: Observable Indicators of Suggested Instructional Practices**

| Instructional Practice | The Teacher | The Learners |
|---|---|---|
| 7. Encourage self-evaluation and reflection. | q. Provides regular opportunities for students to self-evaluate their learning process, products, and results<br>r. "Thinks aloud" to model his or her own meta-cognitive processes<br>s. Provides explicit instruction (when needed) on effective self-evaluation processes<br>t. Provides guidance when needed (such as with prompting questions or a rubric)<br>u. Provides opportunities for students to reflect on their learning and set future goals | • Can describe their preferred learning style and how they learn best<br>• Regularly self-evaluate their learning process, products, and results<br>• Reflect on their strengths and weaknesses as learners<br>• Set future learning and performance goals |

## A Model for Engaged and Meaningful Learning

The Understanding by Design (UbD) model provides a curriculum design framework with an emphasis on developing understanding of big ideas and equipping students to apply their learning in realistic contexts. The seven instructional practices described in this chapter align with these goals. Their use makes it more likely that purposeful teaching will yield more engaging and meaningful learning.

## References

Bransford, J., Brown, A., & Cocking, R. (Eds.). (2000). *How people learn: Brain, mind, experience, and school* (Expanded ed.). Washington, DC: National Academies Press.

Costa, A., & Kallick, B. (2000). *Activating and engaging habits of mind.* Alexandria, VA: Association for Supervision and Curriculum Development.

Erickson, L. (1998). *Concept-based curriculum and instruction.* Thousand Oaks, CA: Corwin Press.

Marzano, R., Pickering, D., & Pollock, J. (2004). *Classroom instruction that works.* Alexandria, VA: Association for Supervision and Curriculum Development.

McTighe, J., & O'Connor, K. (2005, November). Seven practices for effective learning. *Educational Leadership, 63*(3), 15–16.

McTighe, J., Seif, E., & Wiggins, G. (2004, September). You *can* teach for meaning. *Educational Leadership, 62*(1), 26–30.

McTighe, J., & Wiggins, G. (2004). *The Understanding by Design professional development workbook.* Alexandria, VA: Association for Supervision and Curriculum Development.

Reeves, D. (2002). *Making standards work.* Englewood, CA: Center for Performance Assessment.

Spady, W. (1994). *Outcome-based education: Critical issues and answers.* Arlington, VA: American Association of School Administrators.

Tyler, R. (1948). *Basic principles of curriculum and instruction.* Chicago: University of Chicago Press.

Wiggins, G. (1998). *Educative assessment: Designing assessments to inform and improve student performance.* San Francisco: Jossey-Bass.

Wiggins, G., & McTighe, J. (2005). *Understanding by design* (Expanded 2nd ed.). Alexandria, VA: Association for Supervision and Curriculum Development.

Wiggins, G., & McTighe, J. (2007). *Schooling by design.* Alexandria, VA: Association for Supervision and Curriculum Development.

Wiggins, G., & McTighe, J. (2008, May). Put understanding first. *Educational Leadership, 65*(8), 36–41.

# Jere Brophy

Jere Brophy, Ph.D., is a University Distinguished Professor of teacher education and educational psychology at Michigan State University. A clinical and developmental psychologist by training, he has conducted research on teachers' achievement expectations and related self-fulfilling prophecy effects, teachers' attitudes toward individual students and the dynamics of teacher-student relationships, students' personal characteristics and their effects on teachers, relationships between classroom processes and student achievement, teachers' strategies for managing classrooms and coping with problem students, and teachers' strategies for motivating students to learn. Most recently, he has focused on curricular content and instructional method issues involved in teaching social studies for understanding, appreciation, and life applications. He is a member of the National Academy of Education.

In this chapter, Dr. Brophy explores what is involved in helping students to become autonomous learners who appreciate the value of school content and learning activities. He addresses two overarching questions: what are potential reasons for students to find particular school content or activities to be valuable, interesting, or intrinsically motivating, and how can teachers develop the content or scaffold engagement in the activities in ways that enable their students to experience and appreciate these motivational benefits?

# Chapter 12

# Cultivating Student Appreciation of the Value of Learning

### Jere Brophy

Lack of motivation is commonly recognized as a significant problem in American education. Politicians and policymakers frequently express concern that American school administrators, teachers, and students are underachieving, and they call for articulating and enforcing higher standards. Teachers often complain of students who could achieve more if they were more motivated. Underachieving students cite boring or irrelevant curriculum for their lack of motivation, and students who drop out most commonly cite lack of motivation—not lack of ability to succeed—as their primary reason for leaving school.

There is a curious disconnect between formulations of the problem and attempts at solution. Despite widespread student complaints of a meaningless and irrelevant curriculum, reform efforts have focused on pressuring students to work harder, not on improving the curriculum. They also have focused on producing *controlled motivation*—using threats and sanctions to compel desired behavior; however, research shows that better motivation and learning can be expected when learning contexts support *autonomous motivation*—when students engage in learning activities willingly because they see good reasons for doing so. This chapter explores what is involved in helping students to become autonomous learners who appreciate the value of school content and learning activities.

## Motivation in Classrooms: The Big Picture

Three categories subsume most of the issues involved in classroom motivation. First is the *social context*, the classroom climate. Second are the students' *performance expectations* for learning activities (for example, What are my chances for succeeding here? How can I protect my reputation if I fail?). Third is the *value* students place on particular school content or learning activities (for example, Why should I care about this? What will I get out of it?).

All three categories are important, but there has been much more research on social context and performance expectation than on value. Research on social context has established the importance of socializing students to function as a collegial learning community in which they feel that they belong; enjoy a sense of well being because their basic needs for autonomy, competence, and relationships are being met; and focus on pursuing learning goals rather than seeking to impress or compete with their classmates (Ames, 1990; Brophy, 2004; Davis, 2001; Reeve & Jang, 2006; VanSteenkiste, Lens, & Deci, 2006). Research on performance expectations has established that the content and learning activities should be at an optimal level of difficulty (neither too easy nor too hard), and the teacher should orient students toward attributing their learning progress to personally controllable factors (concentration, effort, persistence), developing positive self-efficacy perceptions, and viewing their abilities as incrementally improvable rather than fixed and limited (Dweck, 1999; Pajares, 1996; Whitley & Frieze, 1985).

These principles are useful, but except for difficulty level, they do not identify aspects of curricular content or learning activities that might affect students' appreciation of their value. Students might be comfortable, confident, and ready to learn, yet they may be wondering about a learning activity's purpose, and in particular, what benefits or satisfactions they will derive from engaging in the activity and accomplishing its goals.

Even the theory and research developed to date on value do not take us far in addressing these issues. Expectancy-value theorists have established that willingness to engage in an activity voluntarily requires both possessing good reason for doing so (valuing the activity or its outcomes) and believing that one can accomplish the activity's goals (success expectancy) (Wigfield & Eccles, 2000). Interest theorists have established that individuals tend to engage productively in activities that they find interesting (Hidi & Renninger, 2006). Intrinsic-motivation theorists have established that better motivation and learning can be expected when learners engage autonomously in self-chosen activities rather than when their task engagement is externally coerced and regulated (VanSteenkiste, Lens, & Deci, 2006). These findings are helpful, but they do not address two basic value questions facing curriculum makers and teachers:

- What are potential reasons for students to find particular school content or activities to be valuable, interesting, or intrinsically motivating?

- How can teachers develop the content or scaffold engagement in the activities in ways that enable their students to experience and appreciate these motivational benefits?

## Some Useful Theory

In my own efforts to address these questions, I have found several theoretical models and conceptual distinctions useful.

### Autonomous Motivation

Self-determination theory distinguishes among the following forms of behavioral regulation:

1.  External regulation occurs when our actions are regulated by external rewards, pressures, or constraints (students engage in lessons or assignments solely because they will be rewarded if they do or punished if they do not).

2.  Introjected regulation occurs when we act as we do because we think we should or would feel guilty if we did not (students engage primarily because if they do not, they will get poor grades and disappoint their parents).

3.  Identified regulation occurs when we adopt an activity or goal as personally important and valuable to us (students engage primarily because they view the learning activities as important for their self-selected goal of gaining admittance to college or a particular occupation).

4.  Intrinsic motivation occurs when our actions are experienced as wholly self-determined and performed out of interest or intrinsic motivation (students engage because they find the content interesting or the activity enjoyable).

External regulation and introjected regulation are considered *controlled* forms of motivation, whereas identified regulation and intrinsic motivation are considered *autonomous* forms. Autonomous motivation is associated with better cognitive and affective outcomes. When students are autonomously motivated to engage with school content, they do not require external sanctions or pressures; they engage voluntarily because they see good reasons for doing so (VanSteenkiste, Lens, & Deci, 2006).

### Subjective Task Value

The concept of subjective task value subsumes four major components (Eccles & Wigfield, 2002):

1.  Attainment value is the importance of doing well in order to affirm our self-concept or fulfill our needs (such as for achievement, power, or prestige).

2. Intrinsic or interest value is the enjoyment that we get from engaging in the activity or the interest we have in the content.

3. Utility value is the role that engaging in the activity may play in helping us to achieve current or future goals, such as career goals.

4. Cost is any negative aspect of engaging in the task (such as anxiety), as well as the time, effort, or other resources required to complete it successfully.

Subjective task value is a key concept in *expectancy x value theory*. This theory postulates that voluntary engagement in a task (such as a learning activity) requires both sufficient valuing of the task (seeing it as worthwhile) and sufficient confidence in one's ability to meet its demands (success expectancy). Subjective task value is determined by weighing the anticipated benefits (attainment, intrinsic, or utility value) of task engagement against its anticipated costs (time, effort, and foregone opportunity to engage in an alternative task).

### Eudaimonic Pleasures

Waterman (2005) has distinguished between two forms of enjoyment that may be derived from activities: hedonic and eudaimonic. *Hedonic* pleasures can be experienced through simple participation, without engaging in effortful or goal-oriented action sequences. Examples include dining at a restaurant, watching television, or window shopping at a mall. *Eudaimonic* pleasures result from sustained goal-oriented efforts, especially during activities that challenge us to realize our potentials. Examples include rock climbing, composing music, acting on stage, and writing computer code.

Experiences of flow or of personal expressiveness are two common forms of eudaimonic pleasure. Flow experiences occur when we become completely absorbed in activities. They are associated with a balance between challenges and skills. Feelings of personal expressiveness are associated with opportunities to experience self-realization (especially during identity-related activities that allow us to express our "daimon"—our true self). Some activities offer only the potential for hedonic pleasures, but others offer the potential for both hedonic and eudaimonic pleasures.

### Big Ideas and Authentic Activities

Harking back to concepts introduced by John Dewey, contemporary investigators have been documenting positive motivational outcomes associated with the combination of powerful ideas and authentic activities (Mitchell, 1993; Pugh, 2002; Pugh & Girod, 2007). Dewey spoke of transformative experiences that occur when we learn a powerful idea that enables us to see some aspect of the world in a new way, such that we find new meaning in it and value the experience. For example, if students explore in depth the concept of biological adaptation, they may begin to notice aspects of the appearance and behavior of animals that they did not notice before, causing them to benefit more from activities such as trips to the zoo, and so on. When developed with emphasis on their connections and applications, powerful ideas provide the basis for *authentic activities* that allow students to apply what they are learning to their lives outside of school. The most fully authentic activities involve using school learning for accomplishing the same sorts of life applications that justify inclusion of this learning in the curriculum in the first place (Brophy, 2004).

### Setting the Stage for Motivation to Learn

Motivated learning of school content is purposeful engagement in learning activities with the goal of realizing their intended outcomes—not just doing what is necessary to earn acceptable grades. When motivated to learn, students seek to understand, retain, and use what they acquire in a learning situation because they believe that it is worthwhile to do so; in other words, students value the learning because they recognize it is enriching or empowering.

If students are motivated to learn in this manner, it is likely because they view the content or learning activity as interesting or enjoyable (intrinsically valuable) or as important and worth learning for some other good reason (having attainment or utility value). Consequently, their motivation is primarily autonomous rather than controlled. Furthermore, it is likely that the content is structured around powerful ideas and applied during activities that are both authentic and rich in potential for experiencing flow, self-expression, or other eudaimonic satisfactions (not just hedonic pleasures).

In summary, to support autonomously motivated learning, we need to make sure that there is at least one good reason to learn each knowledge network that we teach, and develop the network in such a way that students can appreciate its value. Otherwise, we will have to rely on rewards and punishments, introjected forms of achievement motivation, or other controlled motivation pressures likely to produce compliance with task demands, but not motivated learning.

## A Model of Motivated School Learning

Autonomously motivated school learning is not the same as intrinsic motivation, which usually is defined with emphasis on hedonic pleasures described in affective terms (fun, enjoyment, excitement, and so on). This affective language is suitable for analyses of motivation during play or recreational activities, but not for motivated learning that requires sustained, goal-oriented effort. The bases for autonomously motivated school learning are more cognitive than affective and more eudaimonic than hedonic. They typically involve either enrichment (via enhanced understandings) or empowerment (via newly acquired action capacities). Rather than *pleasure* or *fun*, they are better described using terms such as *absorption, satisfaction, recognition, making meaning, self-expression, self-realization, making connections, achieving insights, aesthetic appreciation*, and so on.

In everyday language, we commonly speak of engaging in intrinsically motivated activities "for their own sake." This is not true. We do not engage in valued activities for *their* sake; we do it for *our* sake—because we derive pleasure, satisfaction, or some other valued benefit from doing so. As subjective human experience, motivation resides in people, not objects or activities; however, school content domains and learning activities do possess affordances for human activities, and these affordances carry motivational implications for people who engage in the activities.

The potential for valuing school learning lies in the affordances it offers to students. The most notable of these affordances are (1) the insights and understandings that come from the big ideas that anchor content networks, and (2) the information-processing, problem-solving, and decision-making opportunities that stem from activities designed to develop and apply these big ideas. If a curriculum strand has significant value for students, it will be because its content network is structured around big ideas that provide a basis for authentic applications to life outside of school. This implies the need to structure curricula around big ideas and authentic activities, because these two curricular components provide learning activities that students are most likely to value (for their enrichment satisfactions and empowerment benefits).

Note that this argument is not just another call for making curriculum and instruction more relevant to students. It does include recognition of the motivational value of connecting with students' current interests and agendas, but it does not begin with the students. Instead, it begins with curricular aims, purposes, and goals. It calls for articulating the knowledge, skills, values, dispositions, and appreciations that are intended as outcomes of particular content strands, then asking how these strands might be represented and how students' learning of them might be scaffolded in ways that encourage realization of the intended outcomes. Fundamentally, it focuses on crafting curriculum and instruction to scaffold students' development toward those outcomes, not limiting curriculum and instruction to cater to students' current interests and agendas. Furthermore, it emphasizes that intended outcomes include changes in the motivational aspects of learning (such as inducing students not just to acquire the desired knowledge and skills but to appreciate their value).

Teaching for appreciation is very different from "making learning fun" and similar hedonic prescriptions. It clarifies and scaffolds attainment of aims and purposes, emphasizing outcomes of enrichment or empowerment (not hedonic pleasure). It involves doing something "minds on" with the content (processing, reacting, applying, and so on), but this need not involve activities that are "hands on." Making sure that students experience the intended benefits or satisfactions is the key.

## What Will It Take to Accomplish This?

The implications of this analysis are straightforward, at least in theory: make sure that there is good reason for requiring students to learn each knowledge network that we teach, and develop the network in such a way that students can appreciate its value. This agenda is easy to articulate but difficult to carry out, however, for several reasons.

First, curricular purposes, goals, and intended outcomes are seldom clarified by or for educators at any level, including standards setters, curriculum makers, and teachers. Aims and purposes are usually phrased in relatively abstract and remote terms that are far removed from the classroom activities scheduled on a given day, so it can be difficult to connect a given lesson or learning activity to the big picture. Meanwhile, the teachers' editions of textbooks usually do not have much to say about purposes and goals. Instructions to teachers emphasize content coverage and activity procedures, but not learning goals phrased as intended outcomes.

In their planning, teachers typically focus on making sure that they understand what they will need to do in order to implement the lesson or activity, with little or no attention to its purpose or goals. Similarly, when they do implement the lesson or activity, they usually focus on making sure that students know what to do and how to do it, with little or no attention to why they are doing it or what they will get out of it. Consequently, both teachers and students commonly engage in lessons or learning activities without any sense of purpose beyond meeting requirements (Brophy, 2004; Clark & Petersen, 1986).

Even if teachers are aware of the importance of establishing purposes and goals, they may have difficulty doing so. As John Dewey and others have pointed out, most school content originated as practical knowledge derived through situational problem solving, but as content was systematized within what became the disciplines, it got formulated more abstractly and separated from its situated origins (Hansen, 2006). Consequently, for much of what we teach in school, especially the more abstract content and higher order processes, the reasons for learning it are not obvious to students, and sometimes not even to teachers.

### The Need for Curriculum Reform

People assume that the curriculum reflects consensus beliefs about what is important for young people to learn—that it empowers students with knowledge, skills, and dispositions that enable them to function effectively in modern society. However, current curricula have been described as "mile wide but inch deep," "trivial pursuit," or "a parade of facts"—not structured around powerful ideas. Furthermore, even when a content strand does have significant potential value, it may be taught in a way that is too abstract or otherwise ineffective to enable students to appreciate it. With respect to its potential for student appreciation, curricular content might be classified within one of five categories:

1.  Content that has value that students already recognize and appreciate

2. Content that has value that is recognized by curriculum makers and teachers and could be taught in ways that lead students to appreciate its value

3. Content that has value that is recognized by curriculum makers and teachers, but the potential for appreciating it lies beyond the students' current capacities

4. Content that has potential value and could be appreciated by students (at least at certain grade levels), but curriculum makers and teachers currently cannot articulate this value clearly enough to enable them to represent it effectively in instructional materials or scaffold students' appreciation of it during teaching

5. Content that lacks significant value (and therefore does not belong in the curriculum)

I believe that much of what is in current school curricula lacks sufficient justification. We often hear that "learning is its own reward," but this saying assumes that there is good reason for the learning. I submit that there is no good reason for students to learn a lot of the specialized vocabulary, unnecessary detail, and sheer trivia that is included in most school curricula, nor for engaging in activities such as alphabetizing the state capitals. We need to prune this kind of pointless content from the curriculum.

I also believe that much of the school curriculum fits into the fourth category: it does have potential value, but we have lost sight of the reasons for including it. We need to rediscover and articulate the life-application bases for retaining this content and teach it accordingly.

### The Need to Cultivate Students' Content Appreciation

Even if curricula were perfected to the point that all content had significant life-application value, another significant challenge would remain: many of the activities that this content affords serve purposes and goals that are not well represented in popular ideas about motivation. When we talk about motivation, we typically refer to *fun, pleasure, enjoyment,* or *excitement.* These terms and the images they suggest are well suited to recreational activities but not to activities focused on acquiring and using school content.

Even when we talk about the value of school content, we tend to talk about immediate, direct, and specific applications rather than more generic but less obvious applications. It is relatively easy to interest students in topics that most people find captivating or exciting, to whet their anticipation of activities that most people find fun, or to enable them to see the utility value in knowledge or skills that have straightforward applications (for example, the utility of learning to read, write, or swim is obvious to almost everyone). However, it can be challenging to enable students to recognize and appreciate the value of many aspects of the curriculum, especially in the humanities and social sciences.

Instead of physical thrills, basic emotional reactions, or immersion in multisensory overload, the potentially motivating experiences that occur during acquisition and use of school content are primarily cognitive (achieving insights, making connections, and so on). These experiences can come to be very compelling and highly valued, but they usually do not emerge spontaneously upon mere exposure to school content or involvement in learning activities.

Subjective motivational experiences are not observable, so teachers will need to develop the schema networks that make them possible. Doing so will require combinations of explanation, cognitive modeling (verbalizing the thinking that guides autonomously motivated acquisition and use of the content), and scaffolding of students' engagement in worthwhile activities in ways that help the students to recognize and exploit their potential.

It is commonly said of some learning experiences that students "don't appreciate it now, but they will when they get older." I am arguing that this idea is misguided, that the curriculum at a given grade level should feature content that students can learn with appreciation of its value right now. I am also suggesting, however, that scaffolding such appreciation is challenging because it must rely on sources of motivation that are not familiar to the general public and may take a lot of time and effort to develop, even by teachers who have clear ideas about what to develop and how to scaffold it.

At least three steps probably are involved in helping students to recognize and exploit the affordances of K–12 content:

1. Develop good curriculum—Make wise choices about what content and learning activities to include, to ensure that what students are asked to learn is worth learning.

2. Use lesson framing—Introduce lessons in ways that include explaining the value and modeling applications of the big ideas or skills to be developed.

3. Scaffold appreciation—Engage students in activities that give them opportunities to develop and apply content through firsthand experience in ways that enable them to discover the content's value. Scaffold their engagement to help students notice and appreciate the enriching or empowering value of the activity.

## Teaching for Appreciation

Optimally mediated learning experiences raise students' consciousness of the purposes and goals of each activity, thus enabling them to learn not only with understanding but with appreciation and life application. *Appreciation* connotes that students do not merely understand what they are learning but value it because they realize that there are good reasons for learning it. These reasons may include not only empowering practical applications, but ways that the learning might enrich the students' repertoires of insights and recognitions or otherwise enhance the quality of their inner lives. *Life application* requires that students experience authentic activities that will enable them to apply what they are learning to their lives outside of school. Students without much prior knowledge about or development of schemas for exploiting the affordances of a learning domain (drama, for example) cannot generate much appreciation for it because they are unable to see its potential. Lacking knowledge of concepts (for example, foreshadowing) and strategies (such as analyzing plot developments and making predictions based on them) to guide their information processing, they are not yet able to experience many of the insights and satisfactions that the domain offers.

Teachers can mediate the motivated learning of such students through modeling, coaching, and scaffolding processes. Good modeling conveys not only the strategies needed to meet the demands of an activity but also the aesthetic experiences, personal satisfactions, celebrations of new insights, pleasures taken in familiar recognitions, and other manifestations of what it looks and feels like to engage in the activity with appreciation and motivation to learn. When modeling response to a play being studied in class, for example, teachers might make connections between characterization and plot elements depicted in the play and parallel elements in their own life experiences, or put themselves in the place of key characters and model thinking about how they might handle the characters' dilemmas, and so on. Such modeling helps students begin to understand the kinds of worthwhile experiences that await them if they pursue the domain.

Teachers' coaching should include instruction, cues, and feedback about correctness of responses, but should also convey enthusiasm for the activity, help students to experience the satisfactions that it offers, and stimulate appreciation of the nature and progress of their learning. For example, coaching might cue students to think about key aspects of the personalities or motives of the characters in a play, compliment them on the insights they have developed about these characters, or invite them to speculate about what these insights portend about the resolution of the drama or tell us about what the author was saying about the human condition.

Appreciation-oriented scaffolding begins with (1) selecting appropriate learning activities in which to engage students in the first place, then following through by (2) introducing these activities in ways that inform students about their purposes and about what the students can expect to get out of them, (3) providing coaching that includes making statements or asking questions that draw students' attention to the aspects of the learning experience from which they can take satisfaction (for example, helping students to appreciate the activity's affordances), and (4) providing feedback that stimulates students to recognize and appreciate their developing expertise and perhaps identify interests or talents they might pursue further. Such scaffolding communicates in subtle ways the notion that learners are not only doing something worthwhile, but doing it in ways that represent seriousness of purpose, growth in knowledge or craftsmanship, and aesthetic qualities that reflect their individuality.

Scaffolding school content in this manner is crucial for optimizing individual students' motivation. When developed effectively, reading and writing are not just basic skills needed for utilitarian applications, but gateways to interest development, identity exploration, self-expression, and other enrichments to individuals' subjective lives. Similarly, basic geographical, historical, social, and scientific understandings are not isolated bits of inert knowledge but key components of schema networks that students can use to understand and respond to the social and physical world. Well-developed school content not only has narrowly construed utilitarian value (helping people to meet their basic needs and wants), but enriches the quality of their lives by expanding and helping them to articulate their subjective experiences.

For example, a study of mathematics learners found that mathematics majors and nonmajors had similar perceptions of basic mathematical principles and procedures, but the mathematics majors reported more enjoyment of the subject (its rigor and precision, timelessness, abstraction, and unique challenges), more appreciation of its beauty (the elegance of mathematical arguments or proofs, the way that mathematical ideas develop and build on one another, the interrelatedness of its concepts), and more engagement in mathematical activities for recreational purposes (enjoying mathematical games and puzzles, reading about the lives of famous mathematicians) (Meyer & Eley, 1999). All school subjects offer these kinds of opportunities for motivated learning that lead to personal benefits and satisfaction, but these affordances are not likely to be realized unless students are engaged with worthwhile content and their learning is scaffolded accordingly.

## Next Steps

To support this kind of teaching, educators will need to progress much further in articulating which aspects of school content are most worth learning, what makes them worth learning, and how teachers can scaffold students' appreciation of their value. In the meantime, we might go a long way toward ensuring attention to this gap by reviving a practice that was common early in the twentieth century: including *appreciations*—why what is being taught is worth learning—as an intended outcome of instruction, along with knowledge, skills, and dispositions. This would help to ensure that appreciation goals are addressed routinely during instructional planning. It also would serve as a reminder to standards setters, curriculum makers, and teachers that indeed there should be good reasons for teaching each content strand, and that strands should be developed in ways that enable students to appreciate their value.

## References

Ames, C. (1990). Motivation: What teachers need to know. *Teachers College Record, 91,* 409–421.

Brophy, J. (2004). *Motivating students to learn* (2nd ed.). Mahwah, NJ: Erlbaum.

Clark, C., & Peterson, P. (1986). Teachers' thought processes. In M. C. Wittrock (Ed.), *Handbook of research on teaching* (3rd ed., pp. 225–296). New York: Macmillan.

Davis, H. (2001). The quality and impact of relationships between elementary school children and teachers. *Contemporary Educational Psychology, 26,* 431–453.

Dweck, C. (1999). *Self-theories: Their role in motivation, personality, and development.* Philadelphia: Taylor & Francis.

Eccles, J., & Wigfield, A. (2002). Motivational beliefs, values, and goals. *Annual Review of Psychology, 53,* 109–132.

Hansen, D. (2006). Dewey's book of the moral self. In D. Hansen (Ed.), *John Dewey and our educational prospect: A critical engagement with Dewey's Democracy and Education* (pp. 165–188). Albany: State University of New York Press.

Hidi, S., & Renninger, K. A. (2006). The four-phase model of interest development. *Educational Psychologist, 41,* 111–127.

Meyer, J., & Eley, M. (1999). The development of affective subscales to reflect variation in students' experiences of studying mathematics in higher education. *Higher Education, 37,* 197–216.

Mitchell, M. (1993). Situational interest: Its multifaceted structure in the secondary school mathematics classroom. *Journal of Educational Psychology, 85,* 424–436.

Pajares, F. (1996). Self-efficacy beliefs in academic settings. *Review of Educational Research, 66,* 543–578.

Pugh, K. (2002). Teaching for transformative experiences in science: An investigation of the effectiveness of two instructional elements. *Teachers College Record, 104,* 1101–1137.

Pugh, K., & Girod, M. (2007). Science, art, and experience: Constructing a science pedagogy from Dewey's aesthetics. *Journal of Research in Science Teacher Education, 18,* 9–27.

Reeve, J., & Jang, H. (2006). What teachers say and do to support students' autonomy during a learning activity. *Journal of Educational Psychology, 98,* 209–218.

VanSteenkiste, M., Lens, W., & Deci, E. (2006). Intrinsic versus extrinsic goal contents in self-determination theory: Another look at the quality of academic motivation. *Educational Psychologist, 41,* 19–31.

Waterman, A. (2005). When effort is enjoyed: Two studies of intrinsic motivation for personally salient activities. *Motivation and Emotion, 29,* 165–188.

Whitley, B., & Frieze, I. (1985). Children's causal attributions for success and failure in achievement settings: A meta-analysis. *Journal of Educational Psychology, 77,* 608–616.

Wigfield, A., & Eccles, J. (2000). Expectancy-value theory of achievement motivation. *Contemporary Educational Psychology, 25,* 68–81.

# Harvey F. Silver
# Matthew J. Perini

Harvey F. Silver, Ed.D., is president of Silver Strong & Associates and Thoughtful Education Press and was named one of the 100 most influential teachers in the country. He has conducted numerous workshops for school districts and state education departments throughout the United States. He was the principal consultant for the Georgia Critical Thinking Skills Program and the Kentucky Thoughtful Education Teacher Leadership Program. Dr. Silver is the author of several educational bestsellers and creator of *The Thoughtful Classroom*, a renowned professional development program.

Matthew J. Perini, M.A., is director of publishing for Silver Strong & Associates and Thoughtful Education Press. He has authored books, curriculum guides, articles, and research studies on a wide range of topics, including learning styles, multiple intelligences, and effective teaching practices.

In this chapter, Silver and Perini seek to answer three questions: What exactly is student engagement? What is the value of this engagement? And how can we actively engage students in learning? The authors take a close look at the roles that learning styles and instructional design can play in helping create highly engaging classrooms.

## Chapter 13

# The Eight Cs of Engagement: How Learning Styles and Instructional Design Increase Student Commitment to Learning

Harvey F. Silver and Matthew J. Perini

Every day, in every one of the United States' 14,000 plus school districts and in the majority of our 3 million plus classrooms, a small to mid-size miracle occurs. It begins when teachers lead discussions, deliver lectures, organize discovery labs, initiate practice sessions, and conduct student conferences. The success of these activities depends on the work, participation, and effortful engagement of students. Much of this work is challenging, some is necessarily a little tedious, and almost none of it resembles the activities students choose for themselves during the 185 days a year when they are not in school. And yet—here comes the miracle part—students by and large do participate, perhaps with less enthusiasm and more sarcasm than we would like, but often with grace and determination.

Since the mid- to late-1990s, student engagement has become an increasingly important issue among the research community, but teachers have always had engagement near the top of their list of concerns. In fact, the critics most likely to question teachers' power of engagement are none other than the teachers themselves. Our experience in working with teachers for nearly forty years suggests hardly a car rolls out of the school parking lot without a teacher replaying a moment, brooding over a lesson or a student, or wondering how she might engage her students in greater depth so that they might think, achieve, or just plain see "something more" the next time. This chapter is about that something more. In it, we seek answers to the following three questions:

1. What exactly is engagement?

2. What is the value of engagement?

3. How can we actively engage students in learning?

In answering this third question, we will take a close look at the roles that learning styles and instructional design can play in helping create the something more that is at work in all highly engaging classrooms.

## What Is Engagement?

Over the years, we have asked thousands of teachers to describe this "more," this consequence of greater student engagement. Their lists have proved to be remarkably consistent. Below are ten of the most common responses from teachers.

If students were more engaged, they would . . .

- Show more initiative
- Stay focused and on task
- Pay attention
- Ask more questions
- Take more risks
- Find their own mistakes
- Develop their own ideas and perspectives

- Do their homework
- Take time to think
- Show more excitement

Teachers are usually able to step back from these lists and organize their thoughts into rubric-like ladders showing levels of student engagement—what they are looking for in student engagement and what they would prefer to avoid. For example, figure 1 (page 323) shows an engagement rubric developed by a group of teachers from Upstate New York.

Does the rubric in figure 1 clarify what we mean by engagement? Yes, and no. Certainly the rubric gives us a clearer picture of what engagement looks like in the classroom. But engagement is a little like art: you might know it when you see it, but you have a much harder time coming up with a reliable definition. Even the research on engagement shows a kind of conceptual slipperiness, as terms like *participation*, *attention*, *interest*, and *on-task behavior* all seem to be used interchangeably throughout the literature.

This brings us to our next task, and we pursue it with insight derived from the great twentieth-century philosopher Ludwig Wittgenstein. Wittgenstein told us that a word's meaning is not found in its formal definition, but in its use. So we listened to Ludwig. We collected different uses and variations of the term *engage* from everyday life. We did not consult any scholarly journals. Over a two-week period, we recorded nearly fifty-five occurrences of the term just by keeping our eyes and ears open—and by tapping into a few old memories as well. The following are some of our favorites:

- "I'm terribly worried about her, she seems so . . . disengaged."

  —Worried parent of a teenager
- "I'll tell you what engagement doesn't mean. It doesn't mean agreement."

—Political spokesperson on CNN debating establishing diplomatic relations with Cuba

- "Make sure brain is fully engaged before putting mouth in gear."

  —Popular 1970s bumper sticker

- "The board has engaged a young architect who has some interesting ideas about how to handle the mobile classroom situation."

  —School board member

- "Distentic contribulator"
  "Engaged"
  "Fortronic capacitator"
  "Engaged"

  —Old science fiction movie (dialogue approximated)

- "Annie Sullivan was the model of a totally engaged teacher."

  —C-SPAN book talk

- engage.com

  —Website that relies on user voting to make dating suggestions

All these mixed and varied uses of the term *engage* raised an obvious question for us: what do distracted teenagers, diplomatic relationships, mechanisms on a spaceship, and dating websites have in common? Our first answer was *connection*. After all, each of these examples involves subjects that are engaged to, with, or in something beyond themselves. Consulting an etymological dictionary got us a little closer to solving the mystery of engagement: *engage* is from the Old French *engagier*—to pledge. Engagement is something like a promise. And then—as it has a way of doing—life put it all together for us when Harvey's daughter announced she was engaged. That's when we finally got it. Engagement is more than a connection, more than a verbal promise. Engagement means *commitment*. This is our

**Deep Engagement:** Students take full ownership of learning activities, displaying high levels of energy, a willingness to ask questions, pursue answers, consider alternatives, and take risks in pursuit of quality.

**Engagement:** Students begin taking ownership of learning activities. Their involvement shows concentration and effort to understand and complete the task. They do not simply follow directions but actively work to improve the quality of their performance.

**Active Compliance:** Students participate in learning activities and stay on task without teacher intervention. However, their work has a routine or rote quality, and significant thought or commitment to quality is not evident.

**Passive Compliance:** Students follow directions in a rote or routine manner. They may be mildly distracted and thus may need some added teacher attention or direction to remain on task.

**Periodic Compliance:** Students' attention and participation fluctuate. They appear distractible and stall out easily when questions emerge. May require significant teacher attention and direction.

**Resistance:** Students appear "blocked"—unable or unwilling to participate in learning activities. May require classroom management procedures or redesign of learning activities.

**Figure 1: Rubric showing levels of student engagement.**

something more. Commitment—this is what we are looking for from our students, and you will notice that both the teachers' list of "mores" and their rubric described the signs of this commitment nicely: concentrated thought and effort, self-questioning, and an investment in quality. Sounds good, but it leads to our second question: is engagement up to the job? In other words, how much value does it really have in the classroom?

## The Value of Engagement: What the Research Tells Us

Considering what we already know from listening to teachers, the research on student engagement should come as no surprise. Engaging classrooms, however they are defined in a particular study, lead invariably to gains in student achievement. In surveying the field, Fredericks, Blumenfeld, and Paris (2004) found that engagement correlates with higher levels of academic achievement and greater persistence on the part of students. In a more recent meta-analysis compiling the results from over seventy-five separate studies, Robert Marzano (2007) shows that students in highly engaging classrooms outperform their peers by an average of almost 30 percentile points. "Arguably," Marzano concludes, "keeping students engaged is one of the most important considerations for the classroom teacher" (p. 98).

The benefits of engagement go beyond grades and achievement scores. For example, a recent Michigan State University observational study of middle school teachers (Raphael, Pressley, & Mohan, 2008) showed that teachers who used a wide variety of techniques and strategies to engage students experienced almost no behavioral problems in their classrooms: "misbehaviors . . . were so rare in the highly motivating, engaging classrooms that we leave this study still not certain what the consequation policies were in any of the three highly engaging classrooms" (p. 53). This contrasts with classrooms defined as "low engaging" where it took "at least 10–15 minutes to begin class, which was often delayed further by behavioral disturbances" (p. 45).

The reasoning behind all of this is simple: if we do not design lessons and units that will strengthen students' commitment to learn, then we cannot expect them to take an active or in-depth approach to learning. In other words, if we fail to take student engagement seriously, then the best we can hope for from our students is superficial learning. And as Raphael et al. (2008) suggest, it is entirely reasonable to expect much worse.

This brings us to our third and final question: how do we actively engage students in our classrooms? Or, put into terms that align with our new understanding of engagement, how can we better earn the commitment to learn from all of our students?

## Engagement Through the Lens of Learning Styles: The Eight Cs of Student Engagement

For over thirty-five years, we have been working with teachers, administrators, and their schools to help them differentiate instruction and address the needs of diverse learners. At the heart of this work has been a learning-styles model deeply influenced by the father of analytical psychology, Carl Jung (1923), and his groundbreaking theory of psychological types, which emerged from his observations on how people perceive and process information. What Jung discovered is that much apparently random human behavior is not actually random. People tend to develop clear preferences for certain kinds of behaviors and ways of thinking, or personality types. Years later, Katherine Briggs and Isabel Myers expanded on Jung's work to develop a comprehensive model of human differences embodied by their world-famous Myers-Briggs Type Indicator (1962/1998). We have adapted the work of these giants in psychology to the specific educational context of teaching and learning, and over the years we have refined our learning styles model to make it as practical and teacher-friendly as possible. Out of this work, we have identified four styles of learners (Silver, Strong, & Perini, 2000):

- A *mastery* style that learns step by step and focuses on the practical

- An *understanding* style that learns by questioning and analyzing

- A *self-expressive* style that learns through innovation and imagination

- An *interpersonal* style that learns socially and by following personal feelings

As an extension of this work, we began investigating the relationship between learning styles and student engagement (Strong, Silver, Perini, & Tuculescu, 2003; Strong, Silver, & Robinson, 1995). We pursued this relationship between styles and engagement with the intent of helping teachers deepen their awareness of four natural human drives (fig. 2) that are the root sources of motivation for each style of learner.

| Mastery Learners . . . | Interpersonal Learners . . . |
|---|---|
| are driven by *success.* They delight in developing new competencies and mastering skills that will earn the respect of others. | are driven by *relationships.* They long to interact with others, and they hope that their work is of value and interest to themselves and others. |
| **Understanding Learners . . .** | **Self-Expressive Learners . . .** |
| have a drive to *make sense of things.* This drive appears in their tendency to question, their love of puzzles, their passion for new ideas, and their sensitivity to flaws and gaps in logic. | are driven by *originality.* They long to be unique, to have their differences acknowledged, and to express those kernels within themselves that belong to them and no one else. |

**Figure 2: The four human drives at the root of nearly all learning style models.**

Since then, we have continued this investigation by using the *Learning Style Inventory for Students* (Silver & Strong, 2004) and teacher observations to identify students who show a particularly strong preference for each of the four styles. Then, through interviews with the students and their teachers, classroom observations, and analysis of the work students produced, we were able to identify a set of reliable motivators, or "levers" that teachers could pull to engage the drives that are indigenous to each of the four styles. We call these motivators the "Eight Cs of Student Engagement," and they are identified in figure 3.

So how do we use the Eight Cs of Student Engagement to increase our students' commitment to learning? Here are some quick ideas to get you started.

| We can engage Mastery Learners' drive to succeed through . . . | We can engage Interpersonal Learners' drive toward relationships through . . . |
|---|---|
| Competition and Challenge | Cooperation and Connections (to students' lives, feelings, and experiences) |
| We can engage Understanding Learners' drive to make sense of things through . . . | We can engage Self-Expressive Learners' drive toward originality through . . . |
| Curiosity and Controversy | Choice and Creativity |

**Figure 3: The Eight Cs of Student Engagement.**

## Competition

There is no question that competition is motivating to many students, but if too extreme, competition can become a liability in the classroom. To maximize the motivational power of competition, focus classroom activities around mild and friendly forms of competition that allow everyone to experience success. For example, near the end of each unit, you might use well-designed learning games such as Teams-Games-Tournaments (DeVries, Edwards, & Slavin, 1978) or Vocabulary Jeopardy to help your students review and master key terms for the test.

## Challenge

Why do people work so hard to ski down a double-black-diamond slope? Why do students choose to play the most difficult level of their favorite video games? The answer is because they love a challenge. You can increase the level of challenge in your classroom by providing tasks at three different levels and allowing students to choose the task they feel most capable of completing (called "graduated difficulty": see Silver, Strong, & Perini, 2007, based on the work of Muska Mosston, 1972). More generally, you can foster a challenge-oriented classroom by letting your students know that you expect excellence and by daring them to go the extra mile.

### Curiosity

Look for opportunities to puzzle your students, to engage them in solving mysteries associated with your content. For example, why not start a unit on the American Revolution with this question: How did an untested ragtag militia defeat the most powerful army in the world? Or a lesson on insects with these questions: Why do we need pests like insects, anyway? Would we be better off if we got rid of them? Provoke students to inquire, investigate, and go beyond the obvious with "Yes, but why?" questions: Yes, we use the Pythagorean Theorem to solve the problem, but why does $a^2 + b^2 = c^2$? Yes, mammals give live birth rather than laying eggs, but why?

### Controversy

Our content areas are loaded with controversies, arguments, and intellectual disagreements. Invite students into the controversy. Challenge them to take and defend positions on the hot-button issues at the heart of your discipline. For example, Do women and men write differently? Was algebra invented or discovered? Is global warming more a result of human activity or natural causes?

### Choice

You can easily capitalize on this powerful motivator by giving students more opportunities to make selections and decisions about their learning. Learning centers and Shared Interest Groups (small groups of students working together to learn about a topic of common interest) let students explore content in ways that work best for them, while choice-based assignments and projects offer students the chance to decide how to demonstrate what they have learned.

### Creativity

Many students long to express their uniqueness and individuality. Look for ways to invite their creativity into your classroom through divergent thinking activities, nonroutine problem solving, metaphorical thinking (ask, for example, "How is a colony like a child?"), projects, and just about any way you can think of that allows students to put their own original stamp on what they are learning.

### Cooperation

For many students, the greatest inspiration comes in knowing that they are part of a community of learners. Nurture this sense of belonging through cooperative learning activities, learning partnerships, small group work, and lots of classroom discussion. Or, the next time students conduct research, try Jigsaw (Aronson, Blaney, Stephen, Sikes, & Snapp, 1978; Slavin, 1995), which organizes research projects around a highly effective cooperative structure.

### Connections

Why do I need to learn this? Why does it matter to me? These are common questions from students, and in them we can hear students looking for—and not finding—a way to connect what they are learning to their lives beyond the school walls. It does not take much to let students express their own opinions or to encourage them to draw on their experiences before, during, or at the end of a lesson or unit. Include questions and activities involving students' values, priorities, and experiences in your content. For example, When is rebellion justified? Have you ever used fractions to settle a dispute? What do you want to learn about spiders?

### Designing for Engagement

We have sketched out the Eight Cs of Engagement, but the truth is, simply walking into a classroom with some good ideas for how to increase student engagement can just as easily lead to frustration as it can to active commitment from all students. And while the Eight Cs serve as a useful set of guidelines for student engagement, their real power is released through design. This correlates squarely with a key finding from the Michigan State University study of engaging teachers (Raphael et al., 2008). All the highly engaging teachers in that study used a variety of instructional practices, which they coordinated into a well-thought-out plan. While there are several good design models, we believe that the best ones provide a simple but deep way of thinking about lessons and units. Following is the blueprint model we have developed with teachers during Curriculum Writing Camp sessions (Thoughtful Education Press, 2009). The idea behind the blueprint is that well-designed lessons and units include five different types of learning experiences that help students construct knowledge from the ground up:

- **Knowledge anticipation,** or "hooking" students into the unit by capturing their attention, activating their prior knowledge, and preparing them for the learning to come

- **Knowledge acquisition,** whereby students actively make sense of the texts, lectures, and other sources of learning presented in the unit

- Time to **practice and process,** during which students explore content more deeply and master essential skills through modeling and coaching

- **Knowledge application,** which requires students to demonstrate the full scope of their learning through a summative assessment task, as well as track their progress along the way through formative assessments

- **Reflection,** or the opportunity to stand back from their learning so students can personalize what they have learned, form generalizations, and use their learning to develop future learning goals

In the next section, we will look at how a teacher named Mr. Cogito uses the blueprint in conjunction with the Eight Cs to design and deliver a highly engaging unit. Specifically, we will take an extended look inside Mr. Cogito's classroom over the first four days of a two-week unit on the Age of Exploration. These first four days constitute a mini-unit within the unit focused on the cultural, technological, and historical conditions that led to a new era of European exploration.

The following text is divided into two columns. On the left side, we explain where Mr. Cogito and his students are in the blueprint model, and we describe what is happening in the classroom. On the right side, we highlight the specific elements of Mr. Cogito's design—the strategies and tools he is using and the Cs he is engaging.

| **What Is Happening in the Classroom** | **Design Elements** |
| --- | --- |

### Day One

*Day one is dedicated to **knowledge anticipation**. Mr. Cogito gets the most out of this introduction to the unit by capturing students' interest, activating their prior knowledge, helping them preassess their understanding of key vocabulary, and presenting the essential questions that drive the unit.*

| | |
| --- | --- |
| Mr. Cogito begins by writing fifteen key terms related to the unit on the board, one word at a time. With each new word, students consider what they know about the term and make connections between terms to see if they can figure out what topic or "big idea" they will be studying. | **Tool:** Hook—fifteen words, title withheld<br><br>**Engages:** Curiosity, Connections |
| After the fifteen words are written, the class comes to a consensus: the topic has something to do with "explorers." Mr. Cogito | **Tool:** Consensus Building |

| What Is Happening in the Classroom | Design Elements |
|---|---|
| confirms his students' hypothesis by telling them the name of the unit—"Explorers or Exploiters?"—and asks, "What comes to mind when you hear this title? What do you associate with *explorer*? How about *exploiter*?" Using their learning logs, students generate a preliminary definition of both terms. After sharing and discussion, Mr. Cogito explains that this tension between exploration and exploitation will be a defining theme in the unit. "In fact," he says, "near the end of the unit, you'll be participating in a Circle of Knowledge discussion. You'll have the job of arguing whether the defining legacy of this period is exploration of new worlds or exploitation of native cultures. But before we get ahead of ourselves, let's come back to the new vocabulary words we'll be learning." | **Engages:** Cooperation<br><br><br>**Tools:** Associations, Learning Log, Preliminary Definitions<br>**Engages:** Connections<br><br>**Strategy:** Circle of Knowledge (mentioned only)<br><br>**Engages:** Controversy, Cooperation |
| Mr. Cogito returns to the fifteen key vocabulary terms and asks students to assess their initial Vocabulary Knowledge Rating (VKR) understanding of each term using a simple VKR rating scale: | **Strategy:** Vocabulary Knowledge Rating<br>**Engages:** Challenge |

> 1 = I've never heard it.
>
> 2 = I've heard it, but I'm not sure what it means.
>
> 3 = I think I know it but need some clarification.
>
> 4 = I know it well enough to explain it to others.

| What Is Happening in the Classroom | Design Elements |
| --- | --- |

After rating their initial understanding of the terms, students compute and share their average VKR score for all fifteen terms. "Your challenge," says Mr. Cogito, "will be to make sure that by the end of the unit, your total score is at least a 3.5. That way, you'll know you have a good handle on the important terms in the unit."

Next, Mr. Cogito presents the essential questions for the unit:

**Tool:** Essential Questions

- What conditions made exploration possible?

**Engages:** Curiosity, Controversy

- Who were the explorers, and what did they accomplish?

- What happened between the explorers and the native cultures they encountered? Should the explorers' actions be admired or admonished?

"What I want you to do for homework," he tells students, "is to review these questions carefully and to *be* a historian by asking yourself what else you would like to know about the Age of Exploration. Generate at least one more essential question of your own."

**Homework:** Generate a question

**Engages:** Connections

Mr. Cogito also distributes the Assessment Menu for the unit and asks students to review it. The menu contains twelve tasks in all, four tasks for each of the three essential questions, with each task representing one of the four learning styles. For example, for the first essential question—What conditions made exploration possible?—students can:

**Homework:** Preview Assessment Menu

**Engages:** Choice, Creativity

| What Is Happening in the Classroom | Design Elements |
| --- | --- |

- Select the five most important developments that led to Columbus' voyage and create an annotated timeline. (Mastery Task)

- Compare and contrast the time leading up to Columbus' voyage with the Space Race. (Understanding Task)

- Develop a flag that captures the "spirit of the age" and write an explanation of what the design elements represent. (Self-Expressive Task)

- Pretend they are Columbus and write a personal letter to Isabel and Ferdinand that will persuade them that the time is right for their journey. (Interpersonal Task)

Over the course of the unit, students will be able to choose their tasks, provided that they try tasks in different styles.

### Day Two

*On day two, Mr. Cogito focuses on **knowledge acquisition**. Most of the day is dedicated to the Mystery Strategy (see Silver et al., 2007) in which students work to answer the question, Why was the time right for Columbus in 1492?*

Students begin by sharing the questions they generated for homework and working with Mr. Cogito to put them into larger categories. For example, three students' questions relate to what life was like on ships at the time. "These are wonderful questions," Mr.

**Tool:** Group and Label

**Engages:** Connections

| What Is Happening in the Classroom | Design Elements |
| --- | --- |

Cogito says as he records them on a poster. "Let's keep our eye out for answers to these questions during the unit. And let's get started by getting some answers to one of our essential questions: What conditions made exploration possible?"

Mr. Cogito shows a brief video of Neil Armstrong's walk on the moon and reads an excerpt from Kennedy's famous speech about the Space Race. Mr. Cogito then asks his class to consider this question: how could President Kennedy, in 1961, guarantee the American people that by the end of the decade the United States would safely land a man on the moon when the United States had not yet even put an astronaut into orbit? To generate some initial ideas, students use Give One, Get One: they generate two initial ideas on their own and then move around the room to collect four additional ideas from other students.

**Tool:** Hook

**Engages:** Curiosity

**Tool:** Give One, Get One

**Engages:** Cooperation

After collecting all of his students' ideas on the board, Mr. Cogito draws a parallel between the first lunar landing and Columbus' first voyage. "Like landing a man on the moon," he says, "Columbus' journey to the New World was the result of a number of factors that came together at the right time. It's going to be your job as historians to figure out what these factors were using a strategy called Mystery. You'll be working in cooperative teams to figure out why the time was right in 1492 for the Europeans to discover two new continents." Mr. Cogito provides each team

**Strategy:** Mystery

**Engages:** Curiosity, Creativity

| What Is Happening in the Classroom | Design Elements |
| --- | --- |

of students with an envelope of twenty-five clues to read, group, and label (see fig. 4). After grouping and labeling the clues into categories, student teams will generate five hypotheses about why 1492 was an ideal time for Columbus' journey. Before students start working, Mr. Cogito models the thinking process involved for grouping clues. "First I read the two clues carefully. Then I ask myself, 'What is the topic? What does the clue say about the topic?' For example, these two clues both deal with religion."

**Tool:** Teacher Modeling

Most Spanish expeditions carried priests with them.

"We have come to look for Christians and spices."

—Vasco da Gama

**Figure 4: Sample clues.**

Mr. Cogito goes on to show students how he searches for more religion clues and generates a hypothesis about the role religion may have played in Columbus' journey.

As students work to group clues and generate hypotheses, Mr. Cogito circulates around the room to listen in on groups' thinking. The class convenes so Mr. Cogito can

| What Is Happening in the Classroom | Design Elements |
| --- | --- |

explain that they will continue the learning process for homework (see fig. 5): "You're going to read the first two sections of your textbook. As you read, you'll have to collect evidence that either supports or refutes each of your five hypotheses."

**Strategy:** Reading for Meaning

**Engages:** Curiosity, Challenge

> Hypothesis 1: Improvements in technology allowed ships to navigate across the Atlantic Ocean.
>
> Evidence: The science of cartography, or mapmaking, had become more sophisticated and accurate by Columbus' time. New inventions, like the astrolabe and mariner's compass, made longer and more difficult voyages possible.

**Figure 5: Sample student homework entry.**

### Day Three

*On day three, Mr. Cogito pursues several purposes using a brain-based approach called New American Lecture (see Silver et al., 2007). Mr. Cogito continues with **knowledge acquisition**, while also helping students process the content more deeply through questioning and note making (**practice and process**). The questions and students' notes also provide Mr. Cogito and students with good formative assessment information (**knowledge acquisition**).*

| What Is Happening in the Classroom | Design Elements |
| --- | --- |

Students share their hypotheses and the evidence they discovered in the textbook. After the discussion, Mr. Cogito provides his students with a cause and effect organizer (see fig. 6).

**Tool:** Cause and Effect Organizer

**Engages:** Curiosity

### The 5 Cs: Why the Time Was Right for Columbus in 1492

| Causes for Exploration | Possible Effects |
| --- | --- |
| Competition among nations | |
| Control of travel to the East | |
| Commerce and middle-class comfort | |
| Creation of new technologies | |
| Courageous explorers | |

**Figure 6: Sample cause and effect organizer.**

He explains, "The Five Cs in this organizer correspond to the big ideas in your textbook reading." Mr. Cogito uses New American Lecture to describe the critical information about each of the five major causes in small chunks. To both deepen and assess his students' knowledge and understanding along the way, Mr. Cogito stops at different points throughout his lecture to pose a different question from this list:

**Strategy:** New American Lecture

**Engages:** Curiosity, Connections

- Why did Europeans want to travel to Asia? Which influential groups supported this travel?

| What Is Happening in the Classroom | Design Elements |
| --- | --- |

- What was happening in the Middle East at the time that influenced Europeans' desire to find a new route to the East?

- What developments made it possible for Europeans to travel where they had been unable to travel before?

- What other reasons might explorers have had for exploring new lands?

### Day Four

*The fourth day is dedicated to **knowledge application** and **reflection**.*

Students synthesize what they have learned about the unit's first essential question by choosing their first task from the Assessment Menu (timeline, comparative essay, flag, or personal letter) and working to complete it (**knowledge application**).

**Synthesis Task:** Assessment Menu

**Engages:** Choice, Creativity

Before moving on to the next essential question, Mr. Cogito asks students to look back on what they have learned so far (**reflection**). Students review the student-generated questions they recorded on day two and ask themselves if they have found any answers.

**Tool:** Student-generated questions (revisited)

**Engages:** Curiosity

For homework, students continue their **reflection** by reviewing their VKRs to see if their understanding of the key terms has evolved.

**Homework:** Revisit VKR

**Engages:** Challenge

## Making the Commitment to Commitment

These are the commitments Mr. Cogito has made to his students:

First, he has a deep awareness of his students' learning styles and the learning drives that underlie them. More important, he rotates his use of the Eight Cs to engage different styles and drives. As the research of Robert Sternberg (2006) shows, teaching in this multistyle way leads consistently to the greatest gains in student achievement, because it "enables students to capitalize on their strengths and to correct or to compensate for their weaknesses, encoding material in a variety of interesting ways" (pp. 33–34).

Second, Mr. Cogito uses a wide variety of instructional tools and strategies. Mr. Cogito has a minilibrary of references on research-based instruction including *Classroom Instruction That Works* (Marzano, Pickering, & Pollock, 2001), *Tools for Promoting Active, In-Depth Learning* (Silver et al., 2001), *The Art and Science of Teaching* (Marzano, 2007), and *The Strategic Teacher* (Silver, Strong, & Perini, 2007). When it comes to delivering instruction, he relies on the tools and strategies in these texts to do most of the heavy lifting for him—and he is almost always pleased with the results.

Third, Mr. Cogito takes seriously the work of instructional design; he incorporates tools, strategies, and the Eight Cs into a cohesive model that keeps students actively engaged and allows them to make learning their own.

Mr. Cogito has made these commitments because he knows that commitment is reciprocal, that it requires mutual effort and yields mutual rewards. By making these same commitments, we encourage our students to give us that "something more" that we all hope for: their deep and abiding commitment to learn what we teach.

## Acknowledgment

It is difficult to imagine this chapter having taken shape without the wisdom of our dear and deeply missed friend, Richard Strong. Every room Richard entered became more engaging, and his brilliant work in making classrooms and schools more engaging places will continue to inspire us.

## References

Aronson, E., Blaney, N., Stephan, C., Sikes, J., & Snapp, M. (1978). *The jigsaw classroom*. Beverly Hills, CA: Sage Publications.

DeVries, D. L., Edwards, K. J., & Slavin, R. E. (1978). Biracial learning teams and race relations in the classroom: Four field experiments using teams-games-tournaments. *Journal of Education Psychology, 70*(3), 356–362.

Fredericks, J. A., Blumenfeld, P. C., & Paris, A. H. (2004). School engagement: Potential of the concept, state of the evidence. *Review of Educational Research, 74*, 59–109.

Jung, C. G. (1923). *Psychological types*. (H. G. Baynes, Trans.). New York: Harcourt Brace.

Marzano, R. J. (2007). *The art and science of teaching: A comprehensive framework for effective instruction*. Alexandria, VA: Association for Supervision and Curriculum Development.

Marzano, R. J., Pickering, D., & Pollock, J. (2001). *Classroom instruction that works: Research-based strategies for increasing student achievement*. Alexandria, VA: Association for Supervision and Curriculum Development.

Mosston, M. (1972). *Teaching: From command to discovery*. Belmont, CA: Wadsworth Publishing.

Myers, I. B. (1962/1998). *The Myers-Briggs Type Indicator*. Palo Alto, CA: Consulting Psychologists Press.

Raphael, L. M., Pressley, M., & Mohan, L. (2008). Engaging instruction in middle school classrooms: An observational study of nine teachers. *Elementary School Journal, 109*(10), 61–81.

Silver, H. F., & Strong, R. W. (2004). *Learning style inventory for students*. Ho-Ho-Kus, NJ: Thoughtful Education Press.

Silver, H. F., Strong, R. W., & Perini, M. J. (2000). *So each may learn: Integrating learning styles and multiple intelligences*. Alexandria, VA: Association for Supervision and Curriculum Development.

Silver, H. F., Strong, R. W., & Perini, M. J. (2001). *Tools for promoting active, in-depth learning*. Ho-Ho-Kus, NJ: Thoughtful Education Press.

Silver, H. F., Strong, R. W., & Perini, M. J. (2007). *The strategic teacher: Selecting the right research-based strategy for every lesson.* Alexandria, VA: Association for Supervision and Curriculum Development.

Slavin, R. E. (1995). *Cooperative learning: Theory, research, and practice* (2nd ed.). Boston: Allyn & Bacon.

Sternberg, R. J. (2006). Recognizing neglected strengths. *Educational Leadership, 64*(1), 30–35.

Strong, R. W., Silver, H. F., Perini, M. J., & Tuculescu, G. (2003). Boredom and its opposite. *Educational Leadership, 61*(1), 24–29.

Strong, R. W., Silver, H. F., & Robinson, A. (1995). Strengthening student engagement: What do students want (and what really motivates them)? *Educational Leadership, 53*(1), 8–12.

Thoughtful Education Press. (2009). *Classroom curriculum design: How strategic units improve instruction and engage students in meaningful learning.* Ho-Ho-Kus, NJ: Author.

# Robert J. Marzano
# Jana S. Marzano

Robert J. Marzano, Ph.D., is CEO of Marzano Research Laboratory. During his forty years in education, Dr. Marzano has worked with educators in every U.S. state and a host of countries in Europe and Asia. A prolific author, his work focuses on reading and writing, instruction, thinking skills, school effectiveness, restructuring, assessment, cognition, and standards implementation.

Jana S. Marzano has been a psychotherapist in private practice for over twenty-five years. Her specialty areas include post-traumatic stress disorder, mood disorders, marital counseling, and substance and behavioral addictions. She works extensively with children and adolescents. She has coauthored a book on vocabulary instruction published by the International Reading Association and has published a number of articles on topics ranging from classroom management to the role of the self-system in determining human behavior.

In this chapter, the authors address the thoughts and emotions teachers bring to the classroom—how a teacher's "inner world" influences the "outer world" of his or her behavior. They present a model for what they refer to as the "inner game" of teaching and discuss how metacognitive awareness and control on the part of teachers about their inner world can make them more effective in addressing difficult classroom situations and helping students.

# Chapter 14

# The Inner Game of Teaching

## Robert J. Marzano and Jana S. Marzano

There have been a number of attempts to identify the instructional strategies and teacher behaviors that have a demonstrable relationship with student achievement (see Good & Brophy, 2003; Marzano, 2007; Mayer, 2003). This, of course, makes perfect sense. Any collection of strategies and behaviors that have demonstrable relationships with student achievement is a powerful resource for classroom teachers; however, in spite of their documented relationship with student achievement, instructional strategies and teacher behaviors are not the focus of this chapter. Rather, this chapter addresses what is arguably one of the more underemphasized classroom correlates of student achievement: the thoughts and emotions teachers bring to the classroom. Stated differently, this chapter addresses how a teacher's "inner world" influences the "outer world" of teacher behavior.

The relationship between the inner world of thoughts and emotions and the outer world of behavior is evident from many perspectives. In the field of education, one finds direct and indirect support for the inner world/outer world connection. For example, consider the research on teacher efficacy, which might be operationally defined as the extent to which teachers believe they can make a positive difference in their environment and the lives of their students. Goddard, Hoy, and Hoy (2004) found that a collective sense of efficacy on the part of teachers in a school is a better predictor of student success than is the socioeconomic status of students. The expectations literature also provides indirect support for the inner world/outer world connection. For example, in her review of the expectations literature, Weinstein (2002) demonstrates that the beliefs (expectations) teachers have about students influence their behavior towards students, which ultimately influences student achievement. Finally in a meta-analysis of fifty-five studies, Valentine, DuBois, and Cooper (2004) found a significant correlation between self-beliefs and academic achievement even when controlling for prior achievement.

This chapter presents a model of the inner world/outer world relationship designed to help teachers exert more control over their behavior as a consequence of their understanding and control of their thoughts and emotions. We begin with a description of the fundamentals of the inner world.

## The Fundamentals of the Inner World

According to many psychologists, the self-system is the architect of human behavior (Harter, 1980; Markus & Ruvolo, 1990). In effect, the inner world is driven by the self-system. McCombs and her colleagues (McCombs, 1984, 1986, 1989; McCombs & Marzano, 1990) describe the nature of the self-system in the following way:

> The self as agent, as the basis of will and volition, can be thought of, in part as a generative structure that is goal directed. . . . It . . . consciously or unconsciously defines who we are, what we think, and what we do. (McCombs & Marzano, 1990, p. 66)

Csikszentmihalyi (1990) emphasizes the importance of goals in the self-system:

> The self is no ordinary piece of information . . . in fact, it contains [almost] everything . . . that passes through

consciousness: all the memories, actions, desires, pleasures, and pains are included. And more than anything else, the self represents the hierarchy of goals that we have built up, bit by bit over the years. . . . At any given time, we are usually aware of only a tiny part of it. (p. 34)

Using different terminology, many researchers and theorists have attested to the goal-driven nature of the inner world. For example, behaviorists such as Thorndike (1913), Skinner (1953), and Kimble (1967) explained human behavior as a response to some felt need. Maslow (1970) believed that the "inner nature" of humankind is one which is driven by a well-formed system of needs. Piaget (1954) asserted that humans continually try to establish an internal state of equilibrium by creating a match between internal goals and the outside world. Taking a cybernetic perspective, Glasser (1981) echoed this same sentiment noting that human beings seek to match the outside world with internal "reference conditions."

Marzano and Marzano (1988) explain that the terms *goals*, *desires*, and *reference conditions* all refer to mental constructs that "in some way have a causal effect on human behavior or in some way drive behavior" (p. 71). They too contend that the goals in the self-system are organized in a hierarchic fashion with the more general goals at the top of the hierarchy and more specific goals fanning out from the more general. For example, an individual teacher might have a very general goal of being perceived as competent by his fellow teachers. This high-level goal would be accompanied by a series of more specific goals such as, "Never show you can't handle a situation," "Make sure colleagues see your successes," and so on.

### Basic Operating Principles

Marzano and Marzano (1988) further explain that at the highest level of the hierarchy of goals are basic beliefs. They refer to these high-level beliefs as *basic operating principles* or *propositions*. These principles are very general, and, therefore, they influence a great deal of human behavior. For example, a basic operating principle one teacher might hold is "all students can reach high levels of achievement if a teacher knows how to unlock their potential." Any time this teacher interacts with a student, this principle will elicit certain types of behavior from her—regardless of the student's past achievement. On the other hand, if a teacher has a basic operating principle that "students' academic success is determined by their home environment," then she will exhibit other types of behavior as a result of this principle.

### The Role of Situated Goals

While basic operating principles are the architects of human behavior at a very abstract level, situated goals drive behavior from moment to moment. Marzano and Marzano (1988) contend that at any point in time, an individual is executing a *situated goal* (or pursuing a *desired outcome*) that relates to one of his or her basic operating principles. This is depicted in figure 1.

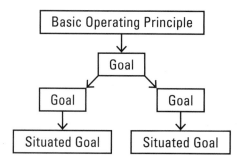

**Figure 1: Basic operating principles and goals.**

To illustrate the depiction in figure 1, assume that a teacher is standing in front of a science class providing students with information about the cell membrane. According to figure 1, at that point in time she is trying to accomplish a situated goal that might be stated as "help my students understand the defining characteristic of the cell membrane." This situated goal is derived from a more general goal that might be stated as "make sure my students learn the science content from the state standards." This goal might be subsumed under a very general goal stated as "give my students the best education possible." Finally, this goal might be subsumed under an even more general basic operating principle such as "life should be led in such a way as to enhance the lives of others."

Situated goals themselves have a substructure called *scripts*. Working from the perspective of artificial intelligence (AI), Schank and Abelson (1977) first popularized the concept of scripts as internal structures that articulate specific actions to be taken in specific situations. Van Dijk (1980) operationalized the working components of scripts. He explained that scripts have *prototypical components* (components that are always executed when trying to accomplish a situated goal) and *free components* (components that might be executed but are not necessary to accomplish a situated goal). To illustrate, consider his description of the components of the script that might be executed for the situated goal of obtaining food in a restaurant:

> Calling a waitress, for instance is a prototypical . . . action that has as its function the prototypical component action of ordering food. Making conversation with her is a free component action or a free auxiliary action to obtain the food more quickly. . . . (p. 235)

The teacher standing in front of the class providing information about the cell membrane is executing a very detailed lecture script. That script might include components like providing a brief preview of the content, presenting small bits of information, encouraging students to interact after each small bit of information has been presented, and so on.

### How the Inner Game Works

Thus far, we have considered the nature of the inner world of human experience—basic operating principles govern general goals that, in turn, govern increasingly more specific goals or desired outcomes that ultimately lead to the execution of a specific script. This inner world is the playing field for the "inner game."

The inner game is in play whenever a person is presented with a new stimulus or presenting event. For example, the teacher executing her lecture script will continue executing that script until something occurs that is typically not associated with the script. To illustrate, assume that the teacher is in the middle of her lecture script, and a particular group of students at the back of the classroom turn away from the front of the room and begin talking. This represents a *presenting event*—an event that does not fit well within the script being executed. All presenting events call for interpretation, and this is where the inner game begins.

### Interpreting a Presenting Event

The immediate reaction to a presenting event is to construct an interpretation. To a great extent, how we interpret a presenting event dictates how we respond to it (the script we execute). Sternberg and Smith (1991) use the terms *triggering condition* and *inferences* to describe this dynamic. They note the following:

> People make inferences only when there is a *triggering condition*. An event or relationship must be problematic, unexpected, or at least interesting, before people begin to make inferences. This fact spares them the unbearable tedium of endlessly calculating relations among events whose conjunction is of no interest. (p. 61)

Metaphorically, one might say that interpreting a presenting event involves answering four questions:

1. What is it?
2. Is it positive or negative?
3. How important is it?
4. How do I feel about it?

The first question—What is it?—deals with how an individual classifies a presenting event. For example, the teacher faced with the group of students talking in the back of the classroom can classify this event in a variety of ways. Her classification might be that the students' behavior is a type of disruption to the integrity of her lecture. Another classification (although far less likely) might be that the students are intently discussing the content of the lecture. Mervis (1980) explains that classifying is an essential aspect of human cognition simply because the world consists of an infinite number of stimuli. Nickerson, Perkins, and Smith (1985) explain that forming conceptual categories is so basic to human cognition that it is essential to human survival. Without conceptual categories the world would present itself as a kaleidoscope of stimuli. Each new event would have to be addressed without the benefit of prior knowledge. One's classification of a presenting event, then, is a function of a deep-seated human mechanism—we organize our past experiences into categories so we can more easily recognize and know how to react to new experiences.

The second component of an interpretation deals with the perceived value of the presenting event. Metaphorically, an individual asks the question, Is it positive or negative? Marzano (1998) notes that it is useful to think of the value assigned to a presenting event as existing on a continuum ranging from highly positive to highly negative. For example, if the teacher providing information about the cell membrane classifies the presenting event as a type of disruption, she would surely assign a negative value to it. Whether it is a highly negative value or a moderately negative value would be determined by the teacher's previous experiences with similar disruptions. If the teacher classifies the presenting event as a type of student discussion regarding the content of her lecture, she would surely assign a positive value. Again, the degree of positiveness she assigns will depend on her past experiences.

The third component of an interpretation deals with the perceived importance of the presenting event. Metaphorically, an individual asks the question, How important is it? This is typically a function of the extent to which the presenting event is seen as related to a high-level goal or a basic operating principle (Marzano & Marzano, 1988). For example, consider the interpretation that the students talking at the back of the room is negative. If the teacher sees the event as an obstacle to a high-level goal such as "help all my students learn the content important to the state test," she will code the event as highly important. If she sees it as an obstacle to a less general goal like "help my students learn about the cell," she will code it as less important.

The final component of an interpretation deals with a person's affective response—answering the question, How do I feel about it? The answer to this question is inextricably connected to the classification of the presenting event. It is also very much of a reflexive response. It is a reflexive response in the sense that it is cued automatically once an interpretation has been rendered. For example, if the teacher dealing with students talking in the back of the room has had some intense and negative past experiences with classroom disruptions, she will have a strong negative affective response once she classifies the presenting event as a type of disruption. Using different terminology, Gilovich (1991) explains that automatic links made between classifications of presenting events and affective responses create inherent biases in our interpretations, "biases that must be recognized and overcome if we are to arrive at sound judgments and valid beliefs" (p. 3).

The importance of affective responses in explaining human behavior has been recognized and discussed widely beginning in the early 1980s (Gazzaniga, 1992; LeDoux, 1994, 1996; Pinker, 1997; Restak, 1994; Sylwester, 1995). This was not always the case. In fact, Pert (1999) explains that in the seventeenth century, Descartes was forced to make an agreement with the Pope that he would not delve into anything that had to do with the soul, mind, or emotions before he was allowed to dissect human bodies. This agreement set the stage for dividing human experience into two distinct and separate spheres—body versus soul, mind, and emotions—for the next two centuries. On a more positive note, Pert explains that in the worlds of modern medicine and psychology, the importance of affective response to understanding human behavior is firmly established. To observe this shift in emphasis one need only witness the popularity of books and articles on emotional intelligence. Indeed, an entire 2008 issue of *American Psychologist* (Volume 63, Number 6), the flagship journal of the American Psychological Association, was devoted to the topic.

## Selecting a Desired Outcome (Situated Goal)

Once an individual renders an interpretation for a presenting event, he or she considers situated goals or desired outcomes for the situation. One might say that after making an interpretation, a person asks himself or herself, What do I want to do about it? (Marzano, 1998; Marzano & Kendall, 2007). The answer to this question does not immediately translate into action. Rather, an individual first considers the likelihood of success for the desired outcome. Metaphorically, once a person identifies a desired outcome for the situation, he asks himself, Can I do this?

To illustrate, consider the teacher who interprets the students talking in the back of the class as a disruption. Also assume she considers it fairly negative and fairly important. Finally, assume that she has negative emotions associated with the disruptive behavior. She will immediately consider desired outcomes. An obvious one would be that she wants the students to stop talking and reengage in her lecture. With a desired outcome identified, she immediately asks herself, Can I do it? If the answer to this question is yes, she then executes her script for getting students to reengage in a lecture. However, if she concludes that she cannot accomplish the situated goal of getting the students to reengage (she answers no to the question, Can I do it?), she then finds another desired outcome she thinks she can accomplish. For example, she might identify the situated goal of completing the lecture and not allowing the problem to escalate. In this case, she will execute a script for "continuing the lecture while pretending to not be concerned about the group of students talking."

## Metacognitive Control of the Inner Game

Whether we are aware of it or not, the inner game is always occurring. One might say it is the way we are hardwired to interact with the world around us. However, we are not always playing the inner game. Rather, for the most part, human beings are simply behaving in accordance with the rules that they have constructed about how to interpret events and how to react to events. As Pert (1999) explains, "The nervous system is not capable of taking in everything but can only scan the outer world for material that it is prepared to find by its wiring hookups, its own internal patterns and its past experiences" (p. 147). In effect, then, the inner game typically manifests as robot-like reactions to presenting events. This fact notwithstanding, it is possible for human beings to actually *play* the inner game by taking metacognitive control over it.

The metacognitive system has been described by researchers and theorists as responsible for monitoring, evaluating, and regulating the functioning of all other types of thought (Brown, 1984; Flavell, 1978; Meichenbaum & Asarnow, 1979). Taken together, these functions are sometimes referred to as exerting executive control of one's life (Brown, 1978, 1980; Flavell, 1978, 1979; Sternberg, 1984a, 1984b, 1986a, 1986b). While metacognition allows humans to take control of their lives, it requires a great deal of conscious thought and discipline. It is the vehicle that allows humans to play the inner game as opposed to being played *by* it.

### Metacognitive Control of Interpretation

Relative to interpreting a presenting event, metacognitive control involves an awareness and examination of how an individual is classifying a presenting event—how one is answering the question, What is it? If the interpretation does not foster the attainment of some high-level goal or is not consistent with a basic operating principle, the individual attempts to change her interpretation. Of course, this strategy is a simple variation of a time-honored strategy from clinical psychology sometimes referred to as *reframing* (see Ellis, 1977; Meichenbaum, 1977). Langer (1989) exemplifies the nature of reframing using the following example:

> Take a couple, Alice and Fred, whom you see quite often. Sometimes you hear them fight a bit. You don't pay any attention; don't all couples quarrel? Now you learn they are getting a divorce. You call to mind all the evidence that explains this outcome. "I knew it; [I] remember how they used to fight. Their fights were vicious." On the other hand, perhaps you hear that they have celebrated their silver anniversary. "Isn't that nice," you say, "they have such a solid marriage; they hardly ever quarrel and when they do they always make up so sweetly to each other." (p. 64)

The example offered by Langer depicts reframing that occurs as a result of new or different information. Here we refer to reframing as consciously changing one's interpretation. Marzano, Marzano, and Pickering (2003) offer the following example:

> As a young man, Mr. Cannady used to experience road rage, feeling incredibly angry when other drivers did things like cutting him off or failing to yield. Then he took a course that taught him to use a technique called reframing. Now when someone cuts him off in traffic, he tells himself, for example, that the person is probably not paying attention because of a sick child and is trying to get home quickly. This new frame immediately calms him down and prevents him from feeling personally offended. When he began to teach, he transferred this technique to the classroom. When students refused to do class work or if they talked back inappropriately or simply do not pay attention in class, Mr. Cannady tells himself that they are probably covering up insecurities, or that they must have had a bad morning at home, or that they just got some bad news. This approach helps

Mr. Cannady keep calm and allows him to perceive students' behaviors as discipline challenges, not as personal attacks. (p. 73)

To practice awareness and control over their interpretations, it is useful for teachers to ask themselves the following metacognitive questions when considering a presenting event:

- How am I interpreting this event?
- Does this interpretation help serve an important goal or an important principle in my life?
- If not, what is a more useful interpretation?

To illustrate, consider again the teacher lecturing while students are talking in the back of the room. The first metacognitive question is, How am I interpreting this? This question is designed to provide the teacher with the awareness that she has interpreted the event as a disruption, which she considers to be negative, important, and with which she has some strong associated negative emotions. This at least makes her aware of her cognitive and emotional state relative to the event that is occurring.

The next two metacognitive questions asked as a set are designed to make the teacher aware of the possibility of reframing the presenting event: Does this interpretation help serve an important goal in my life? If not, what is a more useful interpretation? Cued by these questions, the teacher might realize that she can exert control over her interpretation, and the one she is currently entertaining will most likely cause her anxiety and frustration. She might then consider a more useful interpretation, such as the students' talking, while bothersome, can be viewed as an opportunity to practice some classroom-management strategies she saw modeled in a workshop. Now the presenting event is not seen as an important negative event associated with negative emotion; rather, it shifts to a somewhat positive event in that it is seen as an opportunity to achieve an important goal. In this case, the goal would be "becoming the best teacher I can be." Along with the shift in classification of the event comes a shift in the interpretation from negative to positive and a possible shift in some of the emotions associated with the event.

## Metacognitive Control of Outcome Selection

Individuals can also exert metacognitive control over outcome selection (selection of a situated goal). To facilitate metacognitive control over outcome selection, teachers might ask themselves the following metacognitive questions:

- What would this look like if it turns out well?

- What actions can I take to accomplish a more positive outcome?

These questions are designed to direct a teacher's thinking to a positive possible future. In a series of works, Markus (Markus & Nurius, 1986; Markus & Ruvulo, 1990) has demonstrated the importance of an individual being able to see him- or herself as successful in a given situation. Markus refers to this as creating a "positive, future possible self." In effect, the act of imagining oneself accomplishing a desired outcome creates a possibility that was not previously available.

Again, consider the teacher who has interpreted the students talking in the back of the classroom as an opportunity to practice classroom-management techniques. Using Markus' notion of creating a positive, future possible self, the teacher would attempt to form a brief mental image of how she would like the situation to turn out. This process has been referred to as *mental rehearsal* and *creative visualization* (Murphy, 1994; Orlick, 1986; Suinn, 1972, 1985, 1993) to name a few. Mental rehearsal as a precursor to executing a complex physical routine has been used by elite athletes (Lloyd & Foster, 2006). For example, before executing a dive from the ten meter platform in the Olympics, elite swimmers will visualize the moves in the dive in great detail. This same basic process can be used by teachers when they have reframed a presenting event in the service of a more positive outcome. In effect, the teacher dealing with students talking in the back of the room can mentally rehearse how she would like to interact with students, what she will say as she interacts, the body position and gestures she will use as she interacts, and even how she will feel as she interacts. The teacher might imagine herself talking to the students in a very calm but assertive voice. She might see herself inviting students to reengage in the lecture as opposed to ordering them to do so. Rather than standing at the front of the room, she would see herself slowly moving towards the students. Finally, she would imagine herself feeling confident and calm as she engages in these behaviors. In effect, the teacher would be using mental rehearsal to design and practice the script she will employ with the students.

## Long-Term Work on the Inner Game

As described in the previous section, metacognitive control over the inner game occurs on the spot—while a teacher is addressing a presenting event. This type of metacognitive control is a daily discipline. As presenting events occur, teachers ask themselves the metacognitive questions relating to control of interpretation and outcome selection. In addition to this daily form of practice, teachers can spend time delving more deeply into the workings of the inner game as it relates to specific situations in their lives. At least two areas should be the subject of such focused introspection: classifying events and examining basic operating principles.

### Classifying Events

One area that should be the subject of focused introspection is how an individual typically classifies events. Recall that classifying is the mechanism that allows human beings to make sense of the world. This fundamental human trait is both a blessing and a curse. It is a blessing in the sense that it affords human beings the power to interpret quickly and efficiently virtually anything with which they come into contact. It is a curse in the sense that it frequently biases human beings to perceive presenting events negatively. This is because human beings have a tendency to overgeneralize negative events. For example, a teacher who has had negative past experiences with disruptions will tend to classify events as disruptions that in fact are not. This tendency might be a survival mechanism, since remembering events that are harmful helps humans avoid harm in the future. Seligman (1993) explains that

> the Russian psychologist Bluma Zeigarnik discovered early in this century that we remember unsolved problems, frustration, failures, and rejections much better than we remember our successes and completions. (p. 50)

While overgeneralizing negative events helped our ancestors survive in a world of physically superior predators, it can make modern man overcautious and incapable of seeing the positive potential of presenting events. For example, assume that our teacher has had an experience early in her teaching career in which two students were talking at the back of the room while she was lecturing. At that time, the teacher asked the students to listen to her presentation, but they refused, and the situation escalated to a point where the students physically attacked the teacher. This event would be filed in permanent memory as a primary negative event.

A *primary negative event* is an incident that results in substantial physical and/or psychological harm to an individual. Typically these events occur relatively early in life in situations over which an individual had little or no control. In the extreme, these primary negative events can cause an individual to suffer from post-traumatic stress disorder (PTSD) (Shapiro, 1995). For example, an individual who has experienced the primary negative event of observing a family member being killed might reexperience that event any time anything happens that is even remotely similar to the situation in which the traumatic event occurred.

To break the negative chain of associations with trauma such as this, focused therapy is commonly required (Shapiro, 1995).

Even if a primary negative event does not result in PTSD, it can dramatically affect an individual's ability to address disturbing but manageable presenting events. Again, consider the teacher addressing the issue of students talking in the back of the room. If the teacher has experienced a primary negative event such as the one described earlier that resulted in an attack by the students, every presenting event that even remotely resembles that early experience will trigger an interpretation that is highly negative, highly important, and laced with strong negative emotion. In fact, in a series of work, Anderson (1983, 1990a, 1990b, 1993, 1995) has articulated the *theory of spreading activation*. Fundamentally, the theory postulates that any presenting event, once classified, activates all other events stored in permanent memory that have similar characteristics. This spread of activation occurs in seconds. It is little wonder then why a teacher might have difficulty dealing with specific situations in her class that she interprets negatively.

While focused introspection can help an individual become aware of primary negative events in his or her life, it probably will not alter the influence these events have. However, focused introspection in conjunction with consultations with a trained therapist or psychologist can help teachers identify primary negative events and erase the automatic connections with which they have become associated (Shapiro, 1995). Indeed, in their meta-analysis, Lipsey and Wilson (1993) found a positive and significant effect size regarding the relationship between psychotherapy and success at work. When teachers or any other professionals are plagued with primary negative events that have occurred in their lives, brief periods of therapy can greatly enhance their effectiveness and their sense of self-efficacy.

## Examining Basic Operating Principles

A second area that should be a target of focused introspection is the examination of basic operating principles. Logic would imply that people are always operating in accord with their basic operating principles; if a teacher has a basic operating principle that all students can learn with proper instruction, her actions in the classroom will be consistent with this principle. While this scenario appears quite reasonable, Argyris and Schön (1974, 1978) have shown that there is often great disparity between a person's espoused beliefs and his or her actions. Stated differently, there is oftentimes a difference between what people say or think they believe and how they act. To illustrate, a teacher might say that she believes all children can learn complex content given appropriate instruction. This would be an espoused belief. However, the teacher's actions might contradict this stated belief in that the teacher systematically excludes certain students from instruction in challenging content. Marzano and Marzano (1988) explain this contradiction in the following way: the teacher might think she has a belief that all students can learn complex content, but she has a basic operating principle that is not consistent with this espoused belief.

Focused introspection can help clarify the basic operating principles that truly govern a person's behavior. This type of focused introspection is ontological. In contrast, the focused introspection described previously regarding identifying primary negative events and extinguishing their automatic responses is psychological in that it deals with discovering patterns of behavior and their origins. According to the *Dictionary of Philosophy* (Runes, 1983), ontology is the study of being. Modern work in ontology is commonly traced to Gruber's (1993) work in artificial intelligence (AI). There the term refers to knowledge representation systems that are used to construct AI systems. Over the years, it has been applied to many other domains, one of which is human experience.

Marzano, Zaffron, Zraik, Robbins, and Yoon (1995) note that the ontological approach is designed to provide individuals with (1) an experience of their interpretations as constructed realities as opposed to absolute realities, and (2) an experience of themselves as the author of their interpretations instead of the victims of their interpretations. One of the ways to enact the ontological approach is through a reasoned examination of one's behavior and the logical deduction of the basic operating principle that must be governing the behavior. Thus, a teacher would begin by examining what she actually does (as opposed to what she says she believes) and then deductively determine the basic operating principle that must govern such behavior. With a basic operating principle disclosed, an individual next examines the origins of that principle from the perspective that the principle was created by interpretations of specific life events. At the moment an individual experiences being the author of the basic operating principles governing his life, he simultaneously realizes that he has the power to change his interpretations of events as they occur. Indeed, Frankl (1967) found that this dynamic was a defining characteristic of those prisoners who survived Nazi concentration camps.

Educational programs that provide ontological inquiries into life experiences have been shown to be perceived by those who have gone through them as increasing in their value over time. That is, over time the effect of ontologically based programs are viewed as more influential on participants' lives as opposed to less influential. For this reason, such programs are commonly referred to as "transformative" in that they create a basic shift in how individuals process the events in their lives (see Marzano et al., 1995).

### Greater Awareness and Control

This chapter has addressed an underemphasized aspect of teaching: the relationship between a teacher's inner world of thoughts and emotions and his or her outer world of behavior. We presented a model of the inner world of thoughts and emotions that formed the basis for describing what we refer to as the inner game of teaching. The inner game can be characterized as occurring any time an individual experiences a presenting event that is inconsistent with the current script he or she is executing. Invariably, an individual interprets and reacts to each presenting event. This process occurs with little or no conscious thought on the part of the teacher. To this extent, the inner game dictates the way a teacher will behave in class, particularly in situations he or she interprets negatively. Such automatic behavior might be the root cause of classroom problems between teachers and students. Fortunately, teachers can exert metacognitive control in regards to their interpretations of presenting events and the outcomes they pursue. Ultimately, this type of awareness and control on the part of teachers can make them more effective both in addressing difficult classroom situations and in helping students in a variety of ways.

## References

Anderson, J. R. (1983). *The architecture of cognition*. Cambridge, MA: Harvard University Press.

Anderson, J. R. (1990a). *The adaptive character of thought*. Hillsdale, NJ: Lawrence Erlbaum.

Anderson, J. R. (1990b). *Cognitive psychology and its implications* (3rd ed.). New York: Freeman.

Anderson, J. R. (1993). *Rules of the mind*. Mahwah, NJ: Lawrence Erlbaum Associates.

Anderson, J. R. (1995). *Learning and memory: An integrated approach*. New York: John Wiley.

Argyris, C., & Schön, D. (1974). *Theory in practice: Increasing professional effectiveness*. San Francisco: Jossey-Bass.

Argyris, C., & Schön, D. (1978). *Organizational learning: A theory of action perspective*. Reading, MA: Addison-Wesley.

Brown, A. L. (1978). Knowing when, where and how to remember: A problem of metacognition. In R. Glaser (Ed.), *Advances in instructional psychology* (Vol. 1, pp. 77–165). Hillsdale, NJ: Lawrence Erlbaum.

Brown, A. L. (1980). Metacognitive development and reading. In R. J. Spiro, B. C. Bruce, & W. F. Brewer (Eds.), *Theoretical issues in reading comprehension* (pp. 453–481). Hillsdale, NJ: Lawrence Erlbaum.

Brown, A. L. (1984). Metacognition, executive control, self-regulation, and other even more mysterious mechanisms. In F. E. Weinert & R. H. Kluwe (Eds.), *Metacognition, motivation, and learning* (pp. 60–108). Stuttgart, West Germany: Kulhammer.

Csikszentmihalyi, M. (1990). *Flow: The psychology of optimal experience.* New York: Harper & Row.

Ellis, A. (1977). The basic clinical theory of rational-emotive therapy. In A. Ellis & R. Grieger (Eds.), *Handbook of rationale-emotive therapy.* New York: Springer.

Flavell, J. H. (1978). Metacognitive development. In J. M. Scandura & C. J. Brainerd (Eds.), *Structural-process theories of complex human behavior* (pp. 213–245). Alphen aan den Rijn, The Netherlands: Sijthoff and Noordhoff.

Flavell, J. H. (1979). Metacognition and cognitive monitoring: A new area of cognitive developmental inquiry. *American Psychologist, 34,* 906–911.

Frankl, V. E. (1967). *Psychotherapy and existentialism.* New York: Pocket Books.

Gazzaniga, M. S. (1992). *Nature's mind: The biological roots of thinking, emotions, sexuality, language and intelligence.* New York: Basic Books.

Gilovich, T. (1991). *How we know what isn't so.* New York: The Free Press.

Glasser, W. (1981). *Stations of the mind.* New York: Harper & Row.

Goddard, R. D., Hoy, W. K., & Hoy, A. W. (2004). Collective efficacy beliefs: Theoretical developments, empirical evidence, and future directions. *Educational Researcher, 33*(3), 3–13.

Good, T. L., & Brophy, J. E. (2003). *Looking into classrooms* (9th ed.). Boston: Allyn & Bacon.

Gruber, T. R. (1993). A translation approach to portable ontology specifications. *Knowledge Acquisition, 5*(2), 199–220.

Harter, S. (1980). The perceived competence scale for children. *Child Development, 51,* 218–235.

Kimble, G. A. (1967). *Foundations of conditioning and learning.* New York: Appleton.

Langer, E. J. (1989). *Mindfulness.* Reading, MA: Addison-Wesley.

LeDoux, J. E. (1994). Emotion, memory, and brain. *Scientific American, 270*(6), 50–57.

LeDoux, J. E. (1996). *The emotional brain: The mysterious underpinnings of emotional life.* New York: Simon & Schuster.

Lipsey, M. W., & Wilson, D. B. (1993). The efficacy of psychological, educational, and behavioral treatment. *American Psychologist, 48*(12), 1181–1209.

Lloyd, P. J., & Foster, S. L. (2006). Creating healthy, high-performance workplaces: Strategies for health and sports psychology. *Consulting Psychology Journal: Practice and Research, 58*(1), 23–39.

Markus, H., & Nurius, P. (1986). Possible selves. *American Psychologist, 41,* 954–969.

Markus, H., & Ruvulo, A. (1990). Possible selves. Personalized representations of goals. In L. Pervin (Ed.), *Goal concepts in psychology* (pp. 211–241). Hillsdale, NJ: Lawrence Erlbaum.

Marzano, R. J. (1998). Cognitive, metacognitive, and connative considerations in classroom assessment. In N. M. Lambert & B. L. McCombs (Eds.), *How students learn: Reforming schools through learner-centered education* (pp. 241–266). Washington, DC: American Psychological Association.

Marzano, R. J. (2007). *The art and science of teaching: A comprehensive framework for effective instruction.* Alexandria, VA: Association for Supervision and Curriculum Development.

Marzano, R. J., & Kendall, J. S. (2007). *The new taxonomy of educational objectives* (2nd ed.). Thousand Oaks, CA: Corwin Press.

Marzano, R. J., & Marzano, J. (1988). Toward a cognitive theory of commitment and its implications for therapy. *Psychotherapy in Private Practice, 6*(4), 69–81.

Marzano, R. J. (with Marzano, J. S., & Pickering, D. J.). (2003). *Classroom management that works: Research-based strategies for every teacher.* Alexandria, VA: Association for Supervision and Curriculum Development.

Marzano R. J., Zaffron, S., Zraik, L., Robbins, S. L., & Yoon, L. (1995). A new paradigm for educational change. *Education, 116*(2), 162–173.

Maslow, A. H. (1970). *Motivation and personality.* New York: Harper & Row.

Mayer, R. E. (2003). *Learning and instruction.* Upper Saddle River, NJ: Merrill, Prentice Hall.

McCombs, B. L. (1984). Processes and skills training intervention. *Educational Psychologist, 19,* 197–218.

McCombs, B. L. (1986). The role of the self-system in self-regulated learning. *Contemporary Educational Psychology, 11,* 314–332.

McCombs, B. L. (1989). Self-regulated learning and academic achievement: A phenomenological view. In B. J. Zimmerman & D. H. Schunk (Eds.), *Self-regulated learning and academic achievement: Theory research and practice* (pp. 51–82). New York: Springer-Verlag.

McCombs, B. L., & Marzano, R. J. (1990). Putting the self in self-regulated learning: The self as agent in integrating will and skill. *Educational Psychologist, 25*(1), 51–69.

Meichenbaum, D. (1977). *Cognitive-behavior modification.* New York: Plenum Press.

Meichenbaum, D., & Asarnow, J. (1979). Cognitive-behavioral modification and metacognitive development: Implications for the classroom. In P. C. Kendall

& S. D. Hollon (Eds.), *Cognitive-behavioral interventions: Theory, research, and procedures* (pp. 11–35). New York: Academic.

Mervis, C. B. (1980). Category structure and the development of categorization. In R. J. Spiro, B. C. Bruce, & W. F. Brewer (Eds.), *Theoretical issues in reading comprehension* (pp. 279–307). Hillsdale, NJ: Lawrence Erlbaum.

Murphy, S. (1994). Imagery interventions in sport. *Medicine and Science in Sport and Exercise, 26,* 486–494.

Nickerson, R. S., Perkins, D. N., & Smith, E. E. (1985). *The teaching of thinking.* Hillsdale, NJ: Lawrence Erlbaum.

Orlick, T. (1986). *Psyching for sport: Mental training for athletes.* Champaign, IL: Leisure Press.

Pert, C. (1999). *Molecules of emotion.* New York: Touchstone.

Piaget, J. (1954). *The construction of reality in a child.* New York: Basic Books.

Pinker, S. (1997). *How the mind works.* New York: W. W. Norton & Company.

Restak, R. M. (1994). *The modular brain.* New York: Touchstone.

Runes, D. D. (Ed.). (1983). *Dictionary of philosophy.* New York: Littlefield Adams.

Schank, R. C., & Abelson, R. (1977). *Scripts, plans, goals and understanding.* Hillsdale, NJ: Lawrence Erlbaum.

Seligman, M. E. (1993). *What you can change and what you can't.* New York: Fawcett.

Shapiro, F. (1995). Eye movement desensitization and reprocessing. New York: Guilford.

Skinner, B. F. (1953). *Science and human behavior.* New York: Macmillan.

Sternberg, R. J. (1984a). *Beyond IQ: A triarchic theory of human intelligence.* New York: Cambridge University Press.

Sternberg, R. J. (1984b). Mechanisms of cognitive development: A componential approach. In R. J. Sternberg (Ed.), *Mechanisms of cognitive development* (pp. 163–186). New York: Freeman.

Sternberg, R. J. (1986a). Inside intelligence. *American Scientist, 74,* 137–143.

Sternberg, R. J. (1986b). *Intelligence applied.* New York: Harcourt Brace Jovanovich.

Sternberg, R., & Smith, E. (1991). *The psychology of human thought.* New York: Cambridge.

Suinn, R. M. (1972). Removing emotional obstacles to learning and performance by visuomotor behavioral rehearsal. *Behavior Therapy, 3,* 308–310.

Suinn, R. M. (1985). Imagery applications to performance enhancement. *Behavior Therapist, 8,* 155–159.

Suinn, R. M. (1993). Imagery. In R. N. Singer, M. Murphy, & L. K. Tennant (Eds.), *Handbook of research on sport psychology* (pp. 3–31). New York: Macmillan.

Sylwester, R. (1995). *A celebration of neurons: An educator's guide to the human brain*. Alexandria, VA: Association for Supervision and Curriculum Development.

Thorndike, E. L. (1913). *The psychology of learning*. New York: Teacher's College, Columbia University.

Valentine, J. C., DuBois, D. L., & Cooper, H. (2004). The relation between self-beliefs and academic achievement: A meta-analytic review. *Educational Psychologist, 39*(2), 111–133.

Van Dijk, T. A. (1980). *Macrostructures*. Hillsdale, NJ: Laurence Erlbaum.

Weinstein, R. S. (2002). *Reaching higher: The power of expectations in schooling*. Cambridge, MA: Harvard University Press.

# Index

## A

Abelson, R., 349
Achieve, Inc., 152–153
affective responses, presenting event and, 352–353
alignment, curriculum mapping, 199–200
Ambady, N., 233
American Council on the Teaching of Foreign Languages (ACTFL), 27
American Educational Research Association, 152
analysis, thinking skills, 150, 156, 176
Anderson, J. R., 360
Anderson, L., 172
apartheid system, poor versus wealthier students and, 126–128
appreciation, teaching for, 313–316
Argyris, C. 361
Aronson, E., 73
art and music, decrease in time spent on, 125–126
*Art and Science of Teaching, The* (Marzano), 218, 220
assessments
    for learning, 256
    goal-oriented, 43
Association for Supervision and Curriculum Development (ASCD), 145
authentic activities, 306
autonomous motivation, 301–302, 303–304

## B

backward design, 17, 274–277
Barber, B., 114, 128
Beginning Teacher Evaluation Study (BTES), 39–40
Bennett, B., 1, 3, 64–91
Berliner, D., 1, 3, 46, 112–143
Beyer, B., 145
*Beyond Monet: The Artful Science of Instructional Integration* (Bennett and Rolheiser), 67
Biddle, B., 33
Billings, L., 177
Biological Science Curriculum Study (BSCS), 172
Bloom, B., 32, 171
Bloom's Taxonomy, 74, 148, 149, 171, 172
Blumenfeld, P. C., 324
Blumer, H., 68–69
boredom, handling, 12–14
Bradley, L., 102
brain, patterning and relationship building in the, 178
Bransford, J., 173–174, 273, 289
Bridgeland, J. M., 137
Briggs, K., 325
Brophy, J., 1, 4, 32, 33, 41–43, 300–317
Brown, A., 173–174, 273
Bruer, J. T., 106
Bruner, J., 71, 73, 172
Bryant, P., 102
Bryk, A. S., 153
Buzan, T., 73

**On Common Ground: The Power of Professional Learning Communities**
*Edited by Richard DuFour, Robert Eaker, and Rebecca DuFour*
Examine a colorful cross-section of educators' experiences with PLC. This collection of insights from practitioners throughout North America highlights the benefits of PLC. **BKF180**

**Ahead of the Curve: The Power of Assessment to Transform Teaching and Learning**
*Edited by Douglas Reeves*
Leaders in education contribute their perspectives of effective assessment design and implementation, sending out a call for redirecting assessment to improve student achievement and inform instruction. **BKF232**

**Change Wars**
*Edited by Michael Fullan and Andy Hargreaves*
In the third Leading Edge™ anthology, education luminaries from around the globe share their theories-in-action on how to achieve deep change. **BKF254**

**Designing & Teaching Learning Goals & Objectives**
*Robert J. Marzano*
This book summarizes key research behind designing and teaching learning goals and objectives and translates that research into step-by-step hands-on strategies. **BKL001**

# Wait! Your professional development journey doesn't have to end with the last pages of this book.

We realize improving student learning doesn't happen overnight. And your school or district shouldn't be left to puzzle out all the details of this process alone.

**No matter where you are on the journey, we're committed to helping you get to the next stage.**

Take advantage of everything from **custom workshops** to **keynote presentations** and **interactive web and video conferencing**. We can even help you develop an action plan tailored to fit your specific needs.

*Let's get the conversation started.*

Call 888.763.9045 today.

 solution-tree.com